Detour

To Barbara, the love and joy of my life

ISBN-10:1-4611-4721-2
EAN-13:978-1-4611-4721-3

Table of Contents

Foreword

If your taste in business books is for those that recount the details and secrets of the famous and flamboyant; or books that list the founder's flashes of insight that enabled a wunderkind to leave the competition in the dust while he was at the helm of his Silicon Valley start-up, read no further. This is not that kind of book.

But if your proclivity is to dive into engaging stories of plain-old guys like you and me; women and men who built successful companies through hard work, luck and teamwork; stories of grabbing success from the jaws of defeat on one day; and then grabbing defeat from the jaws of victory on the next; or stories of true entrepreneurship that created successful new businesses within in massive bureaucracies, *keep reading this book.* You will love it, as I did. And you will learn, as I did, extraordinary new things about how to manage innovation.

The plain old ordinary guy is Chet Huber. Chet worked his whole life in General Motors – the stereotypical massive bureaucratic corporation. Pundits and analysts might have differed slightly about GM's next quarter's numbers, but they uniformly believed that GM could not innovate itself out of a paper bag. Yet Chet and his team, under the watchful eyes of Rick Wagoner and Harry Pearce, the Chairman and Vice-Chairman of GM, created OnStar. After growing at about 20% annually for a decade, OnStar is likely this year to hit revenues of about $3 billion – and about 25% of it will hit the bottom line. It has negative net assets. Chet assembled a team to do this not in Silicon Valley, but in Detroit. And GM's two most pressing competitors, Toyota and Ford, have announced *eight times* that they were ready to introduce their own *better* versions to compete against OnStar. They have not yet been able to do it. And after the brand *Toyota,* the brand OnStar has the second-highest unaided recall of any brand in the industry. The brand has been built with minimal advertising. This is *not* a plain old ordinary story.

Chet and his team built OnStar through intuition, trial and error, and calculated risks. I am proud to say that at a couple of critical junctions they actually used some of the theories that have emerged from my studies of innovation, too – theories that Chet absorbed semester after semester, as he spoke to the students at the Harvard Business School as they discussed the OnStar cases. These sessions for over a decade have been the capstone classes of our course, *Building and Sustaining a Successful Enterprise.* Every semester I have been impressed by Chet's engaging verbal style with the students. But as you read this book you will be delighted by his writing. I've never known someone who was such an astute manager to also be such an engaging writer. You will truly *enjoy* reading this book. It is fun. And it is true.

On behalf of the many thousands of people who will read this book, I give my deepest thanks to Chet Huber, for taking the time to teach the rest of us – plain old ordinary people like Chet – about how to be innovators, entrepreneurs, and managers. He teaches us that as long as we follow the rules, we can succeed at this – even in environments where small minds and smaller hearts might be convinced that it is impossible.

From the Harvard Business School in Boston,
Professor Clayton M, Christensen

Introduction

In order to understand what follows in this book, you'll need to have a basic understanding of what OnStar is all about. OnStar is a service that's been built into millions of GM cars and trucks since it first appeared in the U.S. market in 1996. It's enabled by a very unique and largely proprietary combination of core technologies, including wireless voice and data networks, Global Positioning Satellites, voice recognition, crash sensors, digital acoustic correction, geocoded databases, multiple massive software platforms, vehicle integration modules, and an incredibly intricate and highly redundant computer telephony architecture. All of these pieces work together in an amazingly complex and elegantly choreographed manner—something that holds great meaning for the rocket scientists at OnStar who knitted them all together, but in the best of all worlds, they remain mercifully invisible to the customers who they were invented to serve.

To normal humans, the OnStar brand isn't really supposed to be about technology at all; it's about a simple, small blue button in the car that represents a very personal connection to real people when our customers need them the most. Customers have described it as their wingman, a copilot, or "my amazing guardian angel." It started by promising the unimaginable at the time—that it would automatically know when your vehicle had been in a crash and immediately summon help to the precise location of the crash scene. But OnStar has always been about more than that. In its broadest sense, it's about always being there for you and providing peace of mind to you or a loved one while on the road, because life happens while you're driving.

It's the friendly, professional, well-trained voice of an OnStar advisor who is there for you if there's been a medical emergency, if you've got a flat tire or mechanical problem, or if you're trapped in a snowstorm, hurricane, forest fire—you name it, it's happened. It's a connection to the cavalry when you've witnessed a crash and want to be a Good Samaritan, when you've seen a road hazard, or when you have information about a missing child. It's your posse when some lowlife has stolen your car and you want it back and you'd like to see the crook behind bars. It's a convenient, high-power, hands-free calling system that lets you keep your eyes on the road and hands on the wheel if you need to carry on a conversation while driving. It's help in finding a destination, and then in guiding you there safely, turn by turn, without the expense or distraction of a screen in the car. And it's the comfort and peace of mind of having something as technically complex and intimidating as a modern automobile completely demystified by turning a monthly analysis of over 1,600 diagnostic codes, including checking the air in your tires, into a thoughtful e-mail from your car that lets you know that its feeling just fine.

Today, none of this sounds particularly revolutionary or dramatic because we've already been doing it for well over a decade. Millions of OnStar subscribers have interacted with the system hundreds of millions of times, and the brand has become extremely well known for its peace-of-mind mission. But it wasn't always that way because all new initiatives have to work their way through the twists and turns and myriad of life-threatening catastrophes that invariably await those who attempt profound innovation. Statistically, most fail, but the lucky ones that survive will begin to create their own unique history and maybe even a story worth trying to capture. I'm hopeful that's what this book accomplishes.

The following chapters were written immediately following my retirement as president of OnStar, a role I held for fourteen years since the business's founding in 1995. It relies on the best of my memories, supplemented by the observations of many of the individuals involved and otherwise available public information. It tells the story of OnStar's creation, challenges, and subsequent growth into a multibillion-dollar enterprise through my eyes—someone who was assigned to lead the effort without the baggage or benefit of years of experience with the industries, technologies, or laws of innovation that were at the core of the opportunity.

I'd worked for General Motors all of my life, starting at age eighteen as a co-op engineering student at a college that was owned by the company. I assumed that I'd probably work for GM for my entire career, and it seemed like that was going to be the case as I settled into an interesting and comfortable career path working in the company's locomotive business. Over the years, I found the company to have the characteristics that you'd expect to find in an extremely large, decades-old enterprise: massive scale, mature business processes, a deeply embedded culture of historical success, and layers of bureaucracy that had grown up over time to support such a mammoth and geographically diverse corporation.

What I also experienced, and probably valued the most, was the company's "Midwestern personality"—a straightforward, ethical, high-integrity approach to dealing with its business. And while everybody in a company as large as GM didn't behave that way all of the time, I honestly knew I could rely on it as the institutional instinct of the organization. This wasn't a place that made its living by being overly slick or shady or trying to intentionally cut corners or fool people. No, this was a place where you could count on support for demonstrating the appropriate kinds of personal behaviors and for doing the right thing, and that was something that always made me very proud.

It was after nearly a quarter of a century with GM that my career abruptly changed. It took a hard right turn through a sadly brief, but important encounter with an amazing educational institution that provided a unique and invaluable perspective on leadership. Then just as suddenly it veered left and picked up speed as it entered the unmapped territory that was to become OnStar, the professional adventure of my lifetime. It all happened so fast, and with no real warning, that there wasn't time for thoughtful deliberation or reflection.

It was as though my raft had capsized mid-rapids, and navigating the whitewater that was all around me had just become a lot more personal and a lot less predictable. It was exciting, confusing, exhilarating, frustrating, fun, and just plain scary as hell, all at the same time. And what I thought I knew about myself and GM was being challenged and stretched in ways that would have been hard to imagine just a brief time before.

The characteristics that described General Motors were all still there, but now they took on new meaning and held different implications for a start-up business like OnStar. Massive scale, strong processes, and the order and structure of existing bureaucracy were traits that could possibly translate into strengths for a new business to leverage, or they might be burdensome encumbrances that weighed it down and prevented it from being creative and agile – it all depended. And a longstanding culture of success could be very positive if it had a living, breathing nature to it, something that not only tolerated reinvention, but embraced it as a fundamental prerequisite for future success. If, however, success had taken on the calcified rigidity of a historic relic and was more prone to look backward than forward, then it could be a problem—again, it all depended.

As GM was a hundred-year-old car company, it would have been easy to argue polar opposite positions as to whether its age made it the best or worst place in the world to try to do something as off-template from its core business as OnStar. Unfortunately, it wasn't that simple. Everything about trying to answer that question fairly ended up including the ambiguous "it depends." And most of the "it depends" depended on the people involved and the unique context created by all of the other events that were taking place inside and around GM and the global auto industry during those times.

The good news was that the people that mattered most within the corporation were able to turn its potential assets into real ones. And the timing of the initiative intersected with a narrow, but extremely important window of opportunity where GM had both the resources and risk-taking appetite necessary to give OnStar a chance to come to life. The other good news was that the characteristic of GM that I admired the most, an instinct for doing the right thing, fell naturally in line with what this new business was destined to be all about. In my estimation, it took all of these factors, along with patience, tenacity, and a little luck, to have the story turn out the way it did. That didn't mean there weren't countervailing forces, because there were. Some were the natural challenges that confront all serious innovation, and some were the self-inflicted wounds caused by the customs and dysfunctional behaviors too often tolerated within large, mature organizations. But, on balance, it turned out that the timing was right, the key people displayed the requisite vision, commitment and courage to get the job done, and our growing appreciation for the importance of the mission provided ample reserve energy to get us through even the darkest of moments.

Now, with something as interesting and open-ended as OnStar turned out to be, there are many ways to approach telling this story. With over two hundred million service interactions and counting, you could easily fill a book with hundreds of real-life examples of the things OnStar has already done—responding to crashes, medical emergencies, large-scale crisis events, carjackings, or even the more amusing events of freeing a pet monkey that had locked itself inside of its owner's car. That orientation would push the strategic, technological, and organizational issues into the background and focus on the emotion of what OnStar has meant to real people. That would be a fun book to write, and one that I hope someday gets written.

Or this could have been a book about business lessons learned. OnStar has already been the subject of a number of academic papers, including cases now being taught at the Harvard Business School. With all of the interest in innovation in today's business literature, surely there'd be room for one more book that attempted to distill the experiences of OnStar's launch into bite-sized theories that could be useful to future innovators or corporate strategists. Or maybe it could be a book that tried to prove that GM was actually an under-appreciated juggernaut of innovation and had done everything right and that OnStar's success proved it. Conversely different facts, spun in a little different direction, might have confirmed GM's election to the Rust Belt Museum's Hall of Fame because they'd done everything wrong—and that OnStar's survival had been a miracle.

I actually didn't come into this with a point of view to promote, a business theory to evangelize, or an ax to grind. In all honestly, I came to this story with an immense sense of pride and a sincere desire to somehow capture and document an unexpected and amazing personal journey before it was lost to memory. That pride took many forms and covered a very wide range of people and institutions. It was pride in General Motors and many of its senior leaders for their dedication and resolve in bringing OnStar to life—for doing the right thing. It was pride in our customers for their willingness to encourage and support our progress, for their desire to help others, and most of all, for allowing us to occupy a special place in their lives. It was pride in the too often under-recognized contributions of the emergency response community: doctors, nurses, paramedics, police, firefighters, and 911 dispatchers. These people, and the institutions they represent, are truly national treasures. It was pride in our many business partners who took leaps of faith and applied their best efforts to a cause that initially had anything but a certain outcome. And, most importantly, it was pride in the wonderful team of people who made up my OnStar family for their dedication, hard work, courage, and contagious passion they brought to the business every day.

So this story is my best attempt to tell all of their stories, along with my own. It's as real and unfiltered as my memory of the events and the emotions they stirred in me at the time would allow. There are places where many of the people involved might wince, including me, because things didn't always go as planned and because life has an annoying tendency to unfold in unexpected ways. The tumblers aren't constantly aligned, progress isn't linear except in hindsight, and more often than not complex situations aren't black and white, but are more likely to leave a mark that's black and blue. Unfortunately, those moments were as real and important to the nature of the story as the many places where things went right, and to ignore them and only highlight positive events would have been misleading. Including my view of the entire picture—the good, the bad, and the ugly—wasn't intended to needlessly disparage certain individuals in order to further elevate the contributions of others, but to make this story as authentic and unvarnished as real life always seems to be.

But, even in recognizing the reality of those challenges, something really special has happened in the creation of this business—an improbable and heroic accomplishment for GM and the many special people who were so intimately involved. And, for me, the past fourteen years provided an amazing personal opportunity to experience an extremely rare event—something like being swept up inside the vortex of a tornado. I can only imagine that, if I lived through it, I'd feel the need to tell the story, to explain what it felt like, what I saw, and how I survived. Not that it would necessarily add to the science of tornadoes or prevent future roofs from being blown off, but it might be useful to somebody someday—and maybe actually be a little entertaining along the way. So this is my view from inside the tornado, a tornado that formed when a monstrously large company slammed overconfidently into the immutably unpredictable laws of innovation. It's a real story, one part personal journey, one part business lesson, and two hundred million parts that fall into the category of "you can't make this stuff up."

OnStar wasn't conceived and built in a test tube. And it certainly wasn't destined to turn into anything that you'd be reading about today, as it experienced more near-death experiences than Luigi from Super Mario Brothers. It started as a fuzzy idea, bounced around like a pinball inside of what was once the world's largest industrial company, and through a series of mostly unscripted events, it ended up evolving into a business that produced incredible results. There were the financial numbers that made it a very interesting business story and were necessary to keep the skeptics inside GM from shutting us down, but more important to those of us who lived in the business were the results that literally changed peoples' lives. They reinforced the meaning and purpose of the effort and provided numerous compelling examples of what's possible when corporations act on their most noble instincts and engage in courageous innovation.

Now I can tell you for sure that this isn't meant to be a how-to business book—it couldn't be. If the last fourteen years taught me anything, it's that there are no seven rules of innovation or really cool entrepreneurial templates worthy of lamination. No, if I get this right, it will be more like a rambling case study, where life inside and around OnStar provides a view into what happened when an established company tried to do something different—really different.

What I think I've learned to appreciate over the past fourteen years is how vitally important it will be for all enterprises, especially the more mature ones, to embrace the fundamental need to innovate, and how hard that will be. I believe the OnStar story, with all of its twists and turns and hopefully never-to-be-duplicated flaming craters, might provide some school of hard knocks insights into that process and possibly illuminate the rough terrain ahead. The sad reality is that, in a world full of low-cost labor, shrinking logistics barriers, and highly mobile technology and capital, American companies have no choice but to grow their leadership in innovation—and fast.

Will that be easy? No. It's messy, convoluted, uncertain, ambiguous, and non-linear. It's one step forward and sometimes twenty steps sideways. It involves forces outside of your control and will require unimaginable effort. You can't assign it to an existing department or appoint a Czar to make happen. It will collide head-on, at high speed, with existing culture, processes, and reward systems and will lose far more often than it will win. And it will insidiously confound accurate measurement using traditional methods, appearing near death when actually healthy, and vice versa. But I'm optimistic. With all of the challenges, volatility, and risks involved, if a company like General Motors can do this, then many others can, too.

I want to thank you in advance for taking your valuable time to read this book. I hope you find it interesting, useful, and maybe just a little entertaining. And if you've ever been an OnStar subscriber, I also want to thank you for the privilege that you've given me and a very special group of people at OnStar to work on your behalf for a cause that brought meaning to all of our lives. It was a gift and a blessing, the opportunity of my professional lifetime, and something that's left me grateful beyond measure.

CHAPTER 1

A Little Context

The following email was sent to all OnStar employees at 8:02 a.m. on July 30, 2009:

Dear Fellow OnStarians,

This morning, there will be a number of announcements regarding upcoming organizational changes at GM, including one involving my planned retirement under the recently announced GM window program and the appointment of Walt Dorfstatter as my successor as the president of OnStar, both effective October 1.

It's been an interesting process, both personally and professionally, to consider retirement, and something I've actually been discussing with the folks at GM over the past couple of years. In my thirty-seven years with the company, I've seen numerous examples of transitions, some happened too soon, some too late, and some were just right— which is what this timing feels like to me. When I first had the opportunity to become involved in Project Beacon back in 1995, there was an idea, a spark, but nothing tangible or real. There were many close calls for the project in the early days, and the leaders at GM could have easily pulled the plug on this initiative. There were numerous risks and unknowns, but courageously, they stuck with it, which gave us the chance to develop a deeper level of confidence in the idea and a growing personal resolve to take it to the next level.

Fast-forward fourteen years, and a lot has happened. Technology has changed, the world has changed, GM has changed, and our idea has blossomed into what most people in the U.S. and Canada have fondly come to know as OnStar. It's taken a lot of hard work, a little luck, an occasional shoestring catch, boatloads of learning, patience, and strong support from our parent, and the creation of an amazingly talented team of emotionally dedicated professionals who make up the OnStar family. But the family has grown much bigger than just us and now includes our nearly 6 million subscribers who have come to know, appreciate, and count on us to amaze and delight them with our ideas and technology and to occupy a very special and trusted place in their lives.

So I honestly think this is the "just right" time for a transition for me. The challenges are not over, the opportunity is not mature, a plateau has not been reached, but a strong foundation has been laid. Important things are always hard to do and harder to maintain, but gloriously worth the effort. This team has lived that dream for over a decade and is now in a wonderful position to take it to the next level. The extremely good news in all of this is that Fritz and the senior leadership within GM are intimately involved with this business and are passionate about its prospects. The other good news is that we've got an extremely talented and deeply experienced leader in Walt, someone I couldn't be prouder of and who will bring tremendous strengths and capabilities in leading this business through the next important phase of its expansion. I know you'll give him all the support that you've always given me as he steps into this critical role.

In closing, I'd just like to say what an incredible pleasure and privilege it's been to have been associated with this business, and all of you, over the past fourteen years. This has been a gift, and I couldn't be prouder of what we've all labored so diligently to create and the life-changing impact we've already had on so many peoples' lives. And while my days of stalking those unfortunate early customers whose antennas I recognized at the car wash on the corner of Mack and Kerby are over, I will continue whenever and wherever I can to be one of OnStar's most enthusiastic cheerleaders.

I'll be here in support of the transition through mid-September and hope to have a chance to thank many of you personally for all of your support over our time together. But if I don't get that opportunity, thank you and good luck on all of your future successes.
With warmest regards and deep respect,

Chet

So that's how it ended. After nearly four decades at General Motors, the last fourteen years of which were spent working on what had become the professional cause of my life, I announced my retirement from OnStar on an otherwise nondescript Thursday morning in July. What had been over five thousand days (and nights) of eating, sleeping, worrying, scheming, regrouping, celebrating, and worrying some more about a business that had been the focus of my energy and passion for so long was now on the verge of moving into the rearview mirror. What an incredible range of emotions ran through my head as I hit the send button to let my OnStar family know that I was leaving.

My note was actually timed to be part of a broader set of GM leadership announcements that were being made that morning, the first wave of the massive restructuring that was going on within the new General Motors. In an ironic twist of fate, GM had actually emerged from bankruptcy and been reborn a couple of weeks earlier on July 10, my fifty-fifth birthday. That date held significance for me since I'd told GM's CEO, Rick Wagoner, two years before that I was planning on leaving when I reached fifty-five, the earliest age that I was eligible to qualify for GM's executive retirement program.

I'd worked pretty closely with Rick over the past fourteen years, liked and respected him a lot, and was pretty sure he thought he'd be able to talk me out of leaving when the time got closer. But things had changed dramatically over those two years, and none of that seemed to matter much anymore. Rick himself had already left the company, not by choice, but by being forced out by the Obama administration's automotive task force five months earlier. It didn't seem fair, but when your last source of liquidity is the U.S. Treasury, and you need $60 billion to stay afloat, somebody else gets to be the decider. That's just business—in this case, topped with a heavy dose of politics.

But sometimes, if we're lucky, we get to make our own choices, and for a lot of reasons, I had made mine two years earlier. If anything, the turmoil from the bailout and the subsequent jockeying-for-position that was taking place within Rick's former staff to curry favor with the task force was just making my choice easier to live with. But it wasn't about that turmoil anyway. The note to my team was absolutely sincere; for a lot of reasons, it was the right time to turn over the controls to OnStar's next pilot.

The business was in really good shape. We'd beaten the odds and accomplished a lot more than anyone, including me, had thought we could in the past fourteen years. We'd established a new and very successful business, with a strong and entrepreneurial culture, within a parent company not recently known for either success or innovation. We'd built from whole cloth a business model that worked, extremely well, and had assembled a team of professionals that was amazingly talented and deeply passionate about their work. Our brand had become nationally prominent and very well respected, and not because we'd spent zillions of dollars on slick marketing spin. Our message resonated because we'd developed a real track record of listening to our customers, respecting their point of view, and driving technology to do important things—like save peoples' lives. And despite the many doubters within GM over the years, the data now made it overwhelmingly clear that OnStar had become a major competitive advantage for GM vehicles, something that could make a real difference.

So with everything going so well, why leave now? Wouldn't this be the time to take a deep breath, clear your head, and put the helmet back on for the second half? For a couple of reasons that were important to me, I didn't think so. First, earlier in my career I'd worked for a division of GM that made locomotives, and during one stretch, we had the same general manager running that business for over fifteen years. He wasn't a bad guy, but what that taught me was that unless your name is on the building, it's probably not healthy for any business to be led by the same person for that long, no matter how good they might be.

What I had a chance to see in those fifteen years was that where our long-serving leader was strong, we were really good, and where he was weak, we stunk. And the organization had just plain figured him out. They knew what he liked and what would send him through the roof. You know what happens next. Everything got stale and overly templated. Maybe he knew that or maybe he didn't, but it didn't change the fact that the business's compass heading had been stuck on autopilot for years.

Now, in the locomotive business where things didn't change all that fast, maybe it wasn't such a big deal. But in a business like On-Star, where the dynamics of the industry we were creating were in a constant state of change, the need to reinvent something before the paint was dry on the last invention was just a fact of life. The continual churning was something I'd gotten used to—heck, in a warped way, I'd actually learned to enjoy it. But there was no sense in trying to kid myself; I knew I'd developed tendencies and patterns, my own personal idiosyncratic ways of trying to stay on the bucking bronco's back. Logically, it seemed like it was only a matter of time before he figured me out, threw me off, and hurt both me and the business. In other words, a new leadership perspective would be healthy for everyone.

Second, while I loved OnStar and the people I worked with, launching and growing the business inside a hundred-year-old car company had required a ton of energy and presented more than its fair share of frustrations. Some were natural, the unavoidable stuff you get in any start-up situation. Why won't the dealers get behind the product? How come the suppliers are late again? Who broke the software, and why does it cost so much to fix? Why did we have our own customer pulled over by the police? (This actually happened.) Those frustrations build character, provide learning and bonding opportunities, help you sort out the people on the team who have it from those who don't, and give you an excuse to drink—heavily. They're the bottoms of the sinusoids that make reaching the tops that much sweeter.

Unfortunately, in addition to the normal start-up issues, we'd been served up an unending stream of unnatural frustrations that came directly from what could only be described as the darker side of GM's culture. There were friendly-fire incidents, corporate wedgies, bloated egos, and professional incompetence elevated to high art. And the worst part was they weren't necessary, they weren't rational, and with so much that still needed to be done, they weren't anything I had the energy to deal with anymore. The fact that those behaviors were tolerated within the company, despite all of the obvious signs that business-as-usual wasn't working anymore, still surprises and saddens me.

It was a vehicle marketing approach that glorified the deal over the product, preferring to focus on new and different ways to package cash rebates rather than building brands with care and substance and, when given the choice, to advertise the benefits of heated windshield washer fluid and sliding SUV roofs that let you carry a grandfather clock standing up rather than the unique and potentially lifesaving benefits of OnStar. It was a corporate oversight process that was more than happy to have our growing profit stream just so long as we behaved like good team players and cut salaried employees and investment dollars to fall consistently in line with what was happening inside the shrinking vehicle business. It was a schizophrenic attitude toward customers that gyrated between genuine empathy and callus monetization. And, at a much more personal level, it was the hair-on-fire frustration that came from being bounced around inside GM's reporting structure—literally, seven times—with the accompanying distractions and emotional turmoil that came from each new superior's unavoidable need to tinker with what we were doing because they thought it was their job.

No, I'd gotten too old and we'd come way too far by my estimation to put a happy face on that anymore. I'd done what I could to talk openly about those issues over the years; sometimes people listened, but nothing ever really changed. At some point, it ceases to be constructive, and you turn into a whiner, even to yourself. And nobody deserves a whining leader, not GM, or more importantly, not the team that I'd help build and who were working so hard to make OnStar successful. I'd seen and experienced bad leadership too many times in my thirty-seven years with the company—typically in the form of a rationalizing, cynical, grumpy character who felt justified in blaming the system for everything that went wrong, and doing it with a clear conscience. I wanted a clear conscience, and it felt to me like the only way to get one was to leave.

So it was the right time for me to move on. The business was in a good place, and Walt was ready to step in and provide a great balance of intellectual horsepower, fresh perspective, and emotional continuity. And I was stepping down before my personal frustrations had the chance to impact my passion for our mission and turn me into someone that would be unable to lead with the enthusiasm and energy that the OnStar team deserved. So much had been accomplished, but there was still so much to do, so much potential. It's hard to imagine a better ending for me personally, as I'd reached an amazing destination. But life has taught me that it's really a lot more about the people you meet and your experiences along the way than it is about the place you eventually get off the train—so on with the journey!

CHAPTER 2

It Begins

It was a fairly dreary Tuesday in mid-November 1994 when I opened my apartment door in Alexandria and saw a fax on my living room table. It's hard to remember the pre-email days, but back then, getting a fax usually meant that it was something important. Turns out it was an organizational announcement from my boss, Electro-Motive Division's (EMD) general manager John Jarrell. I wondered who'd moved where. Somewhere in the first sentence it said, "announcing my retirement." What? Announcing whose retirement? My boss John's? The guy that was responsible for me living six hundred miles away from home for a year in Virginia? And replaced by Bill Happel? Who the heck was that?

I was stunned, saddened, and then angry all in the span of about five seconds. Stunned because I had no idea John was thinking of retiring. Saddened because John was my boss, and someone that I liked and deeply respected, and who respected me. On the roulette table of corporate reporting relationships, I'd already worked for enough knuckleheads to know how rare that was. My sense of loss was immediate and surprisingly strong. The last reaction, anger, was even stronger. The announcement said this Bill Happel guy was being dropped in to run a global locomotive company after completing a successful assignment in GM's die management organization. *Die management?* What in the world was that, what did it have to do with us, and what could he possibly know about the locomotive business?

The answers to these questions: First, die management is a group dedicated to quickly swapping out the dies in stamping presses that are used to smash rolled steel into car fenders and door panels. The faster you can swap the dies, the fewer stamping presses you need to build the same number of vehicles. The Japanese had mastered this, mainly because floor space in plants was harder to get in Nagoya, Japan, than it was in Flint, Michigan. A few industry analysts picked up on their advantage and used it as another embarrassing example of how much better the Japanese were at running car companies. Our response was to call this a crisis, invent a die management organization to address it, name a leader, create and achieve some internal objectives, and claim success. Second, what does it have to do with us? Nothing. Third, what does he know about the locomotive business? Nothing. Now, I'm familiar enough with big companies to know that this approach to succession is not entirely unique to GM. But I know GM the best, and this is absolutely typical of how a reasonable idea, refined by decades of bureaucracy, turns into corporate insanity. Does it make sense to create "career paths" for your best and brightest talent to experience a wide range of challenges and hone their leadership skills for even more important assignments in the future? Sure it does—*sometimes*. But somewhere along the line someone forgot the sometimes and institutionalized an approach that treated way too many leaders like interchangeable parts. At best, this was a well-intended, yet naive throwback to a time when GM was so dominant that it didn't matter who the caretaker at Stonehenge was; it still predicted eclipses. At worst, it was an arrogant disregard for the brutal nature of capitalism by undervaluing the importance of profound experience and institutional knowledge, while simultaneously demotivating the team inheriting the rotationally assigned leader. Ugh!

The reason why the fax was so important to this story is that while nothing is ever a done deal, I'd actually been encouraged to think that my twenty-two years at EMD had positioned me to be a pretty good candidate to take John's job when he retired at some point in the future, but it wasn't supposed to be happening *now*! This timing was terrible. This decision was awful. It was all wrong. It couldn't have been worse. John had talked me into moving to Washington, DC, spending a year away from my family and out of my career path, and attending a military college at age forty, with the sense that it would help "round me out" and better position me for the future. What could that mean other than getting me ready for his job? Except his job was just taken by a forty-five-year-old graduate of die management who'd probably be in it for a while. What a mess this was turning into—little did I know.

A LITTLE BACKGROUND

I was born in Hammond, Indiana, the fourth of six children, all girls except me. Dad was a World War II veteran, came from a family of eleven, and while he'd never gotten around to finishing college after the war, he had worked his way into a job as chief chemist for one of Mobil's lube plants in the Chicago suburbs. My mom, from a family of eight, was a quintessential homemaker who also occasionally worked outside the home and still made sure everything around the house ran like clockwork. It was truly a "back in the day" family lifestyle. Dad's bacon and eggs every morning must not have done permanent damage considering he's still performing his annual ritual of "the Cubs have a chance" (April) and "fire whoever the manager is" (usually by July) at the age of eighty-eight. Mom always made sure we were together for dinner every night and lined up in the pew at church every Sunday morning. When we're in town, she still does.

Up until eighth grade, I was more or less a B+ student. My early grade school report cards probably captured it best in a grading system I still think works pretty well for most situations. Remember those ratings for scholarship, effort, and conduct? My scholarship was generally near the top rating, my effort one level lower, and for too long, my conduct was in the "needs improvement" category. Apparently, my problem was that I felt compelled to share whatever I was thinking with whoever was in earshot whenever I wanted. I blame it on growing up in a house full of mostly older sisters where I couldn't get much airtime, so I saved it all for school. Anyway, no harm, no foul, B+ seemed good enough to me, and I got pretty comfortable with that self-image.

Then came my first year of high school. But before that came word that my dad had gotten transferred from his plant in the Chicago suburbs to one in St. Paul, Minnesota. Minnesota? That sounded cold, far away, and generally unappealing. But there was no vote. I'm not even sure if Dad had a vote, really, so off we went.

The bad news was that I knew nobody, which may have solved the chronic conduct challenge. Without as many distractions, I actually found myself doing pretty well in school—like straight A's for the first time ever. And it didn't seem terrible. At five feet two inches, I actually made the freshman basketball team, something that would have been impossible in Indiana. I'd like to think it had to do with my emerging jump shot, but mainly, it was because everybody in Minnesota who had any athletic ability played hockey. Whatever. I got to play, and we still had cheerleaders on the sidelines (even if the cute ones were all wearing ice skates).

And at the end of the year came stranger news than the year before. Dad was being transferred back to the original plant that he had been at in Chicago. Again, no vote, but we didn't even get to move back to the same city we'd left since Dad was looking for a shorter commute. I couldn't blame him, but the end result was another complete change of classmates and another place with no base of friends. The added challenge of this move was that the school was huge; Harold L. Richards High School had a thousand students in the sophomore class. And while this wasn't Indiana, Illinois boys played basketball almost as well. I had grown, but five feet six inches wasn't going to make the team at this school, so a lot had changed.

What hadn't changed was my newly acquired self-image as a good student. So I made new friends and spent the next three years growing up and becoming surprisingly competent in math and science. Somewhere around the end of my junior year, I found myself thinking about college, more or less because that's what most of my friends were doing. Nobody in my family had yet gone to college, but at some point, it just seemed like I had to go. But where? And, more importantly, what to be when I grow up?

I'd heard one of my classmates, Dennis, say he was going to be an engineer because that's what his father was. I honestly had no idea what an engineer was, but Dennis was good at math and science, too, and it sounded good. It especially sounded good to be able to say something specific rather than not knowing. I ultimately ended up with really good grades in high school and a very high score on my ACT, so, ready or not, my next stop was engineering school.

I looked at brochures from more schools than I can remember, which back in the day really meant brochures actually sent through the mail. I ended up applying at a number of pretty good colleges and thought I might be headed out east to school. At some point, money was going to be an object, or more precisely, lack of money was going to be an obstruction. That's when my high school advisor, Mr. Latitto, asked me if I'd ever heard of a school in Michigan called GMI. General Motors Institute, or GMI, was something that only GM, in its scale and global reach, could have conceived. Forget the fact that there were literally hundreds of universities around the world that granted engineering degrees, General Motors at some point decided to start their own. Founded in 1919, GMI had evolved into a fully accredited college granting bachelor's degrees in mechanical, electrical, and industrial engineering and a form of a business degree in industrial administration.

GMI was set up as a very unique five-year co-op engineering program. That meant you needed to be accepted by the college and then find a division of GM that would "sponsor" you for your "work sections." The year was set up in alternating six-week sections between the campus in Flint, Michigan, and wherever your division assigned you to spend your time on the job. The concept was actually pretty good: Get drilled with calculus, thermodynamics, physics, and organic chemistry for a month and a half and then head back to some work assignment where there might actually be a place to try it out. It didn't always work that way, but six weeks of Newton's various means of torturing a young mind, even one good at math and science, was probably enough anyway.

All right, thanks Mr. Latitto, but who's ever heard of GMI? Who does their football team play? And what do the girls look like? The answers: People have heard of GMI, just not people that you've heard of. There is no football team, save a version of intramural flag football that could only be appreciated if you wear a pocket protector. And girls? Well, technically, there were some girls in the program (probably 10 out of 250 in the freshman class), but there was a nursing school in Flint. Ouch, ouch, and ouch.

Then he hit below the belt, telling me I could earn enough during my work sections to more than pay my own way through school, GM had a program to pay for graduate school at "real" universities if you did well, and if you didn't like it, you could always transfer out to another school after your freshman year and have enough credits to be a second semester sophomore at most other colleges. That sealed it. The next thing I knew, I had interviewed at the closest GM facility to where I lived in Illinois, something called the Electro-Motive Division, or EMD, was accepted, and on August 20, 1972, began my career with GM.

THIS IS AN INTERESTING COMPANY

In 1924, an entrepreneur named H. L. Hamilton started the St. Louis Car Company to design and build diesel-electric trolley cars. It was back in the era when the big railroads of the day were operating massively large and powerful steam locomotives and controlled the majority of freight service across the country. Hamilton's little business grew and prospered, so much so that it ended up being one of the largest customers of the company that had been supplying them with engines—Cleveland Diesel.

As it happened, Cleveland Diesel sold their engines for a few different applications, one of which was to power large yachts. One of those yachts was owned by GM's legendary first head of engineering and research, Charles "Boss" Kettering. As the story goes, always the engineer even when off the clock, Kettering preferred spending more time in his yacht's engine room tinkering with the diesels than resting on a deck chair sipping chardonnay. After many back-and-forth discussions with the engineers at Cleveland telling them how to change their engines, Kettering felt comfortable enough with the company to suggest to GM's then CEO, Alfred Sloan, that GM buy them. Hey, why not? This was General Motors, for heaven's sake, and this seemed like something general involving motors, or at least engines.

During the formal evaluation of the business, GM saw that Hamilton's railcar business was a big customer of Cleveland's and decided the concept of general and motors applied to that business as well. So, in 1933, GM acquired Cleveland Diesel and the St. Louis Car Company and ultimately merged them into something they called the Electro-Motive Division of GM, or EMD. This was a time of incredible industrial growth and expansion, and GM intended to be a player on as many fronts involving transportation as possible.

So here I am thirty-nine years later, in 1972, driving up for my first day of work at EMD's sprawling 343-acre facility in LaGrange, Illinois. Surrounded on three sides by massive open limestone quarries, but still in the middle of the western suburbs of Chicago, it seemed like its own city, with a few million square feet under roof, somewhere over twelve thousand employees, and the ability to crank out four locomotives a day. Needless to say, at eighteen years old, it was a pretty big step up from my last position as bag boy and occasional back-up cashier at the local Certified grocery store.

And what an amazing next step it was. I decided to study mechanical engineering, mainly because I challenge anyone to think of a more perfect spot for someone to be a mechanical engineer. A locomotive is basically a 450,000-pound, 4,000-diesel-horsepower, DC-motor-powered mobile science project. A standard six-axle long-haul locomotive only has twelve contact patches the size of your thumbnail, where steel wheels meet steel rails with a coefficient of friction about the same as your shoes on wet ice. It's managing to get all of that horsepower, generated from pistons the size of large paint cans, down to those slippery, small contact spots to pull a hundred fully loaded coal cars out of the Powder River Basin in Wyoming, that makes you have to use almost every one of Newton's bloody equations. And just to make it a little more interesting, if it happens to be autumn and some wet leaves have fallen on the tracks somewhere along the way, the whole equation changes. That's either crazy or way cool and was something that caused many people to switch majors from engineering to business.

From almost any standpoint, EMD was massive but, more often than not, got lost in the rounding inside GM. There were times when that wasn't all bad, and thankfully, EMD was so different than the much bigger car business that it was generally left alone to manage its own affairs. The main exceptions were that investment decisions required approval by the corporate folks in GM, and occasionally, someone was sent from Detroit to rotate through the general manager's chair or to be the CFO and watch the money.

And, boy, was there money. EMD had built such a dominant business position over the decades that it was sending cash by the truckload eastbound on I-94 to Detroit. The only domestic competitor, GE, had a much smaller market share of new locomotives and only got that because the big railroads wanted a second source to keep EMD honest. Back then, GE locomotives were deficient on every meaningful performance measure, always had been, and their relatively lower revenue kept them from generating the investment cash flow that would have been necessary to change the situation. It was a fairly stable duopoly. GE made some money; EMD printed money. It worked well until it didn't, which was the result of too many complex factors moving too fast in too many different directions to do justice here.

But I'm getting ahead of myself. In my personal case, my co-op engineering experience beginning in 1972 was actually terrific. Alternating six-week periods in LaGrange were spent on interesting assignments in engineering, manufacturing, quality, service, and personnel, basically every function of the business. And then there was GMI in Flint, where the atmosphere was more factory than college town. But it did have a couple of things that made it tolerable.

First, the people at the school, both students and faculty, were all great to be around. Sure they were all focused and reasonably intense since the whole school was studying to be engineers, but it also led to pretty strong bonding opportunities as we all tried to find ways to play as hard as we were studying. Second, it didn't hurt that the drinking age in Michigan had magically been lowered to eighteen the year before I got there, which meant the playing part was typically lubricated by $2 pitchers of Stroh's on most nights of the week.

GM actually had created a pretty interesting asset in GMI. It allowed them to tailor the curriculum toward the engineering tracks most important to the auto industry, while providing a five-year auditioning period during the co-op phase to evaluate the talent. In the meantime, GM got some pretty productive technical work out of people making student wages and had the chance to institutionalize a type of company loyalty unlike anything else in corporate America. In today's world, with hyper career mobility much more the norm, GMI as an in-house college ultimately made less and less sense, and in the 1990s, it spun out of GM to become Kettering University. Kettering still retains the core proposition of a co-op education, with its student body now connected to hundreds of companies instead of just GM. It's still a great school, but times changed and life went on.

About the time I reached my senior year, my old high school counselor's coaching really came back to pay dividends. GM did indeed have a program called the GM Fellowship to send selected students on to graduate school. Despite the Stroh's, I'd gotten pretty good grades at GMI, and since the folks I worked for at EMD liked me, they supported my application for a fellowship to attend the Harvard Business School and pursue an MBA. Under that program, GM picked up all of my tuition, fees, and books and even gave me a monthly living allowance—with no strings attached. You could go to school for two years, graduate with a master's degree with all of your bills paid, and literally leave the company the next day owing nothing. I certainly felt committed to the folks at EMD who had supported me, and I fully intended to come back, but unfortunately, enough other people over the years didn't, and GM eventually eliminated the program altogether. Well, at least in my case it all fell together, and I was off to Boston.

THESE ARE SOME AMAZING PEOPLE

There's been enough written about the Harvard Business School over the years that I'm sure I won't be able to add much of value. It's a great school with very talented people who have a very clear plan on how to go about doing its business.

Back then, the school was divided up into ten sections of about seventy-five people each, and you sat in the same room, in the same seat, for the entire first year as they shuttled in the professors for each course. Their rules, at least back in the day, were that there would be a forced curve where at least 10 percent of each class, or about eight people, would be given a grade of LP, or low pass. If you collected a modest number of those scores, you would "hit the screen," which meant you'd be reviewed for dismissal from the program.

Now think about this. These were really smart, type A people. More Summa Cum Laudes per square inch than you could possibly imagine, and you're telling them that they have a statistically reasonable chance of catching one of these low passes. And how do you get them? Well, in most classes, 50 percent of your ultimate grade was based on class participation, which made the competition for airtime in class with seventy-five people in the room pretty intense. And while you were frantically bobbing up and down in your chair trying to get called on, you were simultaneously trying to identify the eight people who were dumber than you in each class, whether it was marketing, accounting, finance, economics, or whatever. Just about the time you thought you were safe, one of the folks you were banking on to absorb one of the low passes would say something brilliant, which left you feeling incredibly exposed.

I can't say I really liked that part of the program, but maybe it was necessary to keep that many smart folks focused and engaged. Or maybe it was intended to toughen you up for the realities of capitalism. Or maybe in some deeply nuanced way it was supposed to help you absorb the material. Or maybe it was just because it had always been that way, a part of the hazing ritual for decades, and nobody wanted to change it. It didn't really matter, it was what it was. But it did ultimately give you some sense that you could hold your own with a talented group of overachievers in an environment that was equal parts collegial, competitive, and confrontational.

At around the same time, something interesting and unplanned happened just about two months before I was scheduled to leave for school. One of my older sisters, Sharon, who was a flight attendant for American Airlines, decided to set me up on a blind date with someone that she had recently flown with. I'd been after her for years to introduce me to some of her airline friends, and for whatever reason, she'd always told me the time wasn't right. Well, now, when it was probably the worst time for a distraction that I could've imagined, on the eve of jumping into the unknowns of business school, she thought the time was right.

All I was told was that her friend's name was Barbara Anderson, that she was very nice, and that if Sharon got any bad reports back from her after the date that I would pay—dearly. I called, and we agreed on a Sunday-afternoon tennis game. I knew Barb had a roommate, and when I knocked on the door, an incredibly beautiful woman answered. I was sure Sharon would have described her in more glowing terms than "nice" if this were her, so I assumed I was meeting the roommate. The good news was that it was Barb, and the better news was that she was actually more beautiful on the inside than on the outside. The bad news was that as nice as she was, she still showed no mercy or remorse when she beat me at tennis.

We saw a lot of each other between mid-June and when I left for Harvard in mid-August, and it was clear to me that this was a really special person. Nice was an understatement, as I've often described Barb as the kindest and most thoughtful person that I've ever met. She was smart, funny, warm, caring, cute as a button, and for some reason, seemed to like me. Actually, more than like—she accepted my proposal four months later, and we were married between my first and second years in school the following July. Funny how life works out sometimes, just when you think you've got it all figured out, you really don't. I heard once that the way to make God laugh is tell him your plans for life—it certainly has felt that way to me.

Anyway, so now I was a married second-year student, and life was good. Actually, very good, since unlike almost all of my classmates, I was heading toward a graduation in 1979 debt free thanks to my rich uncle, General Motors. And I was coming back to work for EMD, just like we'd agreed. Maybe it wasn't the highest-paying job compared to my classmates, and maybe it wasn't the coolest-sounding title, but GM had been very good to me, I liked the people at EMD, and I really felt the need to follow through on my commitment. So, ready or not, when school ended, it was back to LaGrange and the locomotive business that I loved.

THE EMD YEARS

GM is a funny company. On the one hand, they go out of their way to provide an amazing gift of a terrific blue-chip education. Then when you're done with school and ready to come back, they look at you like that crazy cousin who shows up on your front porch out of nowhere looking for a place to sleep. While I was spending two years in Boston hanging out with folks who were destined to run major companies, start incredible ventures, or hold significant roles in government, everybody else back at EMD was basically getting on with life. It was time for me to get back in line and back to work. There was no crown-prince syndrome here. The week I got back from Harvard, I was assigned to begin my career as a locomotive delivery engineer. That meant traveling to a railroad shop and helping to put a shipment of new locomotives fresh from the factory into service.

Actually, this was one of the fun parts of the business, especially for a mechanical engineer. You fired up the engine, made sure it worked, and got the railroad to sign the acceptance papers required to transfer the title. It was more of a formality than a significant event since the locomotive had a long warranty and the folks working for the Santa Fe had far more experience with our locomotives than we did anyway. I probably didn't need my shiny new MBA for this, but it was interesting work that had to be done and really good experience to be this close to customers. I was now officially "pledging" the locomotive business.

From here, one job led to another. I spent time in the factory working in the quality-control organization and got a chance to learn the interesting, if not completely rational, rules of the road between GM and the United Auto Workers. I then moved into parts marketing, which eventually led to running the aftermarket business for EMD. It had its own profit and loss statement to manage, with about $500 million of annual revenue and profits of over $100 million, which was not big by GM standards, but with scores of competitors and customers in over a hundred countries around the world, it had enough moving parts to be challenging and fun. And I learned a lot.

Ultimately, I was promoted to oversee all of EMD's commercial activities worldwide—the job that I had hoped would put me in a position to someday get a chance to run the locomotive business, which was something I'd always had as a long-term goal. Working for a big company like GM, or even a little part of it like EMD, you never really know how your career might unfold. I've known a lot of people who were always thinking at least two or three moves ahead of their current job, as if they had somehow "broken the code" and figured it all out; however, they may have gotten it right for the first few moves, but then they developed a very strange and distorted view of their career. The whole thing had turned into a game for them, and they became more interested in "winning" the game than handling their responsibilities. For those folks, it didn't seem like the work itself held any intrinsic value or real meaning; their current job was just a square on the chessboard, and their energy was devoted to moving to another square.

Hey, fair enough. It's not my business to make judgments for other people, but it's a pain in the neck when you either end up working for or cleaning up after folks that are just passing through. All I knew was that I wasn't just passing through. I had been in the locomotive business for twenty-two years, I liked it and the people I worked for and with, and I planned on staying as long as they wanted me. But sometimes your best plans get thrown up in the air. Was that God I heard laughing again?

CHAPTER 3

The Industrial War College

The following was written and submitted for course credit as a second-semester student at the National Defense University's Industrial College of the Armed Forces in May 1995:

It's 7:30 in the morning on August 15, 1994, and I'm sitting in a parking lot at a place called Ft. McNair, somewhere in southwest Washington, DC. My instructions said to report to Marshall Hall at 8 a.m. for something called in-processing, and I didn't want to be late on my first day. Much to my surprise, the lot's pretty full, and as I make my way to the building's entrance, I can see a bunch of people inside frantically doing what could only be described as the in-processing ritual. My stomach sinks. Did I read the schedule wrong? Is this the right place? Who are all these people dressed in uniforms, and why did I agree to come here anyway?

Thankfully, my deer-caught-in-the-headlights expression caught the eye of a sympathetic Army officer at the door, and I'm quickly identified as a confused civilian. He gives me a knowing smile and holds out his hand with a form in it. It's apparently the master checklist of the things one is expected to do at an in-processing, and I find a place out of the traffic flow against the nearest wall to read it over and regroup.

The list is full of letters, more accurately acronyms, most of which I've never seen before. I only realize later that Washington is the center of the acronym universe and that this particular list was mere child's play. Anyway, there's at least one entry on the form that I recognize—ID Photo—so I decide to start with that. When I finally reach the front of that line and get my picture taken, a nice lady behind the table takes my form and puts a rubber stamp mark next to that entry. I've broken the code! Its 7:50 a.m., still a full 10 minutes before I'm supposed to even be here, and I've already been stamped. This must be good! Only ten or so more of those stamps and I'd be finished. I look around and see that most of the other people, especially those in uniform, already had been stamped five or six times. The sweat begins to form on my forehead. I'm already behind the power curve, and they haven't even taught me what that means yet.

To make this a little easier to understand, let me back up about a month or so. In my previous life (which is how I now refer to it), I was an employee of General Motors' Electro-Motive Division and was a locomotive salesman. It was a great business, despite the fact that we sold products (locomotives) that most people thought weren't made anymore to customers (railroads) that most people thought went out of business 30 years ago. It's actually been one of the country's quieter export success stories, selling Illinois-built products in more than 100 countries around the world since the 1930s. In fact, in the past few months I'd been in Australia, Hong Kong, Russia, Brazil, Germany, Ireland, England, and Scotland and had plans to visit Egypt and China in the fall. While business had recently been tough, it was starting to pick up, and it was beginning to feel like a pretty good time to be a locomotive salesman. Then I got the call.

In my case, the call didn't come in the form of a draft notice from Uncle Sam, but from my boss, EMD's general manager John Jarrell, who asked if he could buy me lunch. Now, I like my boss, and he certainly was known as a person of great generosity, but he never asked me to lunch. What was up? We made small talk over sandwiches, and just before we got up to leave, he sprung it on me. GM had been contacted by someone from the National Defense University (NDU) and asked if they would like to submit a candidate to represent the corporation by attending a senior U.S. service (or war) college. Apparently,

Congress had passed legislation the previous year to open four slots for private-sector students for the first time in the history of the school, and they were inviting 25 companies to submit candidates to vie for one of the openings in the Class of 1995's pilot program.

All right, interesting so far, and thanks for the sandwich, but what does this have to do with designing, building, and selling locomotives? And more to the point, what does it have to do with me? EMD was way out of the mainstream of GM's core vehicle business, and we didn't have anything to do with the Department of Defense. We dealt with folks like the Burlington Northern, Union Pacific, and the Korean National Railway, not the Army, Navy, or Air Force. Well, at least not until now.

For reasons that are still somewhat mysterious to me, in the span of about a month, I became GM's candidate, was accepted for admission into NDU's Industrial College of the Armed Forces (ICAF), left my wife and two children on the home front in Western Springs, Illinois, and was stationed at Ft. McNair. Initially, I had no idea what ICAF was, what it meant to be accepted, who I'd be going to school with, or what I'd be learning. Only that it was somewhere in Washington, it would last for ten months, and that if I made it through, I'd receive a Master of Science degree in something called national resource strategy. When it all finally started to sink in, I started to gasp for air. These folks were seasoned warriors, on their own turf—what if there were a testosterone meter, I might not even register! To this point, my knowledge of the military was confined to registering for the draft in 1972 and a father who had served as a private first class in Patton's Third Army as it raced across Germany in 1944. Not exactly a four-star experience profile.

Flashing back to that first day at Ft. McNair, the in-processing cycle was definitely the low point of the year, and it was uphill (in many ways) from there. For those of you as unfamiliar with ICAF as I was, it's one of the DoD's five senior services colleges and has been around in one form or another since 1924. Its mission is to provide an extremely select group of military officers (usually the top 2 percent of those at the level of colonel) and other senior-level government personnel who are destined for positions of significant responsibility, with the skills and perspective to participate in the development of national security strategy.

ICAF's unique mission among the five schools is to work at the intersection between military and industrial strength. Back in the 1920s, it was trying to understand how to better mobilize private industry in support of potential future conflicts after World War I, but now it was taking a much broader perspective. Basically, it was trying to create a context within which to understand how all of the elements of national power could be harnessed to support the achievement of our national security objectives in an increasingly conflict-prone world.

Courses covered a remarkably diverse range of subjects, including strategic decision making, military strategy, world history back to 2000 B.C., macro and micro economics, political science, logistics, acquisition, mobilization, and elements of national industrial power. There were also in-depth studies of strategically important parts of the world (I spent two weeks touring various military and industrial sites in China in a delegation hosted by the People's Liberation Army) and of crucial segments of the economy (where I was assigned to the financial services sector and met with folks from the SEC, the office of the U.S. Trade Representative, the Senate Banking Committee, the Fed, and eventually, spent time in the commodities pits in Chicago and on the floor of the NYSE).

Being located in Washington, and representing the varsity level in the DoD's educational infrastructure, the guest lecturers were an amazing collection of individuals including a Supreme Court Justice, numerous senators and congressmen, well-known media personalities, CEOs from various companies, representatives from foreign governments and Washington think tanks, and many folks from various government agencies.

ICAF's 260 students in the class of 1995 were 70 percent U.S. military from all of the various branches, 25 percent government civilians from 20 different agencies or departments (DoD, State, Commerce, CIA, etc.), 5 percent foreign military representing 13 countries (including a Russian Admiral), and 0.4 percent, or one person, from the private sector—which would be me. Due to a series of unexplained events, I ended up being the only real private citizen on the initial shakedown cruise. They warned me that I might need a sense of humor because they weren't sure they had all of the bugs worked out of the program—they were right.

I'm pretty sure I was the only U.S. citizen on the post (with the possible exception of Ft. McNair's food service employees) without a red background on my photo ID. Who knew what that meant—certainly not me as I innocently accompanied my classmates into the top-secret document section of the library at Marshall Hall during my first week at school. It was at that point that I found out that not having a red background was bad, and I was escorted out in the hall in the company of a polite, but serious woman who made it clear that I needed to stay out of their secret clubhouse. Then there was the time when we were all introducing ourselves on the first day of class, and the guy next to me said he was a Navy SEAL. When I later asked someone from the Army what that meant (so I never saw a Steven Segal movie), his eyes got big and he explained that a SEAL is someone who knew 50 ways to kill me without using a weapon, and if I were lucky, I'd never see it coming. OK, so maybe business isn't so tough after all.

There were many times over the year that I was sure I'd fallen into a warp zone between two parallel universes. The folks on this planet seemed to use the same alphabet that I was used to, but in strange and interesting ways. They were so acronym crazy that they had long since given up trying to spell cute words with them—which meant you really did need a master list (that conveniently didn't exist) to have any clue what was going on. Some of my personal favorites were

OOTWA (operations other than war), LIC (low-intensity conflict), and VUCA (volatility, uncertainty, complexity, and ambiguity). I still defy anyone who lives outside of the 202 area code to use them in a sentence that someone in Iowa would understand.

They also had a curious tradition of standing up and sitting down a lot when people came into the room, while simultaneously counting the number of stars or stripes they had on their shoulder to see how important they were. I think stars beat stripes, but I still might have that wrong. Anyway, the standing and sitting was good exercise, but I think you could develop something of a shoulder fetish if you weren't careful.

All right, enough of that, what did you actually learn at this taxpayer-funded institution? Well, in terms of content, we actually studied some very interesting things, from Constitutional intent in the Federalist Papers, to the teachings of the great, dead military strategists, Sun Tzu and Clausewitz, among others. We were poked and prodded by a series of psychological evaluations that attempted to provide insights into how we thought and how we made decisions, something my lovely wife, Barbara, would love to know (sorry, dear, classified information).

We looked at historical events that shaped the world over the past few thousand years, studied the theory and reality of complex alliance networks, and attempted to connect with the ethereal concept of national will. We dissected the private sector, without anesthetic, trying to understand how a world dominated by transnational corporations could be reconciled with the need for a strong domestic economy and the critical role that the economy played in creating the wealth, power, and influence necessary to preserve our country's ability to advance our national security interests. At some point, that didn't seem to match with the reality of about one in ten cars driving within the beltway being built by American companies, but they must save that conundrum for the more advanced class.

We war-gamed the global economic system, debated the appropriate role for government in the creation and distribution of national wealth, and attempted to clarify the objectives of the military in the currently confused post–cold war world order. Ultimately, this all led to confronting the massive challenge of devising a national security strategy that went well beyond the bounds of military might and forced a connection between our expansive and diverse desires and our ultimately limited resources.

Throughout the year, the exchange of perspective between the public and private sector that this little pilot program was trying to achieve, while limited in size, actually seemed very valuable. The issues surrounding return on investment, global competition, labor relations, opportunity cost, regulatory impacts, commercializing technology, and shareholder expectations were important for my military and government classmates to understand. Conversely, it was very interesting to me to examine the concepts of leadership, vision, and grand strategy through the lens of a government and its military and to see how that framing might have value for the private sector.

Globalization, complex alliance networks, clarity of mission, freedom of action, and solving an enemy during the fog of war while they're simultaneously solving you are only a few examples of the common challenges faced by warriors and capitalists. There were valuable lessons and intellectual frameworks taught at ICAF that presupposed the issues being faced were brutally difficult, constantly changing, and fraught with horrific consequences. All in all, it was an amazing educational experience and a once-in-a-lifetime gift for someone like me to have an extraordinary out-of-culture experience.

Finally, I'd be remiss if I didn't make some comment regarding the caliber of the people who I had come to know during my time at ICAF. If these individuals are representative of the current and future leaders of our military and civilian agencies, then sleep well, America. You've got some wonderfully talented and dedicated professionals dealing with many issues that you don't want to even think about, many times living in places you don't want to know about, and doing it despite being hamstrung by a frustrating and compromise-laden bureaucracy. As a group, they were among the most capable, committed, and honorable individuals who I've ever had the privilege to work with, and they displayed a level of cohesion and mission focus that would put the most progressive private-sector firms to shame. These folks could clearly hold their own with any similarly configured group of leaders from outside of government, and they're doing it while raising families on a fraction of the financial awards that the private sector provides. We are all extremely fortunate as a nation for their service, and I was certainly honored to be temporarily allowed to be misassigned among their ranks.

* * *

What an incredible experience, and fifteen years later, I still can't believe what an amazing gift John Jarrell gave me that afternoon at lunch. What a remarkable group of people, and what an extraordinary opportunity to spend time thinking about and debating such critically important, yet unsolvable issues. It completely recalibrated my expectations and standards regarding leadership—what it meant, how important it was, and the duty and care leaders owed to the people and institutions they were entrusted to lead. This recalibration was a seriously important, cold-water-in-the-face moment that left me feeling both good and uncomfortable at the same time. ICAF had undoubtedly accomplished its mission—at least with me.

When school ended, we all received our diplomas in a beautiful full-dress uniform ceremony held on the lawn of Ft. McNair. It was a bittersweet moment, as I knew I'd probably never see most of these folks again. I'd come to admire and trust and truly enjoy spending the last year with these people, and now it was ending. Life goes on, and it was time to get back to work, for all of us. What back to work meant for one of my friends, an F-14 Tomcat pilot Navy captain and former instructor at TOPGUN (U.S. Navy Strike Fighter Tactics Instructor program), was heading to Europe to plan naval air operations over Bosnia. The Navy SEAL (by now a good friend) was heading somewhere in the world to do the incredible and crazy things SEALs do. An Army colonel friend was heading off to a training command to help equip our soldiers to deal with messy urban warfare scenarios where the enemy didn't wear uniforms. And there were many, many more very similar examples.

These folks were all real players in their world, and for them, the past ten months of relative calm and tranquility and just thinking about tough issues was now over. They were scattering to the four corners of the globe and heading right into the middle of tough issues. This was a different real world than I knew, one with countless rocks and hard places, where accountabilities were deadly serious and consequences extended well beyond next year's bonus treatment. Could I honestly ever think that anything in business was that hard again? And what about consequences and accountability? Those definitions had changed for me forever.

As I left the graduation ceremony, my wife and children flew back home to Chicago, and I flew to Detroit for my first day at Project Beacon. You see, about two months before, I'd gotten my next orders as well. They came in the form of a phone call from GM's then vice chairman, Harry Pearce, who explained to me that the company was thinking of trying something a little different, and he thought I might be a good person for the job. By this time, I'd gotten over the shock of John Jarrell's retirement announcement, and while I wasn't particularly happy about it, I thought I was heading back to EMD to work for a new boss—apparently not.

It all happened really fast. What Harry was explaining to me honestly didn't make a lot of sense, at least over the phone. It was something about Hughes Electronics and EDS and satellites and cars. My head was spinning, and my first instinct was to say no thanks. But, in a moment of blinding sobriety, it occurred to me that telling the vice chairman that his idea was too funky to work on probably wasn't very smart. Hadn't I learned anything at ICAF? This was a classic frontal assault. Harry had me outflanked and outgunned. I could try my new diplomatic skills and negotiate, but he held all the cards. It was probably time to surrender. OK, so what day do you want me there?

The next thing I knew, I was off to Motown, bringing along whatever the last forty years of life experience had taught me. There was a *Wall Street Journal* article written sometime back in the 1960s that profiled little General Motors Institute and called it the "West Point of Industry." Over the years, I've often seen the Harvard Business School referred to as the "West Point of Capitalism." OK, now I'm not exactly sure what any of this means, but I'd just completed one of West Point's (and the Naval and Air Force Academy's) graduate schools. With all of this combat training, I must be ready for just about anything, right? OK, where did that snickering come from?

CHAPTER 4

Project Beacon

It was Wednesday, June 16, 1995, and I had just flown to Detroit after graduating from ICAF the day before. The purpose of the trip was to attend the first board meeting of a recently formed joint venture called GM Mobile Communications Services. The board consisted of seven members, two each from GM's vehicle business, EDS, Hughes Electronics, and me. The reason I was there was that, in GM's wisdom, they'd selected an ex-locomotive salesman to be the first managing director of a start-up wireless-and-GPS-technology-based consumer services business. Don't ask.

The joint venture had been the outcome of a multi-month study project within GM to evaluate the potential to use the two nonautomotive parts of GM, Hughes, and EDS to create a new service-based revenue stream to compliment GM's core vehicle business. In the 1980s, GM acquired Hughes and EDS, with the thought that their technology and capabilities might somehow provide a transformational advantage to GM's cars and trucks. Maybe it would be in computer-based design and manufacturing, or maybe there'd be a space-age technology that could be unleashed to differentiate GM's vehicles.

Over the years of GM's ownership of Hughes and EDS, none of that had happened. Actually, EDS had become the sole source IT provider for GM, taking over a function formerly managed in-house. On the surface, it made sense, like a lot of things do in big companies. And while I'm sure some good came from it, the practical result for those of us at the operating level was the creation of a business relationship that was prone to the predictable challenges of a sole-source, shotgun wedding. Costs went up (EDS needed to make a profit), responsiveness went down (they were the only game in town), and they absorbed nearly everyone in the company that knew anything about computers.

It wasn't really clear what Hughes was bringing to the party other than "technology," whatever that was supposed to mean. There were actually a few attempts to reach into Hughes and use something in a vehicle, examples like night vision and high-intensity discharge headlights, but they never seemed to reach any kind of critical mass. Cost was an issue; new technology, especially the kind Hughes had experience with, wasn't generally mass-produced. Their stuff ended up looking cool in a press release, but the price was invariably too high to generate any real volume. I eventually came to view this phenomenon as "brochure-ware," something the car guys loved to brag about at auto shows, but honestly didn't care if they ever sold. That was great for the vehicle guys, but it had left the folks at Hughes with a pretty empty feeling of doing all the work to develop something worth bragging about that never sold more than a handful—not a great business model. Operating synergies with Hughes were proving elusive.

As investments, the acquisitions could be characterized as having been successful. Both companies were doing well in their core businesses, and with the added revenue EDS gained by getting GM's IT account on very favorable "no bid" terms, the cash GM invested to own shares in both companies was earning a pretty fair return for its shareholders. But, in the view of Wall Street, GM was in the awkward position of looking more like a mutual fund than an integrated enterprise. If they wanted to justify keeping these companies, they needed to find places where the businesses overlapped to make the acquisitions really pay off. So the company was looking for ideas, frankly, any ideas, where they could make a claim that one (GM) plus one (EDS) plus one (Hughes) equaled more than three.

A study group had been formed in the second half of 1994 that was optimistically named Project Beacon. A team with representatives from all three parties had been given the task to evaluate whether an opportunity existed to connect GM vehicles, using yet-to-be-developed wireless telemetry, to a unique portfolio of yet-to–be-invented services. An early proposal had actually come from Pacific Bell, who wanted to work with GM (using GM's money) to build out a national network of microwave towers to allow GM to corner the market on this type of vehicle connectivity.

The initial analysis for this fell to Vince Barabba, then responsible, among other things, for evaluating funky new ideas inside GM. Vince quickly saw that the investment necessary to create such a network, literally billions of dollars, made no sense for a car company. But he did think the idea of wireless vehicle connectivity had potential. And if it could be characterized as creating a unique relationship with the vehicle customer, produce a profitable new revenue stream, and be reframed as finally creating operating synergies with EDS and Hughes, then it might actually get some support.

One thing led to another when Harry Pearce, GM's then vice chairman and responsible for Hughes and EDS in the GM management structure, decided to try a little experiment. The company would build a small organization using the resources and capabilities of all of the players inside GM to pursue this wireless services opportunity. Harry had to convince GM's then chairman, Jack Smith, that the idea had potential and would need to be managed outside of the bounds of the normal organization if it were going to have any chance at success. Jack was skeptical, but the initial investment was relatively small, and Harry was optimistic enough (actually without reasonable cause) that he agreed to let Harry run the play.

An important early decision was where to put the experimental team. If they were initially connected to the vehicle business, an idea this strange coming from a vice chairman whose last job was chief corporate lawyer (not a "car guy"), it would've had a hard time building any momentum. If it worked for either Hughes or EDS, the other one would have pitched a hissy, and the GM guys would've immediately cried foul, citing the million ways they would likely be taken to the cleaners by yet another sole-source relationship. Harry had a Solomon-like decision to make.

So what was the answer? It doesn't report to anybody, or wait, maybe it actually reports to everybody. *What?* The solution that Harry invented was that it would be a three-way joint venture with equal ownership by GM, Hughes, and EDS. There'd be a seven-person board of directors with two from each company and one managing director who would run the business. That is, if the study phase actually confirmed there was one.

This was either the smartest way to finesse the issue and get going or the silliest exercise in corporate politics that had ever been created. But it got better. The fine print on this structure said the new board required unanimous approval for any significant decision that the business needed to make. That provision elevated an otherwise tough structure to the level of the United Nations. But, OK, at least one hurdle had been crossed in bringing something to life. Now who's going to run this thing?

The United Nations analogy wasn't bad, especially when you consider the thought process that went on in selecting the joint venture's managing director. Did you ever notice that in the sixty-plus years since the United Nations was founded, not once did the Secretary General ever come from the United States, Russia, the UK, or Germany? In other words, the organization couldn't be seen as being led by, and presumably favoring, one of the real power players in the alliance. It always had to be headed up by someone from Norway or Sweden or Peru or Myanmar. You know, somebody with no ax to grind, no bias—as famously neutral as the Swiss. That's it, Switzerland! Now whom could they find who would be the human equivalent of Switzerland? Somebody with no preconceived notions or favored technologies, no obvious career path from the home organization to protect, and best of all, no knowledge of anything whatsoever related to this opportunity, so they'd be easier for the board to mold and control.

Where could they find such an uninformed, inexperienced, malleable individual who could start the ball rolling? Oh, and did we mention expendable? Because in the unlikely event that the business did start to roll and become big enough to actually care about, they'd probably need to be replaced with someone who actually knew what they were doing. And suppose it didn't get rolling? Well, no harm, no foul, as it wouldn't have been a particularly valuable career that got bruised in the process anyway.

Now, this is a fairly harsh and cynical way to look at this, and I'm sure not exactly what was going though Harry's mind when he called me at ICAF. But subsequent discussions convinced me that a lot of this was on the minds of the other key players. So that's how it came to be that a very strange list of criteria ended up pointing the company toward the selection of the least obvious and least prepared candidate in the world to take on this leadership role. This should have never happened, but at this point, that didn't really matter. What did matter was that the idea was coming to life, the players were lining up in their respective roles, and a locomotive salesman fresh from military school had just gotten a new job.

That first board meeting was actually uneventful. Since I'd just arrived from Ft. McNair the night before, no one really expected a full-blown review of the business, mainly because there wasn't a business to review yet. It was a chance for the board members to meet each other and have a broad discussion about what we'd be trying to accomplish. We talked at a very high level about how big this opportunity might turn out to be and the types of challenges we were likely to encounter and then agreed on a schedule for how the project would evolve and be reviewed over the next several months.

The board was an interesting cast of characters. From the car business, there was the general manager of Pontiac and the head of research & development (the person Harry had designated as my first official supervisor). From Hughes, there were relatively senior guys from Hughes Network Systems and from Delco Electronics. And, finally, from EDS, there was the person in charge of their global relationship with GM and a guy from their North American GM support team. While none of these individuals were from the very top of their organizations, they were influential in their respective companies and, as expected, brought parochial points of view to the table. That wasn't necessarily bad, since having each organization's important issues openly represented was healthy. That is, if it actually stayed open and constructive and didn't devolve into the more likely political maneuvering that too often happens in big companies—time would tell.

The vehicle guys had seen this story before. Some bright idea, not particularly well thought out, that was supposed to drop out of the sky and integrate seamlessly into a hundred-year-old car company. I'd characterize them as cordial, but highly skeptical. They were very politically astute and didn't want to be openly hostile to an idea that had its roots with the vice chairman, but they also had no real reason to go native with this and push it like the second coming of the whitewall tire. In fairness, this was actually a very reasonable position to start with, considering how half-baked it all was at that point.

I'd say the Hughes and EDS board members shared a fairly consistent point of view; missions number one, two, and three were to sell things they made, this time in volume, to GM's car business. They'd both tried many ways to break in before, especially Hughes, and if the wrinkle this time meant being a part of some joint venture approach to finally make something happen, then so be it. Hey, it might actually be an advantage, or at least less painful, to be a partner with the vehicle guys instead of just being pushed around like common vendors inside their supplier management process.

The other thing that certainly wasn't lost on Hughes and EDS was that this might actually turn into something that had the chance to make a lot of money. If they could fund their one-third ownership investment through the profits they'd earn by supplying their hardware and services to the new company, then that would be all good. Round-tripping money would be hard to pull off, but certainly worth the effort. It would require setting things up in a way that would allow them to retain protected supplier status as the company grew. A tough challenge, but wasn't that what an ownership stake and a seat on the board was for? You could tell this was probably going to cause tension at some point in the future when they'd have to earn the business by being fully competitive. But, at the moment, I certainly wasn't smart enough to make a big issue out of it. That could be left for another day.

So, OK, I'd lived through the first board meeting and had a chance to at least put a few faces and names together. It had also begun to illuminate some of the motivations and politics driving the individuals and organizations and reinforced my initial concerns about the complexity of managing through a joint venture. This wasn't a great structure, but there wasn't much that could be done about that at the moment. Besides, as fragile as this all felt at the moment, putting any more effort into governance when the business might not survive past the study phase seemed like wasted energy. The next day, I headed to Project Beacon's headquarters.

Interstate 75 is one of the country's main north-south arteries, starting in Sault Ste. Marie, Michigan, and ending in Miami, Florida. It's interesting how many places with prominent positions in the history of the auto industry and General Motors are located within a stone's throw of this highway. So it was only fitting that the humble beginnings of OnStar would start about half a mile west of I-75's Exit 71 on Crooks Road.

Arriving in the office my first morning, I found the planning team of about ten people occupying a small suite in a nondescript, low-rise, multi-tenant building. They identified the office as being on the first floor, but it was actually garden level, with windows that were routinely covered by the grass clippings of a passing lawn mower. It was sandwiched between an orthodontist on one side and a tax preparer on the other. Not exactly what you might expect to find at General Motors, but something that seemed to fit the status of the project at that point. Not that it really mattered, but I was technically the only official employee of the venture, with the other people I met that morning being assigned "on loan" from their home companies. Most of them were from EDS and certainly had more experience and skin in the game than I did since they'd already been there for months working on the idea. I was coming in as their version of Bill Happel, except that instead of die management, my useless experience was selling locomotives. I can't imagine any of them were thrilled to see me, but at least they were polite about it.

We all gathered in the main open space in the office and went through introductions. A few of the people fell into the category of always being on special assignments. Big companies do that a lot, sometimes for good reasons, like trying to challenge their high-potential talent by putting them in unstructured situations and having them figure it out. Other times it was for less good reasons, like trying to shuffle people who they otherwise didn't know what to do with off to the hinterlands.

For the people in the second category, it was always sad and unfair because they weren't being told the truth. Managers in big companies are too often conflict avoiders, preferring to pass nonperforming people around the organization and out of their hair, rather than dealing with the issues head-on. And there was nothing better than a big, juicy special assignment where you could tell people that they were "special," while simultaneously brooming them off your team. The problem was some of them actually believed what they were being told and then eventually wondered why their careers hadn't gone anywhere. By the time they'd figured it out, they were frustrated and had wasted years they couldn't get back working on things they weren't ever well suited for. That wasn't being kind to the person; it was a cop-out that disrespected their right to know where they honestly stood so they could get on with their life. Anyway, what this all meant to me was that I'd probably just inherited more than a few folks in category two.

But there were a few bright spots. Fortunately, there were at least a couple of people who you could tell really had a firm grasp on the technologies that we'd be working with. They were smart enough to be confident and also smart enough to admit that they didn't have it all figured out—thank God for those guys. I wish I could've learned how to clone that attitude in technical people over the years because it was amazingly valuable and exceedingly rare. Too many technical folks either froze in their tracks when the bullets started flying or way overplayed their hands and acted like they knew everything there was to know up until it was too late and everything blew up. Then they'd try to convince you that it was part of the plan and was supposed to blow up.

The other early bright spot was Lorrie Robertson. Lorrie had come attached to one of the less capable special-assignment guys from GM in the role of administrative support to the entire business, and she was a real keeper. I didn't know it on that first day, but she'd ultimately have as much of a claim on getting this little business off the ground as any genius engineer or creative marketer or IT professional who we'd bring on board over the next few years. Lorrie was very good at what she did and had great contacts within GM's executive admin mafia, where most of the important things in the company got done. More importantly, she became someone I could trust with anything, including the increasingly difficult task of maintaining my too often fragile sanity.

Anyway, the ball was rolling, albeit slowly. We had a mandate to go figure out everything we could about this little opportunity and report back if there was a real business to pursue. We had a board that got stranger and stranger as time went on, but for now, it didn't seem like it was going to be our biggest problem. We had the beginnings of a team, even though everyone was wearing different color jerseys and probably thought they were playing different sports. And we had the ear of the vice chairman and a little bit of his pocketbook, but we were eventually going to need a lot more of both. What we didn't have was a product, a service, a distribution strategy, a capable supplier base, a viable business model, or market research that said anyone would pay us for whatever it was that we might do. Day two, and it wasn't all falling into place yet—thank goodness we didn't know enough to be as scared as we should have been.

The next few weeks and months were filled with bringing new people "officially" onto the team, sorting through the range of Post-it note ideas that were beginning to make up our list of potential services, and trying to talk to just about everyone I could in a serious role in GM's vehicle engineering, finance, marketing, manufacturing, and planning organizations. If we were going to have any chance of getting anywhere with this business, we'd need the support of a very wide range of people, most of whom I'd never met before.

Almost everyone who I talked to had ideas, suggestions, and rec-ommendations for people who would be "just right to work on your project." Back to special-assignment code, that typically meant "I'd be delighted if you'd take them off my hands." There were questions, encouragements, challenges, suggestions, lessons on tribal customs, offers of resources, multiple explanations of how the "real world" worked, and threats. *Threats?* Yikes, I didn't remember signing up for that, but apparently I actually had.

There were some very early discussions that made a big impres-sion on me and had a real impact on how the business moved forward. Larry Burns, at that point the head of quality for a big part of vehicle manufacturing, was interested, thoughtful, and encouraging. That coming from an operations guy who should've instinctively hated the craziness that we might someday bring to his world was very helpful and reassuring. Unfortunately, another operating guy at GM at an even higher level provided one of my most vivid early memories of the other side of the coin. After waiting outside his office for about a half hour past our scheduled meeting time, he finally opened his door and pointed me toward a small chair that was positioned on the opposite side of his very large desk. As I looked up at him across the expanse, and he was certain that I knew who was the Wizard and who was Toto, he began explaining in a stern voice that was meant to scare the hell out of me that our idea was "just a pimple on an elephant's ass." Say what? What had this adult, this GM senior leader, this business professional just said? Before I could even react, the next statement was a threat that if any of this crap ever disrupted anything at one of his plants, we wouldn't even see the truck that ran us over. The meeting was adjourned, and I was dismissed.

Jim Queen, then in charge of engineering for electronic components in the vehicle, went out of his way to try to explain why we were getting so much pushback from GM for wanting to put our technology (which wasn't proven) into their vehicles outside of the normal process (essentially breaking every rule in the company). He said we were being treated like a disease that had infected the body and that GM's natural immune system had kicked in and was producing antibodies that would surround and eject us from the nearest convenient orifice. Jim wasn't proud of that behavior, but was just trying to be helpful by letting me know what we were up against. He actually liked us, or at least felt sorry for us, and did his best more times than I ever knew to protect us from the worst effects of GM's natural instincts. He had a tough job, anyone who had a serious leadership role building cars did, and all something as strange and funky as OnStar could do in the short term was make his job even harder. But he was way more for us than against us, and that took a lot of courage.

Vince Barabba, the guy behind the Project Beacon study, quickly became an ally and, ultimately, a good friend. Vince wasn't entirely accepted as an insider, mainly because he was always stirring up trouble by suggesting that the company needed to look at the business in different ways. Vince was really, really smart, but not always the most practical. He was creative, but found it hard to deal with the details and constraints and the muck that you have to work through to make things happen. Unfortunately, that made him way too easy to be dismissed by the operating guys and reinforced a long-held view within GM that you could either be a strategist (thinker) or an operator (doer), but not both. That framing was insane of course, but it was easy to find examples of it in many places around the company. At least, in this case, it was going to be different, as we drug Vince down into the muck with us on multiple occasions—we had no choice.

Ron Zarrella, GM's recently hired head of all vehicle marketing, was working his way through the "outsider trying to break in" process, despite arguably being the second-highest-ranking executive in GM's massive North American business. Ron was a no-nonsense businessman who had the edge of someone who expected to get results and the twinkle in the eye of someone who would prefer to do it having fun with people who he liked. While Ron wasn't initially sure OnStar would turn into a big deal, he seemed inherently attracted to the idea of trying to do something different and was instinctively open to taking the risk and figuring it out on the fly. He also seemed to really understand the importance of speed, and not just in the slogan-a-month way it generally got discussed within GM. Ron had really good business instincts and strong leadership skills, traits unfortunately not found in abundance within the company.

Rick Wagoner, GM's then president of North American Operations and the youngest person by a decade to ever hold that job, seemed more interested in what we were doing than almost anyone else. It was really hard to understand why, but with everything else Rick had on his plate, he always wanted to make time for us. He allowed me an hour a month on his couch, wanting to know what we were learning and offering to do almost anything to help. He was smart, extremely quick, down to earth, and genuinely a very nice guy—but in a way that you knew you shouldn't try to take advantage of him. You could always expect a fair hearing from Rick, but you'd better make sure you knew what you were talking about because, unlike a lot of other people in the company, he was always really listening.

And, finally, there was Harry Pearce. I'd intersected with Harry for a number of years based on his connection with the locomotive business, but I'd never really say I'd gotten to know him very well. He was very intelligent, extremely articulate, and thought deeply and with nuance about a wide range of issues. He had an ill-deserved reputation for being dispassionate with people, but paradoxically, he was probably seen as the strongest emotional leader in the company. Harry knew GM needed to take on a different character and personality if it wanted to break out of its decades-long losing streak, but he wasn't positioned to get his hands directly on any of the core parts of the business—so he had to be creative and work on it from the outside in.

Despite his sales pitch to Jack Smith, he couldn't have been certain that we'd ever amount to a hill of lint much less a hill of beans. But even if we suspected that his outward confidence was a little ahead of its time, having Harry's encouragement and support really inspired our own confidence and strengthened our resolve. And the "high cover" he provided, most of which we never knew about, undoubtedly protected us from countless armies of elephant dermatologists who were determined to remove the OnStar blemish from the pachyderm's behind.

So this is what the landscape looked like at the beginning, actually before the beginning. A little foggy, a mixture of motivations and a few emerging subplots, an amazing range of interesting technical and strategic issues to be comprehended, and a colorful cast of characters who covered the spectrum from brilliant and inspirational to vapid and dysfunctional. But with all of the uncertainty and crosscurrents, there was still something at the heart of all of this that you just couldn't let go of, at least not yet. Confusing enough? Just wait.

CHAPTER 5

Getting Organized

So now it was time to get going. The senior folks at GM had been sold on the idea for Project Beacon with an overly optimistic set of financial projections and a description of the technology from Hughes and EDS that far exceeded what they could deliver. We knew the pro forma projections needed work, but we weren't yet smart enough to have any idea how much work the technology needed.

My first real hire into the new joint venture was Jon Hyde. Jon was a relatively junior guy from EDS's finance staff, but seemed to have just the spark and energy for what we'd be facing in those first few months. Jon and I tore into the numbers that had been used to justify entering the business, and even for a locomotive guy and a junior finance person, it didn't take long to find out that they made no sense. I mean honestly, made no sense. I can only speculate that they'd gotten this far with such screwy projections because the project was so unique and such a tweener that it didn't fit into any of GM's standard financial templates. Either that or someone must have thought it was Harry's pet project, and since it was only projected to cost $15 million in the first year, it had basically gotten hand-waved into existence. It didn't really matter. The money had already been allocated, and now it was time to just start spending.

At first glance, that might have sounded pretty good. We already had money set aside without the annoying details of needing a plan to use it intelligently to achieve anything specific. It's the kind of situation that a lot of people in big companies dream about. Accountability is overrated anyway, right? I mean, if you're going to be entrepreneurial and creative, you need to be turned loose with a little cash and see what happens. Thankfully, neither Jon nor I were comfortable with that approach, as we both saw the inevitable hangover that would accompany a "hope for the best" strategy that didn't quite work out. So we called a timeout to dig into the plans and see what we had.

That annoyed most of the folks that had been working on the study team before we got there because, as far as they were concerned, the project had already been declared a "go," which was all they needed to hear. Ditto for my board members from EDS and Hughes since they'd been working extremely hard over the years to get anything going that might open up GM vehicles as platforms to buy some of their technology on favorable terms. These weren't bad business people, and certainly, they wouldn't have supported doing stupid things for long, but their one-third share of $15 million was small enough that they were willing to just get going and course-correct later. A delay would run the risk of the whole thing falling into some corporate black hole, never to be seen again. It was a fair concern since ADD can run rampant in big companies, especially with something as small and funky as this.

But, to me, coming fresh from the locomotive business, where $15 million was a lot of money, it didn't make sense to rush ahead with a silly plan just to get something going. Besides, they were holding my old job open at EMD, which gave me the freedom to be completely objective about the prospects of this new project. That positioning—either this project makes sense as a real business or we shut it down and I go back to selling locomotives—ended up being critical to the future success of the business. If it had been "this has to work or else I have no job," I'm pretty sure we would have put our foot on the accelerator at this point and lurched forward, or sideways, or backwards, with no clear objective beyond staying alive as long as we could—probably not a great recipe for success.

Weeks went by, and we were finally able to reconstruct a strategy and set of financial projections that made some sense. They weren't without risks and unknowns, but gone were the plans to use the technology to monitor vending machines, sheep migration (no kidding), or putting it into hundreds of different types of service like delivery vans, bulldozers, farm equipment, boxcars—you name it. Nobody knew how any of that was going to work anyway. Who would distribute in each of those markets? Was there enough real value being created to justify the cost? Would the technology work? Who would we be competing against? Apparently, the thought was that those details could all get sorted out later. Just make a few dozen simplifying assumptions, and you could easily project the money that we'd be collecting from all of those shepherds in Ireland.

In fairness, in any new venture, there's always going to be a murky zone where the initial vision and brainstorming ultimately have to be reconciled with reality. That's fine. It happens all the time; it's a natural part of the creative process. Get too focused on the details too soon and you run the risk of missing some potentially big ideas. But if you stay in the Land of Oz too long, the balloon can't get you back to Kansas. The problem, in this case, was that nobody had called time-out yet to start the focusing part, but they'd created the illusion that they had by producing financial statements that showed profits from silly initiatives flowing like the lower Mississippi River after a spring thaw. Jumping off into the unknown and committing to these numbers just made no sense.

No, what Jon and I did was narrow the scope to something that seemed to fit with who we were and what we might be able to do. Retail buyers of new cars and trucks would be the target market, and the services would need to be focused primarily in the area of safety and security. This wasn't something that we conjured out of our imaginations; I actually wish we'd been smart enough to have those instincts. In fact, new cars and trucks had been one of the many segments that had already been looked at, analyzed fairly extensively, and included as part of the overall plan. What Jon and I realized was that if we were going to go forward, it couldn't just be a part of the plan, but it had to be *all* of the plan.

This was a good lesson in "more is better," until it's too much. You needed to have enough in the scope of the business at launch to make it big enough to care about, but not so big and unwieldy that it couldn't be executed. Because the original study team was dominated by folks from EDS and Hughes and since their track record of getting the vehicle guys aggressively behind anything they were trying to sell into their cars was extremely poor, they worked around that problem by adding other stuff, like sheep monitoring, to a relatively modest vehicle plan so that the numbers would look better on paper. If they had demanded that the business be based on more cars and less sheep, with an unproven technology plan and no actual market data saying customers would pay for any of this, their concern was that it would've probably gotten thrown out.

I'm pretty sure they knew the vending machines and sheep strategy wouldn't work, but they were hoping that once the business got going and the technology got into cars, everyone would love it so much that they'd quickly get behind a much bigger and faster vehicle rollout. At that point, everyone would have forgotten about the sheep, and the business would be all about cars. The problem was that there were too many moving parts in that strategy, not the least of which that it's terribly complicated to integrate something like OnStar into a new vehicle program, even when the company tries to do it with its eyes wide open. To somehow think you could run a bait-and-switch play on the car guys and have them back into a high-volume strategy without knowing it was asking for a train wreck. And if they were going to try that, I intended to watch the crash from the safety of LaGrange, Illinois, where I'd be the guy selling the replacement locomotives. Thankfully, it didn't come to that.

The good news was that we were able to build a reconfigured plan that focused exclusively on new vehicles, and the numbers (with the magic of pro forma assumptions) actually worked. The problem was that a couple of those key assumptions would require GM's vehicle business to commit a few unnatural acts, like make exceptions to the vehicle development timing rules and commit to a faster than normal volume ramp-up. Unfortunately, there was really no other way, and these weren't the kinds of decisions that were within the authority of my board of directors. Decisions like these would need to be made at the very top of the corporation since they impacted emotionally charged policy issues with high-risk consequences.

All of this led up to a meeting that took place at Detroit's main convention center, Cobo Hall, in the fall of 1995. GM had rented Cobo because it needed a place big enough to host a gathering of the three thousand or so executives that made up its massive North American leadership team. The event was to start with a huge cocktail reception on the first night, with meetings to follow over the next two and a half days. Since Rick Wagoner and his staff had their normal monthly North American Strategy board meeting set for the afternoon before it was all supposed to start, they just held it in a room at Cobo to simplify the logistics. Our little topic, a status update on the Mobile Communications Services joint venture, was near the end of the afternoon's agenda and, mercifully, right before everyone was planning on going down to the main exhibit hall for an adult beverage.

I'd decided before the meeting that I'd try to use this update to get the policy issues on the table, and I thought there'd be a fifty-fifty chance that the whole thing would come unglued and I'd be heading back to Illinois permanently. I got through the early charts, and only a few people were listening, but at least one of them was Rick. The limited engagement wasn't that surprising considering the "pimple on the elephant" analogy was still fresh in my memory. When I got to the point of talking about the need for a revised strategy, the dynamic in the room changed pretty dramatically—all of a sudden everyone was listening.

There were two basic issues I needed to cover. First, we needed to go into this planning on it ultimately being a high-volume program.

If it got going and we learned that it wasn't what we thought it was or we found a major flaw in our strategy that made the business unattractive, then we could obviously throttle back or stop altogether. But we needed to have a base plan that assumed success and included a high-volume rollout, otherwise with the extended product cycles in the auto industry, we'd lose years hanging back with a wait-and-see approach. I paused, waiting for a reaction, but nobody said anything, which felt like a good sign. Anyway, I thought this was going to be the easier of the two issues to deal with, so I might as well plough ahead to the tough one.

The second issue was a lot hairier and open-ended. Car companies typically take a long time to introduce new technology into vehicles, not because they like it that way, but because there's a lot of extremely sophisticated validation required to make sure it's going to work in an environment as complex and variable as a car. There are safety issues, quality concerns, and the potential for massively expensive recall campaigns if something goes wrong. And beyond the technology's initial introduction, once a new car platform is designed and all of its parts are validated to work together, car companies prefer to button them up and not change anything for three to six years while they crank out copies and earn back their investment. The tribe of engineers who worked on launching the last new platform would move on to the next one that was being developed, and the cycle would continue. There just weren't enough resources inside a car company to do it any other way.

OK, these guys knew all this better than I did, so what's the point? Well, the point was that unless GM was willing to suspend the technology introduction process rules for something that was destined to change as quickly as our technology would, we should probably stop now and save the effort for something else. Consumer electronics was at the heart of what OnStar needed to be, and that was a world where rapidly changing technology produced amazing results: lower costs, better functionality, and higher quality. Those laws of physics operated in twelve- to eighteen-month product lifecycles in that world, and you either jumped in and embraced that or risked becoming roadkill. So if we needed to adhere to the normal vehicle rules (basically thirty-six- to sixty-month time cycles), then "we'd run the risk of selling eight-track tapes when everyone else was selling CDs." Basically, we'd have outdated technology, our costs would be too high, and we'd look silly to the outside world. Funny how antiquated that analogy sounds today, but in the pre-iPod world of 1995, it provoked the intended response.

Rick thought about it for a second and then turned to GM's head of vehicle engineering and asked him if he could do it. The engineer, who was probably twenty years older than Rick and a seasoned car industry veteran, said, "Yes, if you make me." Say what? *If you make me?*" Holy cow, what lantern had I just kicked over? Before Rick had a chance to respond, he went on to explain what Rick already knew. The company had historically struggled with vehicle quality and was working very hard to instill the discipline of a consistent, rigorous product development process. It was something the Japanese had gotten a lot of credit for and something GM knew it really needed to get better at. It was starting to take hold, but it wasn't second nature yet and needed constant support and attention. He said if Rick wanted to make an exception with our initiative, he could probably make it work, but he couldn't make many exceptions before the whole process would blow up.

Rick then went around the table and asked everyone else what they thought. I don't remember many other specific comments, except that they were mixed, and there were no emotional arguments one way or another. Back to the pimple analogy, we just weren't big enough to care about. When the conversation got back to Rick, he actually had more to say than I expected. He said that, the way he saw it, GM's North American business had a number of fundamental challenges going forward. The level of competitive intensity in the market was high. There was excess capacity, and more was being added by the transplants. Legacy costs and a strong union were further squeezing margins, and the market was fundamentally mature. A tough view of the future, but what GM did have going for it in North America was its leading share in the world's largest vehicle market—and its sheer size.

When you took that all into consideration, it meant that we needed to be open to business opportunities where we could use our size and scale to extend our business into more attractive space. It also meant that the company was big enough that it could afford to try a few different things and not all of them had to work. Rick said he had no idea whether our little project would be a winner or not, but he said he'd like to try it because it didn't appear to be a large investment, and he also liked the fact that it would challenge the company to do things differently. Since he expected a lot more of that in the future, it might be something we could learn from.

Then he looked at me and said, "OK, if we go forward, why do I need these two partners?" He understood that the real strategic advantage, if there were one, would be unnatural access to GM vehicles as host platforms for embedded services. If his team were going to take all of the risk of disrupting the vehicle development process and his vehicle brands were going to work to promote this unproven service, why would he want to share the profits equally with EDS and Hughes?

I told him that, from what I could see at this point, his instinct was right; he didn't need the other two companies, at least not in the way this unholy alliance had been assembled. They had experience with the technology, but nothing proprietary, and frankly, the joint-venture approach was turning into the management structure from hell. They could certainly participate and earn profits by being suppliers to the initiative on commercially competitive terms, and we could make a Hughes and EDS corporate synergy claim, but they didn't need to be his partners unless he needed their money—which he didn't.

Then he looked at me and said, "All right, we're going to do this. You're the newest division in General Motors. Now where do you want to report?" At this point, my head was spinning. A half hour before, I would have given even odds on the whole thing blowing up, and now, all of a sudden, the dozen or so of us involved on this little study team were a division of GM? This was turning into one of the early "you can't make this stuff up" memories. I answered with all of the clarity and strength I could muster and said, "I'm not sure." Thankfully, his question wasn't an intelligence test, so he just said to get back to him in the next week or so with a recommendation. In the meantime, the lawyer in the room was given the assignment to unwind the joint venture, and downstairs to the reception I went— and headed straight to the bar.

That night I can remember calling my wife, while still a little buzzed from the reception, and trying to explain to her what had happened. She knew I'd had an important meeting earlier in the day, and she also knew that it might lead to my permanent return home to Illinois. I'm pretty sure she would have been happy if that had been the outcome since that would have meant that we could have gotten back some normalcy after a year at ICAF and six months commuting to Project Beacon. But Barb had never been anything but incredibly supportive throughout my entire career, so she waited patiently for me to tell her the outcome. When she understood what had happened, her question was, "Would it be time to start to plan a move to Detroit?" Move to Detroit? Wow, that really seemed like a big decision. Even though the project had just gotten more of a green light than ever, it still seemed to me that the ice was too thin at the moment to uproot the family and hope for the best. So we decided to punt that decision, with me living the life of a long-distance commuter for a while longer, and wait to see what happened next.

Over the next week, I thought long and hard about where I should recommend the business report. On the one hand, there were going to be a lot of internal operational challenges in getting this thing off the ground, particularly within engineering and manufacturing. It might simplify things if we could somehow connect ourselves to them, and that's actually what most folks I asked thought should happen. On the other hand, this was about the creation of a fundamentally new market, a new brand, and a new customer value proposition. There would be new competitors and new market dynamics. Wouldn't it be better to plug into a place that was supposed to be externally focused, like marketing?

For a lot of reasons (not the least of which were my memories of being threatened by the operating guys), I decided that marketing would make the most sense and went to see Ron Zarrella, GM's then head of marketing, to tell him what I thought. To my surprise, not only did Ron agree to take it on, but said he wanted me working directly for him. He said he liked the idea, thought it would be fun to work on, and actually believed it might turn into something meaningful. He also thought that I'd probably get bumped around a lot within the company as we tried to get going and that it would be good to have the leverage that working for him might provide. The leverage comment was really insightful and ended up being critically important to our progress over the next couple of years.

I met with Rick Wagoner a few days later, gave him my recommendation, and told him that Ron had agreed to take it on. Rick was fine with that, but went a step further and asked that I set up regular monthly meetings with him so he could stay close to what was going on. He said he wasn't looking for the preformatted reports that he was accustomed to in the vehicle business; he just wanted me to come in and talk about what was going on. He was interested in what was going right, what was going wrong, what I needed help with, and what I was experiencing trying to do something like this inside of his organization. He'd apparently meant it when he said he wanted to learn from this, and he was taking it personally.

This was getting stranger and stranger. I'd gone overnight from wondering if there was a business worth working on to having it become the pet project of both the vice chairman and the president of GM North America. I went from hating the crazy joint-venture structure that I'd been thrown into to working for Ron, someone who I really liked and thought I could learn a lot from. And from being coerced into signing on to a plan that made no sense to having a strategy that seemed pretty solid and had the clear backing of the company. At the time, it all felt like an embarrassment of riches, but moving forward ultimately required every ounce of that support, and more.

Now it was time for the fun stuff. After we put the initial timing plan together, we decided that we'd target a launch on Cadillac vehicles as a dealer-installed option in the fall of 1996 (at the start of the 1997 model year). Dealer-installed wasn't ideal for a lot of reasons, not the least of which that it would be operationally complicated and position the dealers as independently minded gatekeepers to our prospective customers. But it was the only way to be fast-to-market because there was just no way to jump into a factory-installed program in less than a year and not have everything blow up. Now that we had something to shoot for, we needed to assemble a real team to make it all happen. Beyond Jon and Lorrie and a handful of relatively junior, but highly talented technical folks, we had some really important positions to fill if we were going take on the growing list of tasks that were piling up around the office.

On the plus side, I was able to get Fritz Beiermeister, a GM lifer who'd joined EMD from an international assignment in the car business just as I was leaving for Washington, to agree to move back to Detroit to be part of our leadership team. He did a great job with a very broad range of responsibilities, including getting the service center and advisors all set up as well as sorting out the logistics of getting hardware to dealers and having them trained and ready to install it in cars.

On a recommendation from Harry Pearce, we got Bruce McDonald, GM's recently retired vice president of PR and communications, to join us as a contract employee to help in getting the message out about our new business. Since it was going to be a low-volume launch, it made no sense to spend a lot of money on traditional advertising. So we needed to find ways to get nonpaid media coverage, basically turning ourselves into a news story. Bruce was perfect for the job. He knew everyone in the industry, had more energy and enthusiasm than a room full of college cheerleaders, and was a Major General in the U.S. Army Reserves just for good measure.

Ken Enborg joined from the GM legal staff and was someone I'd worked with years before on an antitrust issue at EMD. There were so many potential deal-breaking legal issues that it still amazes me we got the business off the ground. That was purely the result of Ken's unique and tireless approach to making things happen, with a little high cover from GM's former general counsel, Harry Pearce, when things got too crazy, even for Ken—which wasn't very often. Ken was an ex-Marine who'd served in Vietnam, was a former prosecutor, and saw himself as a CEO trapped in a lawyer's body. Believe me, all of that was good for us. Ken was fearless and optimistic (Marine), scheming and able to see leverage where none existed (prosecutor), and always willing to jump into any business issue with both feet whether he knew anything about it or not (CEO).

Unfortunately, in terms of other top draft choices in those earliest days, that was about it. The remainder of the key positions were filled by various lists of GM's "redeployables." It was almost always the same pitch from the organization that was sending them to us: This person is really dependable (shows up for work most of the time), has a lot of energy and creativity (moves quickly toward the door around 4 p.m. and will periodically invent new sick relatives that they need to visit), is very entrepreneurial and open to risk-taking (has a side job and doesn't wear a seat belt), and is just right for your role (what was it again that you did?).

Unfortunately, assigning less senior candidates to a program like ours actually made sense within the traditional GM template. Using

GM's rules to determine the type of person you needed for any given job, you first needed to calculate how big it was. If you were in a big organization, had a lot of people reporting to you, and had a big budget, then according to the rules, it must be a high-level job. The higher the level, the more you can pay so you can attract a better candidate. This approach makes sense for most parts of a large, stable organization, but what about starting something from scratch? There's no headcount, no organization, no budget, and therefore, by this logic, you must not need really good people. But what about the fact that everything needs to be figured out? There's no established compass heading, nobody has a template, a business model has to be invented, the technology is insanely complicated, and a new brand needs to be brought to life. Does anyone honestly think it was easier to launch Chevrolet than it was to rotate in as its tenth general manager?

Most of GM's HR folks readily admitted to the disconnect between their system and the needs of a start-up organization, but admitting it and doing anything about it are two very different things. Hey, maybe I benefitted from this personally because who in their right mind would've trusted what turned out to be a billion-dollar investment in a high-tech wireless start-up to an ex-locomotive salesman? Anyway, being saddled with some folks who weren't up for the challenge was still harder than it needed to be, but we didn't have a lot of choice. I could hold my breath, but I'd just turn blue, pass out, and wake up in the same place.

Bruce McDonald schemed with the folks in GM's PR staff (who all used to work for him), and they decided that our coming-out party should be at the Chicago Auto Show on February 7, 1996. That decision drew a line in the sand and set a lot of things in motion. We'd just received our first "working" Generation 1 module from Hughes in late December, and we already knew that version 1.0 of its embedded software was full of bugs. We'd also begun building the IT infrastructure to support the service centers, but there was a lot of duct tape holding it together, too. And, oh yea, we needed a name!

Project Beacon didn't really sound that great and neither did GM Mobile Communications Services. How do you do something like name a new company? By this point, we'd hired an ad agency that was pulling together a creative list of what we might call ourselves. The list got to be about five pages long single-spaced, and from there, it was sent to a firm that GM used to see which names were legally available. That narrowed the list down to about twenty-five or so choices, but they were still all over the map. There were literal names like "SaveME," there were artsy names like "Teleramous," and there were technology names like "Orbit Link." Out of necessity rather than concern for the democratic process, I decided to send the list home with everyone over the Thanksgiving holiday and ask them to come back with the consensus vote of their families. That narrowed the list down to three names, which we quickly took out to research, and OnStar came back as the winner.

With a name in place and a rough timetable to launch on paper, it started to feel like things would settle down a little bit. What a mistake that was. Early experience should have tipped us off that there was going to be one struggle after another, but mercifully, at this point, we couldn't see all of the problems lurking just over the horizon. It quickly became clear that this was going to be harder than it looked.

An early lesson I learned, and relearned, and relearned again, over the years was never completely trust what your suppliers are telling you, especially when there's technology involved—and maybe even less if the suppliers used to be your business partners and were still owned by your parent company. Once we got going, it became screamingly clear that both Hughes and EDS had significantly overstated their experience and capabilities with the technologies that were necessary to bring OnStar to life—the things that were supposed to be the foundation of our corporate competitive advantage.

Up until this point, they'd talked a good game, but had mainly been talking to automotive executives who thought all of this space-age stuff was either cool or too complicated to understand, or both. That led to a lot of head nodding in earlier meetings when it was all still a vague idea that most people thought probably wouldn't get off the ground anyway. Now there was a deadline, real money was being spent, and the deliverable wasn't just a flashy press release, but the scary prospect of needing to make sure that an airbag deployment's call for help would always get answered. That's when it became extremely clear to me that the choice of the business's mission—safety and security—was going to be both a blessing and a curse. As I saw it, the curse was that there was no margin for error—period. Trying hard to get it right and getting close but not delivering and blaming it on how hard the technology was just wasn't acceptable. It wasn't acceptable legally, but more importantly, it wasn't acceptable morally.

In one of our earliest meetings, when the idea of the foundation of OnStar's brand being safety and security came up, folks from the GM legal staff went into predictable hunker-down mode. Even with Ken Enborg's best emotional appeal for the ultimate value of the service to our prospective customers, his legal colleagues from central office were positioned to shut down the idea because it involved too much risk. Over the years, I've actually had a lot of people from outside the company marvel at how GM's legal staff ever allowed us to do something as apparently off-template and potentially risky as OnStar. Their sense was right; they wouldn't have allowed it, except for a reframing of the issue that came from someone they couldn't ignore, their boss Harry Pearce.

In one of the "chock full o' lawyers" meetings that was supposed to finally be the end to the project, Harry listened patiently to all of the arguments about why this was such a bad idea. There really wasn't much dissention, aside from Ken's loud and vocal defense. Otherwise, it was more like a feeding frenzy, with numerous one-upmanship examples that all seemed to end the same way—with us somehow causing a car full of nuns to get stuck on some railroad tracks and get wiped out by a speeding train.

When they'd all exhausted themselves, which takes a while with lawyers showing off for their boss, Harry finally spoke up. He asked the room a question: "If one hundred cars crash and they don't have something like OnStar on board, how many of them will call for help?" It was quiet. Then he asked, "Now, how many out of a hundred OnStar-equipped cars that crash will need to call for help before we'd be more wrong for holding back a potentially lifesaving technology like this than we would be for putting it in?" Before anyone could respond, he was emphatic that he didn't mean that anything that even worked once would meet the standard. No, his standard was clear. We would need to do everything we knew how to do to make it as reliable as best-in-class technology and strong operating discipline made possible, and then we would need to fully and clearly disclose those things that might go wrong. If we did all of that, it seemed to him that we'd be compelled to give this a chance. This was an early example of Harry helping to define what "doing the right thing" looked like at OnStar.

That ended the meeting, ended the legal sniping (for a while), and laid a large block in the foundation of the business. And while the "no excuses" imperative could be looked at as a curse, it actually ended up being a far more important blessing. It started everything about OnStar on *exactly* the right compass heading. This mission made as much sense to your heart as it did to your head and gave us a crystal-clear lens that we could use to look at many of the complicated and difficult issues that were ahead. It didn't necessarily make things any easier or the decisions less complex, but it certainly made the tradeoffs more clear and the right future paths to take more obvious. And having a team full of people with both their hearts and heads aligned fueled a passion that became a force of its own within the OnStar team.

So if we were now sure that this was the right thing to do and absolutely convinced that it had to be done right, how were we going to reconcile that with the nagging reality that our suppliers weren't the technology juggernauts that we thought they were? Hoping for the best didn't feel very good, but the only reasonable alternative seemed almost as farfetched. If somebody needed to get his or her arms around all of this complexity and integrate all of the pieces into something that had to work, no excuses, then it would have to be *us*. But us wasn't ready for that. Us hadn't been conceived or built to deal with that. Us's business plan hadn't comprehended the need for the resources to do that. Us had a problem.

That's when I started to learn just how serious Rick and Ron were when they said they really wanted to give this business a chance. This was going to take more resources and a completely different concept of the business if it was going to work. The "virtual organization" that was built into the original business plan had to go. We couldn't trust that our suppliers could work with limited oversight and deliver to a vaguely understood set of interface specifications and that, when we plugged it all together, it would stand up to the "save lives" standard. There were just too many moving parts.

I told Ron we needed to execute, what felt to me like, a self-defense, vertical integration strategy. Bring in more people to work on our own team (not sure how many) who would become the experts in how these various technologies worked together for our unique application. And since there was no application like ours anywhere in the world, we couldn't just recruit them from other companies; we'd have to grow them ourselves while the business was in launch mode. That was a lot for Ron to swallow, but thankfully, by GM terms, the numbers were still small—probably a few dozen or so extra folks to start off with and we'd figure it out from there. Ron thought about it for a minute, and rather than give me the "there's no way I'm going back to Rick to ask for more resources" speech that I was half expecting, he just said, "Makes sense—get going."

At this moment, there were a lot of other ways the story could have gone. If we'd still been part of the joint venture, there'd have been no way Hughes and EDS would have allowed us to hire these extra folks and begin to build this expertise within OnStar. They would have said they were an unnecessary expense, but their real concern would have been that they'd lose leverage by us knowing more about their secret sauce. If my boss would have been anybody other than Ron, I would have gotten the speech I expected and been left stuck in no-man's land. Either outcome would have doomed the business. But I didn't get either outcome; I just got told to get going.

So we began the process to add the resources we needed, a process that played out in one fashion or another for the next decade. At this point, however, the purpose for adding to the team was very clear and very specific—to get as deeply involved in Hughes and EDS's business as necessary to make sure everything was going to work the way it was supposed to when we flipped the switch. As you might expect, this didn't go over real well with those companies, as they much preferred to control the magic that was going on behind their curtains. Unfortunately, that was just too damn bad and only the beginning of not worrying too much about making friends and playing nice corporate politics. There were going to be many, many more bumps and bruises along the way, not because anybody wanted it that way, but because the alternative of trying to do something this different, while not making waves was never going to work. Besides, there were future airbags to respond to.

CHAPTER 6

Those Are Fighting Words

While we were privately making our plans for launch, Ford surprised everyone by announcing that they would soon been offering a service called RESCU, and it sounded eerily similar to OnStar. It would be available on select Lincoln models and was supposed to hit the market before we did. Ouch! During all of the evaluations dating back to the early 1990s, GM was convinced that nobody else was thinking about trying this, and besides, nobody else could do it anyway because they didn't have EDS and Hughes—so much for that intelligence. Our team was floored. What would happen next? I wondered if it would dampen GM's enthusiasm for the program since it clearly wasn't going to be unique anymore; it might have even sent me back to selling locomotives. Wrong. Now that Ford was planning something, the natural Southeast Michigan automotive testosterone kicked in, and it was game on.

Before Ford's announcement, the folks at Cadillac were only casually engaged. They knew about our plans to launch at the beginning of the 1997 model year, but it was going to be a dealer-installed product. To an optimist, that meant fast-to-market, but to people who'd been around for a while, it meant something closer to a mud flap or custom floor mats, accessories sold across the parts counter. Even though this "back end" parts business added up to real money at many dealerships, it was never mistaken by real car guys for the important, sexy side of the new vehicle itself. So up to this point, casual engagement from the Cadillac division folks was understandable.

But now their archrival, Lincoln, had a feature claim that Cadillac didn't, and they just couldn't stand for that. Over the years, this irrational instinct to react to anything somebody else announced caused more confusion and wasted more time than you can possibly imagine, but this time it actually worked in our favor. We were immediately summoned to Cadillac general manager John Grettenberger's office to brief him on the Lincoln announcement and assure him that what OnStar was planning was even better.

John was a tall, silver-haired, handsome man in his late fifties who was straight out of Hollywood central casting if you were looking for the head of Cadillac. He was also smart, experienced, and a genuinely nice guy. The fact that he didn't really care that much about us up until this point wasn't his fault. Why should he? We were still a science project, and a pretty humble one at that, and he was running the largest luxury car division in North America. But now a competitor was starting to make a superiority claim that intersected with our science project, and those were fighting words.

At this point, we didn't know much about the Lincoln RESCU service, but from what we could tell, it was using the same fundamental building blocks that would make up OnStar: a cellular connection, GPS signals, and a call center that would be used to deliver their services. But they were planning on taking a much easier path by completely eliminating any meaningful connection to the car. It would use the vehicle's battery to get power, but beyond that, it was isolated from the real operational side of the vehicle's electrical architecture. In layman's terms, that meant it wasn't going to sense and respond automatically to airbag deployments, and you wouldn't be able to do things like remotely unlock a vehicle's doors. This made their solution way easier to implement, but we'd researched that approach and found it wasn't nearly as compelling to customers. RESCU would've looked really advanced if there'd been no competition, and as far as Ford knew at that point, there wasn't any. That turned out to be a painfully bad assumption on their part.

John liked what he heard, believed we could pull it off (a huge leap of faith at the time), and shoved us into the fast lane. All of a sudden, we were swept up into a series of PR events that were already on Cadillac's calendar. First, there was an embargoed media event planned for late January on an ice track in Michigan's Upper Peninsula. Embargoed meant the journalists had agreed not to publish anything about what they'd seen until a previously agreed upon future date. The original reason for the event was to showcase stability-control technology, and they were using the tarmac of a retired Strategic Air Command base for driving around cones while slipping and sliding on the ice. With John's direction, the Cadillac PR team shoehorned us into the program for our first press demo. The embargo part worked since the public announcement of OnStar's creation wasn't supposed to come until the Chicago Auto Show a few weeks later.

At this point, we probably had version 3.0 of our software in the OnStar module and were finding more new bugs on a daily basis than we knew how to fix. But we worked hard to contain the demonstration to things we were pretty sure wouldn't blow up and candidly told everyone that the product was still in its developmental phase. There were a couple of glitches, but it was so cold outside and the media folks were having so much fun sliding around on the ice with the Stabilitrak demonstrations that nobody seemed to care. The most embarrassing moment came when John Grettenberger asked our "advisor" to pretend we were on I-94 near Detroit and to look in our database to recommend a hotel for the evening. Without flinching, she pulled up the location on the computer screen and offered John the Ann Arbor YMCA. I actually laughed, for a second, but John wasn't amused. A Cadillac customer being offered a place to stay at the Y—we had work to do.

There was a question period after everyone came in out of the cold, and I was actually pretty nervous. I had never, I mean *never*, interacted with anyone from the media in my old job selling locomotives. What if they asked real tough, insightful questions (not likely), or tried to embarrass me (more likely), or misquoted me (very likely), or I had a Turrets moment and said something really stupid (highly likely)? John, who was a real pro at this, calmed me down, and it went fine, with the only notable question coming from a reporter who asked whether we'd use the GPS system to tell the IRS where he was, which was kind of funny, but it actually helped us develop a thoughtful response to an issue that would come up time and time again relative to our technology and privacy.

The next big event was the Chicago Auto Show, where GM had traditionally hosted a media luncheon for several hundred folks during the show's press days. It must have been an otherwise quiet news year because the decision was made to have Rick Wagoner use the venue to announce the creation of OnStar. My role was to stand next to Rick when he made the announcement, say a couple of pre-scripted words about how excited we were to be doing this, and be ready to do demos on cars we had set up in the ballroom.

This ended up being a much more intense event than what we'd experienced in Northern Michigan. As the president of GM North America, Rick Wagoner gets a lot of attention at a major auto show like Chicago. It took a lot of energy and planning, but it was over in a blur and we survived. A fair amount of it showed up in TV news snippets; a couple even made the national broadcasts. We actually ended up in the *Wall Street Journal*, and they didn't say OnStar was stupid. There were more than a few high fives exchanged (and adult beverages consumed) by the OnStarians who had coaxed version 5.0 software (bugs and all) into producing demos that made us look like we had it all under control. Afterward, in a tone that was calmer than it should have been, Rick said there was no turning back now that we'd gone public. That remark certainly got my attention.

Courtesy of Cadillac and the need to respond to Ford RESCU, there were many more PR events over the months leading up to the official launch of the service. In some ways, they seemed like a stream of distractions in the middle of trying to get everything to work right, but it was what it was. I did learn to appreciate how Cadillac did things and was really glad that we weren't paying for it. You could always tell a Cadillac event by the accommodations (a resort that I'd never heard of), the size of the shrimp (mutant jumbo), and the fact that the reception always had an ice sculpture. But they could draw an audience, and in addition to the shrimp, that audience was being served up a growing dose of the OnStar story.

The New York Auto Show in April had another series of firsts: our first drivable demos (with version 20.0 of the software), our first real coverage on mainstream shows like *Good Morning America*, and my first live TV interview. It was a business-oriented cable show scheduled to be on at about 5:45 a.m. Eastern time, which meant very few people were going to be watching. I was so scared I don't think I slept at all and was relieved to be getting it over with when the car picked me up at about 4:45 to take me over to the studio. Our segment was just supposed to be a short filler piece on the program, mainly because the auto show was in town.

I sat through a short makeup session and then really started to get nervous when they walked me onto their set during a commercial break. The hosts barely looked up from the papers they were reading, but one of them must have noticed how pale I looked through the fake tan makeup I was wearing. He said, "Don't be nervous, and whatever happens, don't look directly into the camera." Someone backstage was counting down the seconds, and all at once, the lights were on and the host started talking, not to me, but just introducing the segment. I had no idea what to do, so I panicked and looked directly at the camera. Eventually, he was talking to me, asking questions about OnStar, and then it was over. I think I got a few things right, but it'd all happened so fast that all I remember is taking the microphone off and heading out the door in about thirty seconds, with Bruce McDonald at my side. He patted me on the back and told me I'd done a great job, but he was always so positive that he'd have said that to the tobacco executives if he'd been with them when they testified before Congress.

A week or so later, Bruce proudly gave me a tape of the interview. Wow, my own tape—I'd already forgotten how bad it felt to be there and, for a moment, wanted to believe Bruce's original review of my performance. I stuck the tape in my briefcase and forgot about it until I was home with my family in Illinois the following weekend. I pulled it out and thought, "Why not impress my wife with my newfound media skills?" She politely agreed to watch it with me, so in the machine it went. The segment started with the host on camera introducing the topic. Hey, I remembered that. And then they switched cameras and turned on the one that I was *staring* into with the most vacant, terrified look on my face that I'd ever seen. Oh my God, how embarrassing. Unfortunately, we were now committed to watch the next one minute and fifty-four seconds of the interview, and it didn't get any better. I'd never heard myself talk so fast and hadn't realized how much uninteresting and unintelligible technology jargon I'd already accumulated. At one point, the host tried to help by stopping me mid-sentence and asking what all of that meant to real people—like maybe could we someday help save peoples' lives? I think I answered "probably."

Mercifully, the tape was over. My loving wife, Barbara, in the most supportive voice she could muster, just said, "You looked a little nervous." I broke out laughing and said, "You think?" This was one of those humbling moments that everyone needs from time to time, and Barb was doing her best not to pile on. But it taught me a couple lessons. First, calm down, be yourself, and don't try to impress anyone with what you think you know. Second, never *ever* collect or look at any of those kinds of tapes again. There'd be more media encounters (there had to be if we were going to get the OnStar story out there with our nonexistent advertising budget), but they weren't there to turn me into the star of the show—that was a bridge too far.

Meanwhile, between the media events, we were still only beginning to appreciate how hard this was to actually do. We were grinding on the hardware readiness, the back-office service technology, advisor hiring and training templates, the supply chain that would get the unit to a dealer, early connections with the 911 community, and our relationship with the wireless industry. Not only was there no existing path to follow, too many of the paths we were inventing were ending up in the wrong place.

Getting the OnStar module ready for production had been sold to us by Hughes as one of the things we wouldn't have to worry about. They were smart, experienced, and had it figured out. Sure, there'd be a few bumps (remember, this actually was rocket science stuff after all), but they had it under control. Well, maybe, but if under control looked like this, then what did flaming chaos look like?

We'd started our validation process for the OnStar module in December 1995 with version 1.0 software running inside the box. When all was said and done, our first production installation in September 1996 was being powered by version 55.0. I wish I could say we had a numbering system that skipped versions, but we didn't. That meant there were fifty-four distinct versions of the pre-production module over those nine months that had something (or many things) in them that didn't work. There was one where if you touched the car's door handle with static electricity on your hand, the system thought its airbag had deployed and made a call for help.

There was another part of the system that was designed to automatically go to "sleep" to save power when you were out of the car, but wake up for one minute out of every ten so that we could interact with the vehicle if you'd locked your keys in the car. I was still flying home to Illinois every weekend, leaving my prototype OnStar-equipped DeVille sitting in the parking lot at Detroit Metro Airport, and unfortunately, there were many times when I would find myself needing a jump start on Monday morning because OnStar had eaten my car's battery. This happened many times for many different reasons until, one Monday morning, the OnStar system finally outdid itself. By this time, I think, partially out of pity, GM was letting me park in the private lot at Metro that was attached to the hangar that housed their fleet of corporate aircraft. When I stepped off the shuttle bus that Monday, the guard at the gate said that I'd probably need to make other parking arrangements in the future. Apparently, sometime late on Saturday night, my Cadillac had become possessed and scared the daylights out of the guard who was on duty. The system woke up just as it was supposed to, but instead of going back to sleep for another nine minutes, it decided to throw a party for all of the electrons on the car. The OnStar module turned on the radio, started flashing the lights, kept locking and unlocking the doors, and began honking the horn. The commotion didn't last long, but it ended the same way, with another dead battery and another software version that needed to go back to the drawing board.

We were experiencing similar drama on most of the other work streams as well, with gremlins seemingly in charge of the call center, the dealer ordering process, the marketing materials— almost anything that moved was moving in the wrong direction. We kept hiring people in all areas of the business and were probably batting a little over five hundred in terms of their ultimate fit for what we needed. Part of it was because we weren't very successful at attracting GM's best talent, and part of it was that it was hard to convince really good people from outside the company to join GM and move to Detroit.

At that point, OnStar was an unknown commodity stuck inside a corporation without a track record of innovation located in a city that most folks didn't want to visit, much less live in. The unknown part was unavoidable; there was nothing yet to know. The stuck inside of GM part was unavoidable as well. We could try to merchandise it otherwise, but there was no hiding the fact that we were a very small part of a very large corporation that was seen as bureaucratic and uninterested in anything that didn't convert fossil fuel into torque. In many ways, the Detroit part was and still is a bum rap.

Sure, the city of Detroit itself had problems. Coming from the Chicago area, the comparisons between the two were really sad. While both had their share of issues and places that you probably needed to steer clear of, Chicago had another side: a beautiful lakefront, downtown shopping, and shows; a vibrant and well-balanced economy; and a strong base of residential taxpayers. Detroit had a riverfront, but back then, most of it was filled with abandoned buildings, parking decks, and even a cement factory. This once magnificent city had fallen on long-term hard times, in many ways because its prospects were inexorably linked with a domestic auto industry that had been in a gradual state of decline for decades. While you had to admire the grit and determination that Detroiters displayed for "making a comeback," the challenges facing the city made the eventual outcome of the renewal efforts questionable at best.

No, you wouldn't mistake Detroit for Chicago. But once you got out of the city and into the suburbs and beyond, the scales actually tilted the other way. There weren't as many suburbs as Chicago had because it was a smaller city to start with. But the ones that were there were every bit as attractive as anything you'd find in the Chicago area. And beyond the suburbs, what you found in the Chicago area was basically flat farmland. Michigan, on the other hand, was a beautiful collection of inland lakes, rolling hills, and more freshwater coastline than the West Coast of the United States had on the Pacific Ocean.

Now, shoreline aside, you'd never mistake Detroit, or even Michigan, with San Diego—particularly in February. But we ultimately found that if we could solve the first two issues, turning OnStar into something people knew enough about to want to join and having evidence that being a part of GM wasn't a hindrance to a start-up business, then we could get people past the knee-jerk stigma associated with being located in Detroit. But we weren't there yet.

Sometime earlier in the year, somebody from EDS had asked if we'd be OK being nominated for a technology award. I didn't think they were serious because, at that point, there wasn't really anything to nominate, but as long as it didn't cost anything, what the heck. With so much else going on, I'd completely forgotten about it until May, when EDS got a call from the folks who made the award selections and were told we'd been named a finalist in the transportation category. All right, we were a finalist; that sounded good. What was the award again? What did it mean? And when would we find out if we actually won?

The award was the Computerworld Smithsonian Award. It was meant to honor the year's most significant use of information technology in eight different categories like medicine, education, entertainment, and transportation. Previous winners had been companies like Federal Express and Pixar Animation, so it sounded legit. And the only way to find out if you won was to attend the black-tie awards ceremony gala in Washington, DC, and see if your name got called.

How in the world did we ever get to be a finalist in something like this? We needed to hire the person from EDS who wrote our nomination, because from the quality of our early marketing materials, we were in no danger of winning Jiffy Lube's Golden Dipstick Award, much less something from the Smithsonian. Anyway, on June 23, 1996, literally three months before we had our first customer, we flew to Washington, got all dressed up, and went to the ball. It was an incredible event, with hundreds of very well-dressed people mingling in the National Building Museum. I can't remember who the other four finalists in our category were, but it didn't matter. There was no way we could win, so I began practicing my "being nominated is award enough" line.

The dinner ended, and the awards ceremony began. I don't know why, but the merlot they were serving that evening was particularly smooth and had gone down very easy—in quantity. Anyway, no worries. Sit up straight for the next hour or so of awards and go home a proud nominee. It was finally our category's turn. They had nice sixty-second videos on a thirty-foot-wide screen for each finalist, followed by the envelope opening. Our video actually looked pretty good, and if you didn't know that we were struggling to get version 39.0 of the software to stop eating car batteries, you'd be pretty impressed. You know what happens next.

The envelope opened, and OnStar was announced as the winner. It took a second for that to sink in, and before it did, a spotlight hit our table. It now occurred to me, as I was weaving my way toward the stage, that I should've spent more time on that acceptance speech. Thankfully, the merlot kicked in and made me forget, among other things, how nervous I was. Blah, blah, thank you, thank you, blah, blah, and I headed back to my seat carrying the hardware. It was so cool. The award itself is awesome, a fairly large crystal cube with some sort of hologram image floating inside, mounted on a piece of stone that was supposed to look like it came from the ruins of a Greek temple. And it says Smithsonian on it—*Smithsonian*, for heaven's sake. I don't know much about branding, but my guess was that our little brand just got a big shot in the arm.

I flew back to Detroit the next morning with great memories and only a slight headache from the night before. Coincidentally, I was supposed to attend Ron Zarrella's staff meeting that afternoon and provide them with an OnStar update. This was my lucky day, and up to this point, I hadn't had many. I'd just bring my newfound prop to the meeting, and these guys would be blown away. There was no telling how excited they'd get to be able to associate the GM brand with winning an award from the Smithsonian.

Another life lesson I learned, along the same lines of watching my TV interview, these guys couldn't have cared less. What was the award again? Something from the Smithsonian—aren't they the guys that have stuff like George Washington's wooden teeth on display? Wow, for a second there, they thought it might be something really important like the Motor Trend Golden Caliper or Car and Driver's Pewter Piston. But an award from outside the car industry—who would care about that?

You have got to be kidding! I was shocked, disappointed, frustrated, and just plain pissed off. Ron thought it was pretty cool, but not cool enough to make a big deal about it to the other guys. This is when it became clear, crystal clear, that we had to accept that most of these folks would just never get it. Hey, look, I was as surprised as anyone that we'd won, considering the current state of our little adventure. But people, extremely smart people who knew their way around technology, had looked at what we were up to and acknowledged its significance by placing one of the most respected brands in America on it.

It was starting to sink in to me just how important all of this might actually be, and I would've thought (or hoped) that this might have triggered an instinct in at least one of these guys that we had something that might change the game a little bit. And since the way the game was currently going had led to years of sustained market share loss, didn't we need a disruptive innovation to change things in our favor? This was a chance to fundamentally lead in something meaningful and profoundly important. Isn't that what marketing is supposed to be all about? Isn't that what business is supposed to be all about?

As hard as it was to swallow that afternoon, it was good to learn this lesson early. Their reaction had been so outrageously wrong that even a recently displaced locomotive salesman knew that their perspective in this area was awful. Believe it or not, this helped a lot over the subsequent years. Whenever we'd get pushed around and marginalized by the traditional marketing guys in the company, it was easier for us to stand our ground with a clear conscience, knowing that their product leadership instincts were horrible. No, heated windshield washer solution and sliding roofs that let you carry a grandfather clock standing straight up inside a SUV were not as important as something that was completely unique and could save your life—and they honestly shouldn't have needed the Smithsonian to tell them that. But they had, and they still weren't listening. Unbelievable.

The last couple of months before launch were spent in whack-a-mole mode—you remember, that arcade game when you were at the Chuck E. Cheese's restaurant for your kid's preschool birthday parties. You'd drop in a quarter (in our case a few million dollars) and mechanical moles would randomly pop up their heads on a large flat table. The objective was to protect your front lawn by whacking them with a large padded club before they could escape and pop up somewhere else. If only real life were so straight forward and fulfilling, but the metaphor was perfect, save the satisfaction of hitting something with a club.

Moles took the form of never-ending software glitches, missed pieces of the ordering process, late and poorly executed dealer training materials, uncompleted contracts with numerous wireless carriers—the list went on and on. My recent training at ICAF would have called this the "fog of war," basically the concept that even the best battle plans never survive the first shot because stuff happens. Except that, in our case, it was worse. We didn't have a great battle plan to begin with, and no shots had been fired yet. Who knew what would happen when somebody really shook the snow globe hard?

This was one of the many times where my lack of experience with something this new could have really hurt a normal start-up, maybe even sunk it. Typically, companies at this stage are really fragile and always run the risk of running out of time and/or money before they figure out how to get it right. But, this time, some of the things that were so frustrating about GM, being bureaucratic and not having a lot of experience with early-stage ventures, actually worked in our favor. We were so small and GM's expectations were so low that there wasn't a robust external oversight process in place. In essence, they were leaving us alone, which, in retrospect, was either brilliant and gutsy or something else—like being preoccupied with the issues in their much larger automotive business. It was probably some of both.

Had the circumstances been different and had OnStar been started as someone's core business instead of a small science project inside of a massive corporation, I probably wouldn't have survived the run up to the launch. But I was trying as hard as I could, and as long as they were OK with keeping me in the job and letting me figure it out on the fly, I certainly wasn't going to volunteer to be relieved. It was turning into another graduate program, the third and most expensive one that GM had sent me to so far—the OnStar innovation school of hard knocks. I was beginning to appreciate just how hard this program was likely to be and somehow wished I'd signed up for more of the prerequisites. Sorry, you play it where it lies. I guess I didn't know what VUCA meant until I spent a year at Ft. McNair. I just didn't know how quick I'd get a chance to live it.

CHAPTER 7

Launch

So now it was time. The game was afoot. All of the preparations for the launch were as ready as they could be, and at this point, we were still clinging to the naive, but comforting allusion that you really could have it all figured out. Wow, was that wrong. Anyway, the past fifteen months were now behind us, and they'd been either the fastest fifteen months of my life or the slowest—I wasn't quite sure.

While we knew the technology part of this was going to be hard, things were actually feeling pretty good at this point. Version 55.0 of the module was stable, as was the software at the OnStar center. And the new advisor training had produced a small, but enthusiastic band of newly minted OnStar advisors. The one area that seemed to be bogged down was our sales and marketing activity, especially our relationship with the dealers. But it didn't seem like that was going to be a showstopper, and besides, with something as unique and com-pelling as OnStar, I was confident that we'd be able to refine and course-correct in that area once we got up and running.

The early suite of OnStar services consisted of everything that we were technically able to execute at that point. Since the research said safety and security services were highly appealing, we anchored the ser-vice portfolio with automatic crash response triggered by the detection of an airbag deployment and emergency services that could be sum-moned at the push of a button. We also had automatic stolen vehicle response, remote door unlock, and a vehicle finder service, where we could remotely trigger the car's horn and headlights if you had lost it in a parking lot. Rounding out our safety and security category was roadside assistance, where the press a button would summon a tow truck if you'd run out of gas or had a flat tire.

In the area of convenience services, we offered an early form of route assistance and a very open-ended catchall category called concierge services. Under that category, we had instructed our advisors to try to accommodate any requests our customers might have, as long as they were legal. That meant everything from making hotel reservations and flight arrangements, to sending flowers, to planning parties, to singing happy birthday, and to settling in-vehicle trivia disputes. Hotel reservations we'd thought about, but singing songs and looking up the names of the Seven Dwarfs hadn't been baked in the training materials, so it was live and learn.

Our first customers needed to be real pioneers since buying OnStar required a little faith and a lot of determination and perseverance. Faith because there was no awareness of a brand called OnStar, and there was no frame of reference to understand our services. So somebody had to think about why they would want something like this in the first place and then decide why they should trust an unknown company like us to deliver it. We ultimately wanted what every new company in any new industry wants—to become the Kleenex of whatever our emerging industry would ultimately be called. Only, there were two problems: (1) We hadn't delivered anything yet, and (2) people didn't know that they had our version of a runny nose.

The determination part came in how hard it was to actually get OnStar once you'd decided you wanted to buy it. The dealer-installed option, which had helped us finesse a number of internal process issues that would have otherwise delayed the launch by at least a couple of years, was actually a train wreck in many other ways. First, it put the dealers in the position of gatekeepers to our prospective customers. This meant that the only way that a potential customer would even know that there was such a thing as OnStar was if the dealer decided to talk about it when the vehicle was being sold. On some level, we knew that, but we were relying on the fact that this new technology and service was such a unique and compelling competitive advantage for Cadillac. Surely the dealers would be excited to talk about it to help them sell more cars. How often does something like this come along? And it was exclusively available on Cadillac vehicles—what a no-brainer.

This is one of the many places where my personal lack of experience and the fact that we had been assigned a "redeployable" executive from Cadillac as our head of marketing almost derailed the business. Rather than completely understanding the reality of the dealership dynamics, we relied on a flawed theory of how this would work. Sure, dealers wanted to sell new vehicles, but what they're more interested in is making as much money as possible—can't blame them for that. In their view, it was up to the manufacturer—in this case, Cadillac—to market the important and unique features of their vehicles to the point where they attracted real prospects into their dealerships and away from BMW, Lexus, and Lincoln, also called "driving showroom traffic." Typically, that's done with a mix of feature and call-to-action advertising, something GM and the other manufacturers spent billions on every year. Once in the store, it was the dealer's job to "close the deal" and, where possible, bundle as much other high-margin stuff in the transaction as they could without having it unwind.

So now we come in and tell them, here's what we think you should do: You should talk to every prospect who comes into your showroom about this new thing called OnStar, never mind the fact that neither you nor they have ever heard of it before. Why? Because we've got research that says that people will want to buy your Cadillac more if it has OnStar, and if you don't tell them about it, they won't know. If they're interested, we want you to sell them the system at an MSRP of $895 plus installation (approximately another $100 or so). Then you need to order a parts kit, schedule a time for them to bring their new car back in for installation, and sign them up to separate OnStar and cellular contracts so that the whole thing will work.

What was supposed to be in it for them? First, it would help them sell cars. Second, the safety benefits of OnStar would be good for their customers; it might actually save their life. Third, we'd priced the system so they'd make a fair profit; essentially, the normal factory option margin on the hardware (roughly 15 percent) and the installation would generate some profitable work for their service bay. And, finally, it would give them a technology leadership claim, something that could provide a much-needed halo to their entire Cadillac franchise. To us, this didn't seem like an unreasonable way to start.

From their standpoint, their response was simple. We're not going to bring this up to most customers, because if we do, we'll just confuse them and maybe cause them to have to think about it rather than just buying the car (remember, the average age of Cadillac customers was well over sixty). By the way, if it's so good, why don't you advertise it yourself? And while this might help sell a car or two on the margin, by the time we get customers in the showroom and ready to sign, it's all about price, and we'll risk losing the deal if we add anything to the monthly payment. Oh, and by the way, if we can add anything to the monthly payment, it won't be something that gets a 15 percent margin. Remember, we have many other things we can sell, like rust-proofing, vinyl tops, pin stripes, and extended warranties. They may not save a life, but they'll produce a 50 percent margin. And one more by the way, your process is a royal pain in the neck, so either pay me or my salesman an extra "spiff" for the trouble (commonly $50 to $100 per transaction), or don't expect any help.

That's pretty much an unvarnished view of the landscape, as it existed shortly after we launched. I wish we'd been able to see it that clearly ahead of time because maybe we could have done something different and avoided a lot of the ensuing hassles. Not that it matters, but I can say that our motives were pure, and we honestly thought what we were doing was reasonable and fair for everyone. In retrospect, I have to say that the dealers' perspective was also fair and reasonable, which left a pretty gaping hole in our strategy.

Beyond all of that, which was enough, we were thankfully small enough to be able to avoid a head-on collision with another religious dealer issue regarding who "owned" the customer. From the first time I heard it characterized that way, I have to say I really hated the arrogance in the notion of customer "ownership." Sure, you need to understand and respect how the distribution chain worked and the roles and responsibilities of each of the players; that just makes sense. But, for some reason, over the hundred-year history of the auto industry, this ownership issue had created a strange dynamic, which resulted in way too many processes that were internally focused and didn't serve the needs of real customers at all. While we were playing Hatfield's and McCoy's with each other, no matter who "owned" them, more customers than not routinely described their car-buying experience as "going in for a root canal."

But it was what it was, and in the auto business, it was clearly established that the factory was the factory, and its customer was supposed to be defined as the dealer—period. And everything that had to do with a real customer, the person with the actual choice of where to spend his or her money, needed to run through the dealers. The conceptual question was why should OnStar be treated any different? OnStar was just another label for something from the GM factory, and there were rules for how things like that should work. Shouldn't the customer just be told that they needed to buy the subscription from the dealer, at whatever price they wanted to set? The dealer had sold the car, so it was *their* customer, right?

This issue came up time and time and time again over the years, but thankfully, we were so small when we first ran into it that it didn't turn into a war. We were on the wrong side of the theory, but there wasn't enough money at stake back then to make it worth the dealers' time to pick a fight on this issue. It was probably one of many examples of where the expectations for our future survival were so low that we got left alone—which was really fortunate.

It wasn't without some drama, though, even if it was mainly caused by folks from GM's own dealer contact organization. Too many times these guys saw their role as defending the dealers' point of view, rather than trying to factor in what would also be good for customers and GM. Why not just make it "easier for everybody" and follow the car model? We'd deliver the service wholesale to the dealer, and they'd take care of everything. They'd mark it up and resell it to the customer at whatever price they chose, and everything would work out fine. What could be easier?

Easy maybe, but I wasn't sure *easy* was the objective. If GM's auto business had been so outrageously successful, then, fine, don't screw up something that was working so well. But, come on, unless you'd been living in a cave for the past twenty-five years, you couldn't have missed the fact that this business model was straining at the seams. All the profit—no, actually, more than all of the profit—was being earned by an increasingly narrow group of vehicles, mainly trucks. And while nobody wanted to talk about it, we were skating one Middle East oil disruption away from much higher gas prices and a predictable evaporation of that critical segment. No, this probably wasn't the time to leave well enough alone because it wasn't well enough.

In all likelihood, had this turned into a real showdown issue, Rick and Ron would have probably acted like the adult supervision that they were and done the right thing. Thankfully, for them and for us, we didn't have to use the cavalry for this uprising. The few passionate voices in the field vented, and there were some tough discussions and low level threats of retribution, but it never reached critical mass. But it was a really, really important thing to have gotten through. If the business would have been forced to do the "easy," natural thing, GM never could have justified taking this on. There just wasn't ever going to be enough money in what customers would be willing to pay for our service to be able to divide it up into multiple pieces and have enough left over for GM to compensate for their risk and investment of starting OnStar—it wasn't possible.

Had the decision actually gone the other way and taken the easier path, then there wouldn't have been anything to write about. OnStar would have quietly launched, run into all of the challenges that came later, and GM would have concluded that the business model just wasn't going to work. It would have started and ended as a small science project, much like GM's EV1 electric vehicle. The conclusion would have gone something like, "This was a nice idea that was just a little ahead of its time," and then it would have been shut down and dismantled.

I'm not sure how many things come and go inside of big companies like that, not because they were destined to fail, but because the strategy or execution was flawed and caused them to fail. That's real life; it's sometimes unavoidable. Probably the best you can hope for is to learn and move on. The problem is that inside of big companies, there's a lot of inertia that works against the candid introspection necessary to really understand *why* something failed. The learning would have likely stopped at a superficial version of "I told you nobody really wanted this stuff," and the company would have just moved on. Maybe I'm wrong, and maybe that's why Rick wanted to stay personally involved to avoid that outcome, but thankfully, we'll never know.

Anyway, we were able to stick to our guns on the service-revenue issue, hunkered down, and began to comprehend the next range of challenges. As I said, we had a different model in mind than the dealers did. Instead of everybody being told about OnStar, probably one in ten folks were hearing something about the service at the dealership. And instead of $895 plus installation, we were hearing of prices approaching $3,000 in some instances. To the dealers, this was just, "Hey, if somebody really wanted this stuff, why not make them pay?" The gatekeeping had begun, and if the intention was to test the resolve of the early customers, it worked.

I had drawn a bull's-eye on a sheet of paper with a fifty in the middle and concentric circles going all the way down to ten. We'd get daily reports of how many kits had shipped from the warehouse, and in the month of November, I'd put a small X on the target corresponding to that day's the volume—fifteen one day, six the next, twenty-one, and then nine. I dreamed of the time that we'd ever get to fifty new customers in a single day, but it wasn't feeling likely. This was hard work with ugly results and few encouraging signs from anywhere. I continued separate, periodic meetings with Ron, Rick, and Harry, and while nobody was thrilled with the sales, my sense was that they were all somewhat amazed that we'd actually gotten the airplane off the ground.

Harry was the most philosophical and continued to characterize things in respect to the long-term vision. Rick was interested in what else we were running into and learning as human pin-balls bouncing around between GM's internal organizations, the dealers, and real customers. Ron was more interested in the specific strategies and tactics that we were using, what was working and what wasn't, and what we planned to do about it. He was always optimistic about what might be possible, but also very realistic about the challenges we'd face trying to get there. First and foremost, he wanted to win, not just play a good game, and later rationalize why we hadn't—that just wasn't his style.

One early example of that was a meeting about three months or so after we'd launched. The sales were struggling, and there was absolutely no momentum, but we had started to find very isolated pockets—in some cases individual dealers—where penetration rates were approaching 25 percent. That was huge considering that the average at that point was below 5 percent. I'd gone to Ron's office to show him some of those results and to ask for his help in getting more support from Cadillac to actually promote the service with advertising and better dealer engagement. Ron listened patiently but really didn't get too excited, at least not to me. But, after the meeting, he must have twisted somebody's tail because, the next thing I knew, Cadillac had decided to offer OnStar with one year of free service as one of the choices a customer could make during their upcoming annual spring special promotion. This was a big deal.

Spring specials are traditional events on most automakers' promotional calendars and usually involve extra discounts, free options like leather seats or sunroofs, and unique advertising to support the call to action. Spring is an important selling season, when people emerge from the doldrums of winter and start thinking about buying a car. And it's the last chance the auto industry gets to sell the vehicles at reasonable prices before they go into clearance mode in the "Summer Sell-Down," which occurs just before the new-model-year vehicles are being introduced in September. It's Detroit's circle of life and extremely important to the overall performance of every company.

The good news for us in being included was that this would be our first encounter with a national, varsity-level selling event. That meant there'd be a big national advertising campaign to make people aware of OnStar without costing any extra money since there would be special promotional advertising anyway. And even though it was being "given away," it was no more costly than the extra $1,000 discount that was one of the alternative choices, and in this case, it actually had the potential to earn back some of the cost if the customers stayed with the service.

The second benefit was in helping to align the dealership network. If there were enough interest generated with the advertising, the Cadillac dealerships that'd been completely ignoring us would have to become engaged. If people saw the ads and came in asking about it, the salespeople would need to be able to talk knowledgeably about OnStar or be embarrassed, which nobody wanted. And if OnStar's penetration rates increased, the dealers would get much needed experience at ordering and installing the vehicle hardware kits. It was brilliant—and better yet, it worked. New subscriber sign-ups went from less than two hundred per week before to four thousand per week during the promotion. Everyone at OnStar went on high alert. It stressed everything in our little business and required a lot of energy and creativity to pull it off, which was just what we needed.

Beyond the flow through the dealers, the promotion also added early critical mass to our subscriber base. It was still very small, but at least we were starting to get a regular flow of different call types into the OnStar center. We'd experienced our first real airbag deployment call months before, everything had worked as planned, and we spent a fair amount of time afterward debriefing everyone involved and learning as much as we could. But an occasional airbag deployment and the few door unlocks that we were delivering meant that we were really just biding our time. We needed more volume to bring the business to life. There was an unimaginably rich range of customer interactions to be experienced, and we were itching to get at them.

This is about the time the story changed. The mechanical part of getting everything organized included extremely important milestones, such as delivering a few kits, running a few call types through our infrastructure, knitting together a national cellular network, and starting our interactions with the 911 community. It was essentially setting up the first version of the business's plumbing, and while it looked and felt more like the Flintstones than the Jetsons, it worked. But now we were starting to understand what the plumbing was actually capable of doing, and not just technically. This plumbing had a higher purpose than to just generate press coverage in *Popular Science* magazine; it was supposed to positively impact peoples' lives.

We'd decided early on that if our service was going to be focused on safety and security, then our brand needed to be thought of as personal and approachable—something our customers could rely on and trust. We also knew that if we came across as big, impersonal General Motors, especially since our services required using GPS to know the location of the vehicle, then we'd have every conspiracy theorist from here to Montana thinking that Big Brother had just come to life. So our marketing agency came up with the idea that there should be a person behind the brand, at least for the direct materials that we'd send to subscribers when they first signed up.

At this point, it could have gone in a number of directions. Maybe it should be a celebrity since GM was certainly very familiar with that approach. It could be a sports icon or a movie star, or someone actually suggested a former astronaut. Or maybe it should be John

Grettenberger, the general manager of Cadillac, since everything would be initially going to Cadillac customers anyway. There were challenges with each approach, not the least of which that we had no money to spare. And what would happen if the business failed? Who would want to risk having egg on their face?

One thing led to another until we decided we needed to find someone who was unknown, cheap, and expendable. Hmmm... Where have we seen those traits come up before? The next thing I knew, the choices had been narrowed down to Sam Sample or me. OK, it would have been pretty silly to have a fake person represent our first contact with real customers, so I agreed that my signature could be used in the correspondence. I just had no idea what would come next.

In early 1997, I received a letter addressed directly to me from one of our early subscribers. It was handwritten and had taken a little while to get to me since it was sent to the return address on our marketing materials. The letter started out by saying that the subscriber and his wife had been driving their OnStar-equipped Cadillac on a trip to Florida when, out of nowhere, his wife experienced a heart attack while sitting in the passenger seat as he was approaching Atlanta. The next sentence simply said that she had died one week later.

This was the opening paragraph in what was a much longer letter, but at this point, my hand had begun to shake so hard that I had to put it down on my desk. A million things raced through my mind. I began to sweat, and my eyes started to water. What had we done wrong? How could this have happened? Would there be a lawsuit? What was I going to tell Ron, and Rick, and Harry? I knew we'd worked very hard to make sure that everything was ready, but what did we really know? We didn't have anyone to copy or benchmark or to really check our work. We were hanging out there doing the absolute best we knew how, but in this case, it obviously hadn't been enough. I was starting to get a really bad ache in the pit of my stomach, my head hurt, and I probably would've curled up in the fetal position under my desk if I'd been thinking clearly. But, at that moment, I wasn't thinking clearly.

At some point, I don't know how long it took, the engineer in me finally kicked in. The rational thing to do, the only thing to do, would be to pick up the letter, finish reading it, and then deal with the consequences. Somebody had to, and anyway, it had been sent to me. So I cleared my eyes and kept reading.

The letter went on to say that the subscriber remembered that he had OnStar and pushed the button. He said he was connected to a wonderful woman who found the nearest hospital, gave him directions on how to get there, and then called ahead to the hospital to alert them that he and his wife were on their way. He said that the doctors later told him that the quick response and the hospital being prepared for the emergency were the only reasons his wife had lived for a while longer. He wanted to thank OnStar and the advisor for the extra week with his wife because he said he needed it.

I put the letter down again. My hand was still shaking, I was sweating, and my eyes were waterier than before. All of my emotions were upside down. I was relieved, profoundly sad, grateful, proud, and humbled all at the same time. This man had just experienced a terrible, life-changing tragedy and, for some unexplainable reason, felt the need to reach out to someone he didn't know, thousands of miles removed from the event, and express the most heartfelt thanks that I could have ever imagined. It was at that exact moment that I began to understand what we were really doing and what this was really going to be all about.

Didn't we know we'd be involved in seriously important events like crash responses and emergency services? I mean, they were even listed in our brochure. Sure we did, intellectually, but not emotionally, not like this. In hindsight, it should have been obvious that it was only a matter of time before we got a faceful of what the real OnStar was destined to be all about. It wasn't going to be about technology, or business models, or brand management, or dealer relations, or any of the other challenges in getting the business going. It was going to be about the reality of promising to be there for our subscribers when they needed us most and then delivering on that promise. It wasn't always going to end well—it couldn't. By the time we got involved, something bad had already happened. But, many times, we could help change the outcomes for the better, and when we did, we'd have accomplished something awesome and made an important contribution to someone's life.

After this, the idea that we'd ever need a lawyer or anybody else from outside the business to tell us that we had to be careful, work hard, and make sure we were doing the best we could for our customers was absurd. We already knew that, and there'd been no law written that would've been more motivating than the moral obligation we felt to get this right. Also, after this, the idea that we'd ever let someone tell us to cut costs or do something stupid in any part of the business that might impact our ability to be there for our customers was equally absurd. I'd crossed a line; no, we'd all crossed a line. This was the day a career assignment ended and a personal mission began, and not just for me.

It's really clear to me now that I should have kept that letter, mounted it in some sort of indestructible case, and put it in the OnStar museum. But, back then, there was no OnStar museum; there was just a small, struggling group of people working on an idea that was clearly bigger than all of us. It did occur to me, though, to share the story with everyone working in the business, particularly the advisor who had taken the call. She remembered the event, but had no idea of what had happened next. How could she? She'd lost touch with the couple when they got to the hospital. It was always like that and still is. Our advisors have a brief, but extremely important intersection with a serious event; we run our leg of the race and pass the baton without seeing how it ends. When it's over, the advisor is teleported into another vehicle in another state, and he or she does it all over again. Even now, over a decade and millions of interactions later, the individual stories still feel just as emotional to everyone involved. But, back then, when we were so small and still just figuring it out, this feedback was extremely rare and precious.

I did send the letter, along with a brief note, to Harry Pearce. Harry had been so courageous in getting the idea of OnStar off the ground and spoke with such passion about why it would be so important that I thought he deserved to read it himself. My note simply said, "We don't have it all figured out yet, but we're doing the right thing." Harry understood and appreciated the comment. There were still many more unknowns than the traditional GM would ever be comfortable with, and we were creating enough problems that we were probably never going to make many friends inside the company, but this was important and the right thing to do. I think he was proud, but I never asked him—there wasn't time.

So this wasn't a bad way to summarize our first year in business. PowerPoint slides yielded to real customers. The technology turned out to be more bleeding than leading edge, but we had enough tourniquets in the form of a growing band of emotionally committed professionals that we could control the blood loss and keep moving forward. Many people in the core vehicle business could find ten reasons to stop and call it a day for every one reason to keep going, but we were generally no more than a mildly annoying gnat, so they left us alone. Our many shoestring catches and near-death experiences taught us humility, tenacity, confidence, and resolve—critical cultural traits that we would need in abundance in the years ahead. And, finally, we'd come out of the first year with a real identity, not one made up in a focus group. We might ultimately end up doing more than safety and security, but that would always be the soul of OnStar, which set a very high standard for everything else we ever did.

CHAPTER 8

Fred and Walt

With the first year behind us, everything we'd experienced pointed to the fact that there was a lot more that we didn't know than what we did. This was a living, breathing example of the "slippery slope," "in for a penny, in for a pound," or whatever other cute way there was to say that we were being drawn farther and farther out into deeper and deeper water. This sounded more ominous than it actually was; frankly, not knowing all of the things we'd run into next probably actually helped. In blackjack, who in their right mind would hit a twelve if they knew the next card was a king? There's no fun in that, only pain. Better not to know sometimes and just play it as it lies.

But even playing it where it lies requires clubs, a ball, a tee, shoes, and maybe even some skill. It was great to survive the first year, mainly because it's the only way you can get to a second year. But getting through the second year was going to require a lot more. It was now excruciatingly clear that we needed a few more clubs in the bag, probably some new spikes, maybe a lesson or two on the short game, and perhaps a glow-in-the-dark ball since we seemed to be playing so many holes in the dark. In other words, we needed to completely retool our game to have any chance of keeping up with the business we'd just started.

Some of the gaps were painful and obvious. Despite the progress we'd made getting our arms around the technology, there seemed no end to the challenges we were having getting it to behave on a regular basis—and that was before we started trying to teach it any new tricks. Life would've been so much simpler if we could've launched the first year and then just said, "Stop, no more changes until everything settles down." That was laughable because nothing ever seemed to settle down. And it was even more laughable to think we had the power to hit the pause button and think it was connected to anything that would make any difference.

Whether we liked it or not, everything around us was rapidly changing, mostly for reasons that had nothing to do with us. New vehicle models were being introduced every year. Included in the new models were separately evolving subsystem architectures, things like radios, airbag modules, stability-control systems, and power train controllers that might or might not have an effect on what we were doing. Every time any of these changed, the complex interactions of the technologies created an unexplored set of permutations that could either be benign or inadvertently turn loose another tribe of hostile gremlins intent on wreaking havoc somewhere within OnStar. The problem was you could never tell, so you were safer betting on the gremlins.

Outside the auto industry, technology was moving even faster. We knew that, but it was just our luck to land smack-dab in the middle of the then emerging wireless category that was moving hyper fast, even by consumer electronics standards. The cellular industry of 1997 looks tame today, but back then, it was as close to cowboy capitalism as you could imagine. Literally, hundreds of separate cellular companies, competing with loosely defined interface standards, were just emerging from the early 1990s constraints of large and costly devices. Remember when everything used to be called a car phone? A range of portable handsets were starting to hit the market in quantity, but were notable in their bulky size, lack of sophistication, and short battery life. The overall industry had a subscriber base of about twenty-five million, which seemed large at the time, but was nowhere near as big as it needed to be to make its massive infrastructure investments payoff. The industry was simultaneously driving for fast growth and deep cost reductions, which meant devices were changing, technology was changing, and business models were changing.

And all of these were the changes that OnStar had to deal with if all we wanted to do was play defense. What if you wanted to play offense? Actually, the fact was we had no choice but to play offense. In the world of technology-based start-ups, a company that stands still lasts about as long as a Cadillac ice sculpture at a July PR event in Phoenix. I'd seen the results of that, and they weren't pretty. We kind of knew that, but honestly, none of us had any real personal experience in actually living it (remember, I was only recently removed from selling choo-choos).

At one point early on in my days with the business, Vince Barabba schlepped me along to a small, invitation-only conference on innovation. One morning at breakfast, we ended up sitting next to a classic "master of the universe" technology guru who loved to hear himself talk. Vince was always interested in getting other peoples' points of view, so he told him about OnStar and asked what he thought. The guy put down his fork, looked me straight in the eye, and with a big smile on his face said, "If you aren't waking up every morning with an ache in the pit of your stomach knowing that you might read in the paper that somebody was doing something you hadn't expected, something that might put you out of business, then you don't know what business you're in." He went on to say that if GM really thought it was ready for that reality, then, fine, strap it on and jump in the game with the rest of the big boys.

All I could think was "What an arrogant jerk." I'd taken the lecture on the pimple and the elephant and had been told that nobody cared about the Smithsonian. Those comments had been bad enough. I took them because I had no choice; they were "family." Who the heck did this guy think he was? But Vince seemed to know him and had asked for his opinion, so all I could do was nod my head and feel myself turn a bright shade of red. It was only later, after a few more bumps, bruises, and life lessons, that it became annoyingly obvious that he'd been right. This world was crazy, outrageous, unfair, and extremely hard to predict, but if you could get it right, it had the potential to be exciting, rewarding, fulfilling, and extremely profitable.

That was the trick. How do you get it right? In the midst of all of this change, locked inside a company that was at best mildly hostile to jumping through new hoops, we somehow had to carve out a path that kept us alive. No, just staying alive wasn't good enough; we had to be relevant. No, relevant didn't sound very inspirational. Go big or go home. We had to find a way to be leaders in every real sense of the word. This was starting to feel a little overwhelming, and clearly, this wasn't the time to be undermanned. We needed some top draft choices, maybe even a Sherpa or two, but where in the world were we going to find them?

Thank goodness, at this stage, we added two extremely different, yet equally critical human pieces to the OnStar puzzle. I wish I could say these two were handpicked from a masterfully orchestrated recruiting process, but this was another example where my background had left me ill-equipped for the role of leading a start-up organization. My fifteen years in leadership roles at Electro-Motive had been all about downsizing within an established, mature environment, basically how to shrink, not grow. Now I was living in the bizarro world of OnStar where the business's prospects would be determined by how effectively a high-performance team could be assembled and a culture created that fit with our unique mission. Recognizing the challenge was important, but solving it wasn't going to be easy.

Up until this point, almost all of the folks working at OnStar had been sent to us on long-term loan from other parts of GM. While there were exceptions, it was painfully obvious that many of the people we were getting weren't GM's best and brightest future number-one draft choices. In the short term, it was what it was, and as long as the folks were trying as hard as they could, I couldn't complain—much. But if there really was something here and we were going to get really good at it, then things would need to change. That meant getting people from outside the company where we'd have a better selection of talent and becoming increasingly picky regarding the people we'd take from other parts of GM.

I didn't realize it at the time, but my newly emerging courage regarding not just taking whoever got dumped on us was about to be tested. I'd just finished a meeting with Harry Pearce and was leaving the old GM headquarters building on West Grand Boulevard in Detroit when I ran into Greg Lau in the parking garage. Greg was responsible for GM's global executive compensation and career planning, a job he'd held for a number of years, and he was someone who had more power and influence for his level than just about anyone else in the company.

I wouldn't say I knew Greg very well, but I'd met him on a couple of occasions and knew he'd participated in the process that had led to my assignment at Project Beacon. More importantly, I knew he'd be involved in any future discussions regarding my compensation and career path, so he was someone who was either good to run into in the hallway or not—I was never really sure.

Anyway, on this occasion, he stopped me, asked how things were going, and said he was about to call me to talk about someone he wanted me to consider for a position at OnStar. The person's name was Fred Cooke, he was the same level in GM's system as I was (he actually made more money), and his background was mainly in finance. My first reaction was to say I didn't have any openings for someone at Fred's level and that I was happy with Jon Hyde as my CFO. I was also somewhat suspicious that this Cooke character was either another problem child being assigned to the OnStar leper colony or someone who was being positioned to come in and take my job. We'd survived the first year OK, but I was pretty sure I hadn't earned any merit badges for my performance, so anything was possible.

Greg said there was no problem with Fred's level because he could make that problem go away by "red-circling" whatever position we put him in. Red-circling was a strange and mysterious process that was sometimes used to soften the blow to someone who was being demoted. If someone high enough in the company liked the person, they let them keep their level and perks even if the new job didn't technically merit it. It was a nice gesture that was a throwback to kinder, gentler times, but red-circling generally meant red flags.

But since every job at OnStar was a small role by GM's scheme of defining job levels, for all I knew, I was red-circled. That's how silly it was to impose GM's HR system on a start-up. We had no revenue, few people, and very small expenses; therefore, we must not have been doing anything very important. In GM's system, my job would've probably been ranked about the same as a second-shift general foreman at an assembly plant. But maybe this was the time that the system might inadvertently work in our favor. If I had asked to bring someone like Fred into the business, at his level, they would have laughed me out of the room. But since they were downsizing somewhere else, and it was their idea, he might be able to come on board through the back door of red-circling—ah, the wonders of bureaucracy.

Greg also said Fred didn't need to land in the CFO job and that he'd be open to anything for Fred that might make sense. He described Fred as someone with an interesting and different background (I'd heard that before) who was pretty versatile and might be able to help in a number of different places. On that basis, I couldn't immediately say no without looking like I had it all figured out on my own, which I didn't. I also knew that if we kept growing, there was no doubt that I'd need Greg's support with many more issues in the future. So I agreed to meet Fred and see where it went from there. I didn't read Greg as insistent that I take Fred into the business, which was good because I honestly didn't think anything would come of it. I was just playing nice and hoping I'd get credit for checking the "cooperates with others" box.

A few days later, Fred showed up at my office for a meeting. He seemed like a nice enough guy, probably ten years older than I was, about my same height, hair a little grayer—more or less the physical description of 80 percent of GM's executives. Fred was working as the executive director of planning and business development for the Inland Fisher Guide Division of GM, one of the many component manufacturing groups that would shortly be bundled together and spun off from GM to form Delphi. Why Fred was leaving his current job wasn't quite clear; I didn't ask, and he didn't tell. I figured if it were important, I could find out later.

Fred was indeed a "finance guy" by GM's standards, having worked in the infamous GM Treasurer's Office back in the day; at one point, he actually worked for a supervisor in the T.O. named Jack Smith. Yes, that Jack Smith, GM's then current chairman of the board. There were a number of mafia's within GM, sales guys, engineers, plant rats, executive admins, but none stronger or more influential than the finance guys. Fred was, or at least at one point had been, in the mainstream of that fraternity—a "made man," if you will. And now he was available for something as funky as OnStar. What had he done wrong?

All Fred would say was that he'd heard about what we were doing, thought it sounded interesting, and was open to considering a change at this stage of his career. He was amazingly candid about the fact that he wasn't looking for anything to come out of the assignment other than getting a chance to spend some time working on something that was growing before he retired. I did learn that Fred was a Hoosier, which meant that as a fellow Hoosier I had to believe him, so I did.

Fred's background was fascinating. While it was more or less in finance roles for his entire time at GM, many of his assignments were way off the beaten path. Of particular interest was Fred's involvement in a number of asset sales for GM, including the divestitures of Terex, Detroit Diesel, and Frigidaire. He even had an intersection with the early evaluations of selling Electro-Motive. Wait, did he say EMD? My EMD? That's how strange and large this company could be sometimes. I thought I was an insider on that deal, and I'd never heard of Fred before. That's OK, he'd never heard of me, either. But he did know his way around financial statements, could easily range between tactics and strategy when discussing almost any issue, and had a track record unlike anyone within GM for doing deals. And not just deals where he had all the leverage and hammered people into whatever he wanted; the kind of "shooting fish in a barrel" deals that many big companies are famous for. No, these were deals where Fred had the pig and the poke and had to somehow sell them to someone who didn't like pork.

I wasn't smart enough at this point to realize what a critically important skill set Fred actually had for what we were about to encounter, but sometimes you just get lucky. What I did know was that we'd need more smart people as we grew, that Greg Lau would be happy if I had a place for Fred, and that I really liked this guy. He was down to earth, warm, funny, and seemed genuinely interested in coming on board. Whether that was because I was such a good salesman or that he was just so fed up with what he was doing, it didn't really matter. We left the meeting with an understanding that I'd process the paperwork for him to transfer over. We shook hands, he left my office, and later that day, his first grandchild was born—which must be a lucky sign in some culture because it sure was for us. If there'd been stock in the OnStar Corporation, it would have gone way up that afternoon.

Speaking of stock going up, around that same time, another franchise player was about to intersect with our wobbly little orbit in an area where we desperately needed some help—managing technology. Again, this was another example of where my background as a mechanical engineer was of no use to the business, but, nonetheless, something we'd need to be extremely good at if we were going to stay alive. The first year taught me how important this would be and how unskilled we were at it. It also taught me that we'd need to import a lot of talent to have any hope of staying ahead of the bow wave that we were beginning to create.

We'd already brought enough GM engineers on board by this point to know that we needed to find some additional sources of talent. We were using local recruiters and were getting interest from folks working for Southeast Michigan's auto industry electronics suppliers. And we also started to hear from people at other car companies, most notably Ford. Well, that couldn't make any sense, could it? I mean, we already had more than enough carmaker experience with the engineers sent over from GM, so why use up any more of our openings to bring in people from Ford?

After thinking about it for a minute, it was obvious why. The candidates we'd be looking at from Ford wouldn't be from their internal redeployable list like many of the folks were at GM. We'd get a chance to look at their best and brightest, at least the ones who'd made the decision to leave their company. At GM, we couldn't talk to the best talent because their management had the right to block them from talking to us unless the jobs were promotions. But we had few higher-level jobs, so we had no leverage to break the folks loose. And, besides, who in their right mind would think of leaving cool jobs with great futures at places like Oldsmobile, Pontiac, or Saturn for something as fly-by-night as OnStar? It was certainly a different world back then.

When I'd have these kinds of discussions with my boss, Ron Zarrella, he'd just shake his head and say he didn't get it. He said that wherever he'd worked at before, I'd have been stepping over the bodies lined up at my door trying to get a chance to work for the new and growing part of the company. It would give great people a place to show what they could do, an open playing field that would let them escape the templates of the hundred-year-old car business. I couldn't disagree. It should've been like that, but it wasn't. Anyway, we did look at a number of resumes from Ford engineers, interviewed a few, and ended up hiring a couple. One in particular, Walt Dorfstatter, ended up making all of the difference in the world.

Walt had spent fifteen years at Ford, most recently as a manager within their electronics components group. In that assignment, he was overseeing all of the technical aspects of the Lincoln RESCU project and was as familiar as anybody in the world with the types of issues we'd be facing at OnStar. The reason he was interested in us was that he'd become passionate about what he thought RESCU had the potential to become, but didn't have confidence that Ford was committed to follow through on the opportunity. They were treating it the way a traditional car company would, with engineering disconnected from marketing and instinctively outsourcing everything they could in order to make a vehicle claim—brochure-ware. Walt knew that there was so much more it could be, but there was no Harry Pearce at Ford to push the car guys into taking it more seriously.

Walt had seen some of our announcements and felt that if he really believed in the idea, he probably needed to be working at OnStar. In the interview, Walt seemed smart, enthusiastic, passionate, and just a little bit nerdy. It felt like a pretty good combination for an engineer, so maybe this guy was worth taking a chance on. We had no idea how critically important Walt would turn out to be in our future, but we made him an offer that included a modest salary increase, and he accepted. OnStar stock was on a roll.

At some point, he must have given the Ford folks his notice, and when they realized they couldn't talk or buy him out of the decision to leave, I got a call from a guy in their personnel department. Now, this was a new experience, and something I wasn't expecting. He basically started the call by screaming at me for stealing Walt, claiming that I'd put a blank check in front of him and told him to fill in whatever number he wanted. He said that two can play that game, and if we wanted to start a bidding war for people, we could expect double from them.

At that point in the conversation, it occurred to me that this guy wasn't just a jerk, he was a misinformed jerk. I told him that I had no idea what he was talking about and explained that not only had we not bought Walt away from them, we'd actually responded to a resume that he had sent us! In other words, while it may bruise your corporate ego, you need to deal with the fact that he doesn't love you as much as you thought he did. He's so over you.

The conversation ended as abruptly as it started, and I actually didn't know what to think. Did I just start a war between GM and Ford? I didn't scream first, but in the heat of the moment, I'd pushed back more aggressively than I expected—and actually enjoyed it. The next time I met with Ron, I mentioned the call, half expecting him to lecture me on how to keep my cool and stay professional if anything like that happened again. Not. He said if I got another call to tell the guy to stick it. Apparently, Ron knew that there'd been some recent cherry-picking of engineers between the two companies completely unrelated to OnStar and thought that might have been the reason behind the call. But, bottom line, it was too damn bad. It was just business, and they'd need to get over it. But he did say that we must've hit a nerve by hiring Walt, which meant we'd snagged a pretty good guy—little did we know.

There were certainly many more people added to the team during this period, a process that continued throughout the next decade. There were holes to plug, moles to whack, gremlins to vanquish, and a future to create. Our batting average in getting the right people wasn't great at the beginning, but it improved over time. I proved to myself over and over again that GM's approach of moving people around like interchangeable parts didn't work at all in our business. It surely didn't work if you were taking parts out of GM (experienced in the automotive world's customs and steeped in a culture that went back to Alfred Sloan) and force-fitting them into something as seemingly chaotic as OnStar.

The other thing I learned to really appreciate was that the seemingly soft and subtle issues of chemistry matter a lot. It's a given that everyone needs to be smart—really smart. I have no problem with that. It's much easier to make progress when you're working with smart people, and thankfully, finding smart people isn't really that hard. They're not a dime a dozen, but they're also not a particularly rare commodity. What's rare is finding people who have the perfect wrapper around their smart center, one that fits with the unique circumstances of your business and is compatible with their teammates on the mission.

That doesn't mean everybody has to be best friends or the godparent to their children, or that the team doesn't need people with diverse opinions, personalities, and backgrounds, or that everybody has to get along with each other for every minute of every day. But it probably does mean that people with outsized egos who carry around personal agendas won't be very valuable no matter how good their three-point shot is. And it also means that character, integrity, and trust matter— a lot. Not just because it sounds good, but out of practical necessity. This was all hard enough to deal with, and things moved way too fast in unscripted ways to have to try to decode someone's motives in the middle of the battle. You needed people who both had serious game and were equally serious about having each other's backs.

So how do you deal with that? What kind of Myers-Briggs or Rorschach test can you give to make sure that the people you're bringing on board are built like that and that when you add them into the mix they won't end up spoiling the recipe? If there was a test, I certainly never found it. It was trial and error, learning to listen to your gut, and most importantly, having the courage and resolve to act on what your gut was telling you when you'd gotten it wrong, which was invariably going to happen.

In some cases, that meant celebrating the successes when you made the right choices and brought in people like Greg Payne, Kathy Murphy, Scott Kubicki, Rick Lee, Joanne Finnorn, Don Butler, Bill Ball, Steve Schwinke, Debbie Frakes, Terry Inch, Jocelyn Allen, George Gulliver, Gary Gumushian, Debbie Rough, Tim Nixon, Nick Pudar, Lois McEntyre, and Joe McCusker, just to name a few. These people, and many more like them, brought big brains and big hearts wrapped with a passion for the mission and a professional and personal dedication to each other. These were truly amazing individuals, but more importantly, they provided the living, breathing foundation for a culture that bound us all together.

There was also the need to celebrate at other times, like when I made four extremely bad choices in marketing leadership before I finally got it right and brought in Tony DiSalle. That celebration was for learning to listen to my gut, each time a little quicker than the last, and because it was important to the business for me to get this right. And if I didn't step up and clean up after my own mistakes, then how could I expect that from everyone else? It became clearer over time that if we didn't have this constant attention to making sure we had the right people on the team at every level across the entire enterprise, then we'd have very little chance to keep the good ship OnStar afloat and pointed in the right direction. Good strategy, tangible assets, technological expertise, and effective branding were all important, but unlikely to create sustainable success and long-term value in the hands of the wrong people going about their business in the wrong way.

So spending time nurturing the culture and stressing over having the right team on the field were both critical as the enterprise grew, but most of that was still ahead of us. At this point, the team was still small and fragile and just starting to get its sea legs. Adding Fred and Walt was extremely important and would make a world of difference for OnStar's prospects for many years to come. It was time for the second year.

CHAPTER 9

The First "What's Next"

Moving into our second year of production meant we'd survived getting started and were now entering the "what's next" part of our little adventure. I've since learned that the "what's next" phase in a start-up business in a newly emerging category can be very long, seemingly never ending. Again, that's either the fun part of being involved with something like this or it'll make you want to pull your hair out, so better to consider it fun. It's during this phase that the business needs to work hard to develop a split personality by demonstrating its vision and creativity in translating an unknowable future into a continuous series of relevant new services, while simultaneously being deeply introspective and self-critical on the services it's already launched. It's a difficult, but critically important trick to pull off, like using one eye to stare directly down at your feet as you take each tactical step while keeping the other eye trained somewhere out on the horizon so you don't find yourself surviving the journey, but somehow ending up at the wrong destination.

Being introspective and self-critical was something that needed to become an essential part of our team's personality. That meant that everyone at OnStar had to just accept as fact that everything they were already doing not only could be done better, but had to be done better, much better, or we'd have no chance of keeping the lead that we'd worked so hard to build. It's where you needed to believe in the concept of a learning curve and further believe you weren't entitled its benefits unless you worked for them. Just because you're first and have more cycles of experience than anyone else doesn't mean that you automatically learn and somehow get better. So, as hard as it felt, whatever process you'd just invented to make your part of the business work, whatever technology that you'd just deployed, whatever insight you thought you had on subscriber behavior, they all needed to be declared obsolete, and you had to immediately be thinking about a way to replace them. No whining, no rationalizing, and no defensiveness. It was simply the only way to have confidence that your biggest competitive advantage as a first-mover, what you're learning that nobody else knows, will quickly translate into performance that keeps you ahead of your would-be competitors. It just was what it was, and for most people, what it was was hard.

Before you develop a track record as an organization of being able to do this, which at this point we certainly hadn't, it's really difficult to establish any real momentum on this behavior because it goes against human nature. Why did I work so hard to get this all set up and running just so somebody can criticize it and say my baby is ugly? Won't I look bad if the work I just finished, work I thought was really good, now suddenly is considered bad? I'm a professional, I know what I'm doing, and I can defend the approach I just created to anybody! But wait a second, take a breath, and think about this for a minute. Our team was generally made up of really smart, very rational people. Now, what exactly were the statistical odds that, with no experience, nobody to benchmark, no existing templates to follow, whatever it is we were doing just happened to be the best way it could ever be done? Who hits a drive three hundred yards the first time they pick up a club? Heck, I've seen people grab the driver by the wrong end. No, you just had to accept the fact that you must be able to simultaneously take pride in what you've just done to get the business going and understand that your very next job was to blow it up and replace it with something better.

This was another place where our mission really helped people wrap their mind around this imperative. First, since our services required that we always be there for our subscribers when they needed us most, like immediately after a crash, then didn't we owe it to them to leave no stone unturned in our quest to improve everything that we were doing? Second, if we really believed in the ultimate vision that OnStar needed to be installed on as many vehicles as possible to make its maximum contribution to society, then we'd need to produce business results that convinced GM to not just keep going, but to expand our penetration. That meant dramatically driving down hardware costs, becoming more efficient in the delivery of our services, and completely re-architecting every major business process until we'd built a strong and sustainable business model.

This wasn't mindless "hamster running on the wheel" effort of working harder because you were supposed to. We needed to see this as the lifeblood of the company and necessary to maintain and grow our leadership position. And, at this early stage of the business, we were doubly blessed because our getting better didn't need to be a zero-sum game with our subscribers. This didn't need to degenerate into a process where we'd look for places to skimp on service, or cut corners on quality, or take something away from our customers and hope they didn't notice. The laws of nature in the consumer electronics industry said if we got our hardware on the right path, each new generation would be more reliable, have more features, and cost less than the one before. The same was true with almost everything else. If we could search databases faster and more accurately, we could deliver higher-quality routes to our subscribers in less time. If we could somehow figure out a way that each customer didn't need a separate cellular contract to make OnStar work, then we'd lower their cost, eliminate an ugly process at the dealership, and reduce the complexity of needing to have hundreds of separate contracts with all of the different carriers. I wasn't sure how long the win-win-win phenomena could last, but at least, for now, institutionalizing the "do over" mentality in the business was honestly good for everybody. But it was still hard, especially for the folks who'd spent most of their careers at GM.

At this point, still a decade before the bankruptcy filing, GM was trying hard to sell the traditional organization on the need for "continuous improvement." The idea was to get everyone in the company to acknowledge the competitive requirement to get a little better at everything we were doing a little bit at a time. That meant singles, walks, fielder's choices, and bunts were going to be the keys to success—steady progress, not necessarily swinging for the fences. This was intended to fit with the mature state of the automotive business by presumably setting reasonable expectations for gradual progress instead of demanding anything more radical and unsettling.

The problem was that things that more or less fit the description of "continuous" had surrounded us for so long that we'd become numb to them. We'd continuously been losing market share in the United States for the past three decades, with its predictable effect of continuously reducing our profitability. And the continuously reducing profitability had touched off a continuous stream of management initiatives to continuously reduce spending and continuously eliminate headcount. The initiatives went by many names; frankly, the names continuously changed as well just to make it interesting. It was rightsizing, process reengineering, lean and common, waste elimination, the quality network, benchmarking, the plan to win, and zero-based staffing, just to list a few. And the unfortunate dynamic it created in the company was continuous as well.

There was continuous sandbagging of budgets so that when the very predictable word came down that what had been submitted wasn't good enough, you could cry and moan and talk about the sky falling while cutting the number to what you really thought you could do in the first place. It was the continuous process of inverting the zero-based budget line items so that the most important things to the business looked like what you'd need to cut first if someone demanded another continuous pound of flesh. And there was a continuous ability to rationalize why you were fresh out of bold and creative initiatives to pursue because there weren't going to be any new resources approved to work on them anyway, so why waste the time? It was pretty clear that we had to distance ourselves as much as humanly possible from that kind of thinking. There was nothing continuous about OnStar. Maybe there would be in a hundred years, but not now. We actually toyed with the idea of calling our approach "discontinuous improvement" to reinforce the difference to the growing number of GM folks joining the OnStar team, but decided not to call it anything to avoid the risk of turning it into another slogan. It had to become a natural way of doing business, part of the culture. Thankfully, these kinds of behaviors were highly visible, so it was very obvious who got it and painfully obvious who didn't. All of that led to a fairly high boomerang rate of GM folks who came for a while, didn't really feel comfortable with how things were being done at OnStar, and ended up going back "home," either on their own or with a little encouragement. And while we didn't need the extra churn, in some ways, it was actually healthy. It reinforced our leadership team's need to stay on top of performance issues and quickly take action and helped set the same "no excuses" tone in managing our suppliers. This place was different, and if you weren't up for it, you really needed to be someplace else.

This was all good in theory, but now it was time to put it all into practice. The good news and the bad news was that the first year of operations had left us in an extremely target-rich environment in terms of opportunities to dive in and hone our new culture because everything needed improving. First off, almost every element of our technology plan had turned to mush. The emergency services part of the hardware module was functioning reliably, but there were problems with voice recognition, the logic that let us unlock doors, our automatic stolen vehicle notification, and silly things like antennas not sticking to the cars' rear windows. The call center software was proving to be equally flakey, with calls going to the wrong advisors, vehicles that would randomly appear on advisor screens in the Atlantic Ocean, and databases that could find a Chinese restaurant in Omaha but didn't know where O'Hare Airport was located. And, beyond the technology problems, we were stumbling with the human challenges of selecting the right types of people to be OnStar advisors, training them effectively, and providing them with great supervision and coaching. The problems were all fixable and, in fact, all got fixed, but for every one that got settled, we'd always find two more that just seemed to pop up out of nowhere.

Then there were the issues at the dealerships. The Cadillac Spring Special had done a great job getting everybody focused and aligned and had actually produced some pretty amazing results. But when it ended six weeks later, rather than building any momentum, things quickly slipped back to their pre-promotion performance. Not completely back, as sales volumes had moved up some, but the rocket certainly wasn't off the pad. Cadillac's promotion machine needed to move on to Summer Sell-Down mode; we had no role in that and were somewhere off in their rearview mirror.

It was normal practice for car companies to make a big deal about something that was new and then move on to whatever sizzle they could find to talk about next. Things needed to stay fresh. Ad agencies looked for the next-big-thing to talk about, and dealers would get their next set of priorities at introduction events that happened every year just ahead of the arrival of their new models in the fall. Those shows were typically held in places like Las Vegas or New Orleans, were for dealership employees only, and usually involved elaborate theatrical productions where the new-model-year vehicles would drive out on stage accompanied by extremely loud rock music and dazzling light shows. Eventually, the lights would dim and a spotlight would illuminate the car division's general manager, who would give the dealers a pep talk about why it was a great time to be a Cadillac (or Buick or Chevrolet or fill-in-the-blank) dealer. That would be followed by a string of lower-level GM folks taking the dealership personnel through the new model year's changes in styling and advances in things like fuel economy or antilock braking systems. If it was a real slow year and nothing much had changed, the music would be louder, and you'd eventually be hearing about accent-painted door handles or how many cup holders were in the backseat.

We'd had our turn at being the cool new thing last year, but since the volume had been so low and we hadn't really broken through, I'd hoped we'd get another kick at it. Ron was supportive of that, as was John Grettenberger, so we got to participate again, but it felt somewhat unnatural and awkward. The reaction was "Didn't we just talk about this?" and "What new tricks do you have up your sleeve?" New tricks? How about the tricks we already do that nobody knows about, like say respond to crashes? It was so frustrating because we'd gotten ourselves stuck in just the wrong place in the dealers' minds—not new enough to be interesting, but not established enough to be part of their natural sales pitch. Dealers and the marketing divisions had a lot of challenges on their plates beyond us, so this was a problem we needed to solve on our own—and we weren't very good at it.

It also didn't help that the process that we'd invented to support the dealer-installed option strategy had made the whole transaction stick out like a very sore thumb. It was the kick-me sign that seemed to pop out every time we'd start building any positive momentum at a dealer meeting. Invariably, there'd be someone in the crowd who felt compelled to vent about how they weren't making enough money on something that was this hard to do, and besides we had no business messing with *their* customers anyway. That would generally set off a feeding frenzy that would send the OnStar guys in the room, including me, looking for asylum in the witness protection program. It was a complicated set of dynamics, and unfortunately, none of them seemed to be running in our favor.

Oh, and by the way, the dealers were right. Our process really was terrible for the dealers, and the only thing that a year's worth of experience had done was make that painfully obvious to everyone. It started with how hard it was to explain OnStar to customers in the showroom. Was this hooked to satellites or to cell phones or to somebody at a call center? Did someone always know where the driver was? What happens if there's a crash that doesn't make an airbag go off—will the customer still get help? Can someone listen to me in the car without me knowing about it? If I already have a cell phone, why do I need to sign up for another plan? There were a million questions that could potentially distract the customer from buying the car, and unfortunately, sometimes salespeople made up their own answers just to get it over with. Does my Cadillac really have a satellite phone inside if it has OnStar? "Sure it does" was the wrong answer, but one that got used often enough that we ended up having to invent a process to uninstall OnStar when the disappointed customers got home and found out otherwise.

Then there was the installation process. Order a kit for over $700, wait a couple of days before it gets delivered, and then have the customer bring in his or her new Cadillac for half a day to get it installed. And that was only the start. How about needing to take out the backseat to run the wires, using a hacksaw to cut a hole in the tops of some vehicles' center-console armrests to stuff the handset in, and having to carefully install a GPS antenna in just the right place between the rear speakers so it could reliably pick up signals from outer space? Oh, and then the dealers needed to get each customer to individually sign up for a cellular contract, preferably with the company we had a deal with in their region so that we could claim the cellular commission on the sale.

Holy cow, had we honestly known what we were asking these guys to do when we put this plan together? There wasn't a good answer to that question. If we'd told them that we really did know how bad this was, but did it anyway, they'd have declared us insane and then shot us. If we'd had said we'd built this whole approach in little pieces and really hadn't stepped back and seen how ugly it had gotten, they'd have declared us incompetent and then shot us. The real answer was closer to the second than the first, but the results were destined to be the same, and we probably did deserve to be shot.

So now we have technology problems, people problems, dealer problems, and just for good measure, supplier problems. Unfortunately, the more we got into it, the more we confirmed our worst concerns about our former partners, now suppliers—they really weren't as good at this as they said they were. Thankfully, we'd started to bring in our own folks to get deeper into the details, but it was still too early for that to make any real difference. In the meantime, it ended up being a constant struggle to get their attention focused on the seemingly endless stream of issues that were piling up all around us.

It didn't help that they were still irritated that they'd been pushed out as partners and were relegated to the role of supplier, and it also didn't help that our volumes for the first year had been much lower than we'd projected. We were in business and shipping product and delivering services, but we were quickly developing the reputation of being difficult to deal with and a bad customer. We were demanding, critical, seemingly never satisfied, and didn't buy as much from them as they wanted us to. We were borderline not worth their effort, and they were starting to treat us that way.

One example involved the contract we had with EDS to manage our call center. Aside from their core IT-related services business, EDS also had a small practice area in call centers. They weren't nearly as well known in that industry as their much larger competitors who specialized in call center outsourcing, but it was a business that they thought they could make some money in, particularly if they could bundle it on top of their larger IT relationship with their existing customers. They had a few small accounts at this point, but their main volume was in running call centers for General Motors' car business. GM needed a number of call centers for dealers and customers, things like the 1-800 Roadside Assistance service that came as part of a new vehicle's warranty. Since they were already doing that kind of business for GM and considering that our original business plan was looking for synergies with Hughes and EDS, it seemed only natural that we'd start the business with them running our OnStar call center.

It became clear during the first year of operation that running call centers wasn't really EDS's strong suit. I don't know the history, maybe GM had asked EDS to take the roadside business on as a favor, or maybe they were awarded it because they were part of the family. Either way, it couldn't have been because they'd earned it competitively. Not knowing any better and not needing another moving part to have to manage as we were trying to get launched, we'd taken the easy way out and just piled in on top of that existing GM relationship. But it soon became painfully obvious that they didn't have the professional tools or operating discipline to consistently deliver a reliable, high-quality customer experience. We needed to get this fixed.

I eventually elevated my concerns up the EDS chain of command, starting with our account manager, then to his boss, then to his boss's boss, and eventually, I realized I was getting nowhere. The people I was talking to had bigger and bigger titles in EDS's GM account management structure, but the real operating resources at EDS reported through another chain of command—in this case, their call center practice organization. They made it extremely hard to get to those people, preferring to use their GM account interface team to act as the intermediary. But I'd finally had enough of the "who's on first" discussions and made myself enough of a nuisance that they finally relented and let me meet their Mr. Big of call centers.

I knew I had a really tough message to deliver to this guy, but I honestly held out hope that he'd be the kind of person who might actually want to know what his customer was thinking. Sometimes, if you connect with the right person in the right way at one of your suppliers, it can almost be like magic. Everybody's got problems; no organization is perfect. That's just a fact of business life. If everything always ran perfectly on autopilot, companies wouldn't need organizational structures or high-priced managers. But when things weren't perfect, it gave the right kind of leaders a chance to step up, take accountability, roll up their sleeves, and get things fixed—magic! And if magic wasn't possible, good leaders typically at least had the guts to level with you about their problems and be honest about what you could expect to happen next. So maybe I'd get lucky, and this would be the start of a beautiful relationship—I sure hoped so.

I started the meeting by saying that I was sure that he'd heard about the challenges we'd been having in getting our little business off the ground. I was sure because why wouldn't I be sure? I'd practically had to set off a bomb to get a meeting with this guy, so somebody must have briefed him on the issues, right? In a fairly casual and detached way, he said, "No, I'm not really up to speed. Why don't you just fill me in?" Did he just say that? He wasn't up to speed? Fill him in? OK, this didn't seem like it was starting very well, and he was actually giving off a vibe of being mildly annoyed that I was taking up his time. All right, time for plan B.

I spent the next five minutes delivering a high-volume, emotionally charged, fact-filled monolog that started to fog the glass walls of the conference room. We'd found problems, serious and systemic problems, with many things in their operation. They had issues with the capabilities of their supervision, their training materials were deficient, their workforce management tools were nonexistent, their advisor quality-assurance process had big holes, and they seemed way more interested in finding ways to manage to the letter of the contract than to the spirit of the business. And those were just the obvious, call center 101 things that they were doing wrong. We weren't experts in this area, at least not yet, but they were supposed to be. If they were going to claim to be good at this business, and they certainly weren't bashful about charging us like they were, they had to deliver—and they weren't.

I'd said what I needed to say, probably actually a little more than I needed to say, but something really did need to change, so I kept going. We were small at this point, but the plan wasn't to stay that way for long. Growth in size and complexity was coming, and it certainly wasn't going to make any of this any easier. And, besides, remember what we were doing again? These weren't calls to renew magazine subscriptions or sell aluminum siding, we were the people inside of vehicles with our subscribers moments after a terrible crash. If somebody didn't get energized, passionate, emotional, or heck, even angry when we weren't as good as we could be, then we definitely weren't the right people for these jobs.

At this point, I stopped to give him a chance to respond. I could see this wasn't going over too well, but in fairness, it was a tough message to hear. He took a deep breath and said he'd heard what I said and understood most of it, but had a question that was bothering him. He said, "You know, I've got dozens of clients that I do call center work for, and all of them love what we're doing for them except for you. So I'm wondering what's wrong with how you're looking at this." *What?* He must've been kidding me, right? But the sad part was I think he really meant it, either that or he thought I was a moron.

I lost it. I said, "Look, I used to sell locomotives for a living, and if I'd ever told a customer that had serious problems with one of our products that I wondered what *he* was doing wrong, there would have been yellow police tape outlining the hole in the wall that I'd been thrown through. Then, when they were sure they had my attention, they'd have run me over with a train." There was a little more yelling, and I'm not exactly sure how the meeting ended, other than awkwardly. We bumped along with them for a while longer, all the while hiring more and more of our own people to provide sufficient management oversight to protect us from their shortcomings. We eventually needed to fire them and find someone else, which we did, but it would've been a lot easier if they'd just performed the way they said they could so we wouldn't have had to. But they left us no choice.

This might have been the first time I used the word "crash" in anger with a supplier. Being there for our subscribers in the event of a crash was beyond vitally important. This wasn't a business imperative; it was a moral imperative. And if they didn't get that, then they needed to get out. We were an interesting customer. On the one hand, we had great growth potential, were defining the cutting edge of some pretty interesting technologies, were the leaders in our category, and were ultimately developing a very strong and powerful brand. If you were a supplier and were prospecting for a new client, those would all be pretty attractive characteristics. On the other hand, things at OnStar were always in a constant state of change. We were inventing and perfecting almost everything on the fly, there were a lot of risks and unknowns, and you could literally cost someone their life if you got your part of the program wrong. So if you were thinking clearly, deciding whether you wanted our business wasn't really a no-brainer.

What I learned to do over the years was to characterize working with us as a great opportunity for a potential supplier, but only if they came into it with their eyes wide open. This wasn't the place to assign the junior varsity, or expect that there'd be a lot of tolerance for pulling out contract language to dodge responsibility, or to try to hide the peanut and make excuses when things went wrong, which they were inevitably going to do from time to time. If the business was attractive, it came with accepting and respecting OnStar's unique mission almost as much as we did. If you couldn't do that, no problem; not everybody was cut out for this. Just be up front about it and step aside, or it wasn't going to end well for anyone. But if you were up for it, you'd be in for a real adventure, one that would be good business, and more importantly, one that you and your team would probably end up being very proud to have been a part of.

I realize that this makes us sound like a bunch of know-it-all maniacs, but we honestly weren't. We certainly didn't know it all, far from it, and that's why we needed to be working with suppliers that really knew what they were doing. We might have been maniacs, but I hope in the kindest and gentlest definition of that word. The second meaning of maniac, according to *Merriam-Webster*'s online dictionary, is "a person with inordinate or ungovernable enthusiasm for something." Well, if you would allow the substitution of "organization" for person, then that was us. We had ungovernable enthusiasm for something—our mission. And it was possible to find other organizations, actually wonderfully talented and committed organizations, that eventually shared at least a small slice of that mania for the same mission.

They were companies that not only said they were up for the challenge, but proved it time and time and time again. We came to characterize these companies as alliance partners and developed very strong relationships with them at the very top of their organizations. They were companies like Verizon Wireless, LG Electronics, Convergys, Qualcomm, Navteq, Minacs, Campbell Ewald, Mapquest, and Digitas, just to name a few. These companies jumped in with both feet, helped establish the business, and took getting it right as personally as we did. It certainly wasn't always easy, or without bumps and bruises, but it became a living, breathing team effort and something of a quest for everyone involved.

There were also other types of organizations that weren't really suppliers at all, but whose much longer-standing missions wrapped around ours. These were people from emergency medicine, the 911 community, law enforcement, fire departments, paramedics, and national, state, and county governments. We were the new kids on their block and spent a lot of time and effort working to earn their support and respect by listening to what they needed from us and putting our best efforts into helping in any way we could.

Examples included organizations like the National Emergency Numbering Association, the National Association of EMS Physicians, the International Association of Fire Chiefs, the National College of Emergency Physicians, the National Center for Missing and Exploited Children, many organizations representing law enforcement like the Fraternal order of Police and the International Association of Chiefs of Police, the Centers for Disease Control and Prevention Foundation, and the National Highway Traffic Safety Administration. These groups represented thousands of highly dedicated and deeply experienced professionals who were generally under-resourced to accomplish their vital missions. Over time, we learned to appreciate that they deserved to have a voice in the "what's next" phase of our business to help shape our technology and plans in ways that could contribute to their societally important work.

So that was the first part of the "what's next" phase of the business: continuously evaluate everything we were doing, fix what was broken, and try to make everything that was working work even better. That meant we were crawling through every piece of our current technology platform, starting to get our arms around the wide-ranging and important issues that had surfaced with our dealers, and we were rapidly bringing in OnStar-badged talent to better manage underperforming pieces of our supplier base. But if that's all we did, which already seemed like a lot, then in a year or two's time, we might have everything fixed, but we'd still only be where we wanted to be a year or two ago. Not only did that sound depressing, hadn't we already decided that we couldn't stand still? So the real challenge was figuring out how to do all of the fixing and improving while simultaneously conceiving, inventing, and executing the new things that would keep us from turning into a sitting duck.

We ended up spending countless hours sketching ideas on white boards, and I could never tell if we were making progress or if it was just the fumes from the markers that were making me feel better. At one point, after a lot of drawing and erasing and redrawing and re-erasing, it felt like a plan was coming together. It was going to be hard to execute, would involve creating something that had never been done before, and would require a "bet the business" strategy since we weren't big enough to run any real risk mitigation plays in the background if we couldn't pull it off. What had happened to me in the years since I'd left LaGrange? Since when was I comfortable (well, if not really comfortable, then at least not panicked) having the preferred plan be something with this many risks, unknowns, and moving parts? Maybe it was the magic marker fumes, but thankfully, Fred and Walt were breathing in the same things because they were going to need to be a big part of pulling it off.

The essence of the play was to replace the $700-plus Gen 1 system with Gen 2 at half the cost and 50 percent more capabilities. It also needed to be half the size to save vehicle weight and make it easier to install at the factory. In addition, it needed to be set up to work right out of the factory, basically preprogrammed and active to eliminate the added subscriber cost and dealer complexity of a separate cellular contract for each car. And, finally, it had to be able to do a couple of new tricks for customers, like allowing us to remotely do diagnostic checks on the vehicle and changing the way we handled our stolen vehicle recovery service.

OK, so getting all of this accomplished was going to be hard, maybe real hard, but at least the theory was supposed to work in our favor. Harnessing the consumer electronics cycle was going to be critical to our future success; we'd told Rick that at the meeting back at Cobo Hall, and we really meant it. Back then, the question wasn't "Could we do this with the hardware?" but "Could the GM vehicle development process deal with how fast things were going to need to change once we had the cool new hardware?" Well, now we had to hold up our part of the bargain and prove we could actually deliver the next-generation system with much more capability and much lower costs. If we could do that, we could then go back to the vehicle engineers and start the hard work of trying to break their rules and quickly shove it into vehicle production without getting killed. If we couldn't do that, then we ought to stop now anyway because we'd just spent the last couple of years wasting our time. So it was put up or shut up, no time like the present to confront those demons, and see if we had the game to pull it off. All right, Walt, all yours—no pressure.

Now, suppose we actually can come up with a box that can magically do everything we want it to do, what about the part of having them all come pre-attached to the nation's wireless network? Again, the theory was good and really important if we were ever going to end up installing these things in high volume on GM's assembly lines. The problem was, however, that this was more of a business-strategy decision than a technical challenge, and the decision wasn't ours to make. Each separate cellular company, and there were literally hundreds of them around the country back then, had their own strategies and policies and the absolute right to manage them as they pleased. While what we needed from them wasn't necessarily bad for them, it wasn't obviously good, either. And, at this point, we had no leverage. We had no volume and no brand awareness. We were just a speck, and the pimple analogy seemed sadly appropriate. But if we could get this done, it could change everything. It could help get us out of jail with dealers, it would significantly lower our subscribers' costs of having our service, and it would massively simplify the path to factory-bundled service. I could almost see the American flag waving over the amber waves of grain. All right, Fred, time to suit up and win one for the pimple.

OK, and as long as we were still dreaming, why not dream big. We might as well add a couple of new services to the list of things that needed to be in the next hardware box, but how were we going to decide what those would be? That seemingly simple and innocent question, what to add to our existing service portfolio, was actually the most complicated, vexing, and risk- and opportunity-laden challenge the business was ever going to face, and face continuously for the rest of our life. This is where you needed to be in tune with your customers, with today's technology and tomorrow's, with trends that were put in motion by others, with the unanticipated second- and third-order effects of things going on in other industries, with competitors' anticipated future actions, and with the parallel universes of government regulations and emergency service provider protocols.

Oh, and by the way, being in tune doesn't mean just being able to read English. It means being able to interpret what it all means, developing instincts that turn facts into roadmaps and timed initiatives. It means profoundly understanding what your brand stands for and using it as a framework to provide context to your strategy. And it means developing judgment that allows you to shoot ahead of the existing target, in some cases even leading it to where you want it to be. And, finally, it means consciously resisting the urge to shoot every bullet at once, because you know if you do, one of them will end up in your foot.

This was really, really interesting and really, really important to get right. And getting it right didn't just mean picking the smart initiatives to pursue and getting them in the right order. It also meant executing them professionally and immediately getting them on the path for future improvement, just like everything else that was going on in the business. This was one part tick-tack-toe, two parts checkers, and one part chess, if you were lucky. Tick-tack-toe meant you had something that customers wanted and were willing to pay for. Checkers meant that you were planning sequences of interrelated moves that meaningfully built on top of each other and had preconceived fallback plans if you'd somehow missed the target and had gotten something wrong. Chess meant you were conceiving new services for their value in shaping the landscape to your future competitive advantage, war-gaming the likely moves of currently nonexistent competitors in an effort to anticipate their entry points and blocking them before they could get there.

At this stage, with all of the bullets already flying, I have to say, we were lucky to find a pencil and piece of paper to play tick-tack-toe. Our first two wish-list items actually came the old-fashioned way, listening to customers, with one telling us what we were doing was wrong and needed to change and one telling us something she'd love to see us do next. First things first, which one of our services had we gotten wrong?

One thing that we thought was a really cool way to show off our deep connection into the vehicle's electrical architecture and distinguish ourselves from what Lincoln had with RESCU was to use Cadillac's existing theft alarm system to automatically tell us that a subscriber's car had been stolen. Knowing the instant a car had been stolen would give us a head start in contacting the police and improve the odds of being able to recover the vehicle. It all sounded great, fit really well with our brand, and seemed pretty high-tech. And, better yet, the Cadillac marketing guys loved the edge that it brought to their vehicles. "A Cadillac was tough enough to take care of itself"—what a great claim. Now, if all we'd intended this to ever be was brochure-ware (make the claim, but not actually include it in many vehicles) then it probably would've been fine. Kind of like the tree that falls in the forest that nobody hears, so it didn't really make a sound, right? But, unfortunately, whenever trees fell around us, they usually seemed to land on the roof of our car, and this was no exception.

The problem with this service ended up being that Cadillac's theft system was standard on every one of their vehicles, meaning that it was out there in volume. It was also very easy for a Cadillac customer to accidentally trip their own alarm, which they also did in volume. In a non-OnStar-equipped Cadillac, the horn would honk and the headlights would flash for about a minute to draw attention to the vehicle and then they would automatically stop, and that would be that. You could interrupt them before a minute was up if you knew how, which meant digging into the owner's manual and learning the secret handshake, but not many people made that effort. What usually happened is they'd set off the alarm, deal with the horn honking until it stopped, and then get on with their business. Aside from a little embarrassment and a lot of noise pollution, that was no problem.

If you had OnStar, the world was different. Actually, to the customer, it felt the same, at least for a while. The horn and lights would do their thing, and if the owner waited patiently until they stopped and didn't do the secret handshake that our OnStar module needed to register an official reset, then the car thought it was stolen. It would then automatically send a distress signal to the OnStar center and alert the advisor that it was time to come apprehend the bad guy. We'd then call the appropriate local police wherever the vehicle was, and they'd go looking for the "stolen" Caddy.

It was probably our lucky day, although it didn't feel like it at the time, when this process played out early in our history in Wisconsin, and long story short, the Cadillac's owner was ultimately placed face-down by the police on the hood of his DeVille. It thankfully all got sorted out, but the inadvertent perpetrator was actually the CEO of a company who had high-level connections inside GM. Yada, yada, yada, and the next thing I know, I'm on the phone with this guy sweating bullets. Thankfully, he had a sense of humor and actually really seemed to like our technology, but his strong suggestion was that this service was probably a little ahead of its time. OK, ouch, thanks for the feedback. As you might expect, we immediately put in a work-around process at the OnStar center that involved calling into the vehicle first to try to determine if the driver was friend or foe, but that was only a Band-Aid. What we really needed was a fundamental change in the definition of the service and a corresponding change to the specs for the Gen 2 system. OK, this makes the cutline.

The other new idea that made the cut for Gen 2—remote diagnostics—traveled a different path into production. We'd been covering the walls since my first day in the business with Post-it notes full of ideas about what we ought to do next. The engineers always wanted to be junior marketing experts and typically had more (and generally better) ideas than everyone else. Early on, the concept of getting diagnostic codes wirelessly out of the vehicles and doing something meaningful with them was a real favorite of the techies, but I kept saying no. My sense was that nobody cared if their oxygen sensor module was bad since most people didn't work on their own cars anymore. This really made no sense to spend any more time on, so leave it alone and move on to something else. That was until a nice woman in a Phoenix focus group told us differently.

Focus groups are tried and true tools of the auto industry. They're places where new concepts were tested, new designs were reviewed, and where opinions were solicited on everything from a manufacturer's quality to the effectiveness of their TV ads. I know it's hard to believe it when you see some of the crazy stuff car companies do after they've presumably tested the concepts, but the idea of talking to real people, especially your existing customers, really does make a lot of sense. By this time, we were running focus groups with new subscribers, and there was one particular woman at a session in Phoenix who really helped us understand just how valuable listening to our subscribers was always going to be. We'd probably taken twenty different new service ideas to that particular group to test, and one of them was diagnostics. I was hopeful that when we got the predictable "I don't work on my car, so I don't need any of that nonsense" answer, the engineers would finally drop this one and move on to something more productive.

The moderator finally got to diagnostics, explained what it was, and this nice, somewhat older woman stopped him and said, "I don't really understand or care too much about diagnostics, but have you ever seen the TV show *MASH?* You know, where all of the soldiers that have been wounded are lined up on stretchers outside of the tent for surgery, and the doctors decide which ones are hurt the worst and take care of them first? That's what I want for my car—triage. I don't care exactly what's wrong with it, just whether it's bad enough that I need to stop now because it's about to blow up or the wheels will fall off, or whether it's really not that serious, and I can keep driving and bring it to the dealer in a couple of days." That was brilliant, and as usual, my instincts had been proven wrong again. Actually, not completely wrong, because this woman didn't want the diagnostics so she could work on her car, but she'd taken the technology and looked at it like a real person. She wasn't an engineer or an auto industry insider, which actually made her much more qualified to render judgment on this concept.

What I'd missed, what we'd all missed, was that there was a chance to use the technology not mechanically, but emotionally. Peace of mind was the third of the three concepts in our brand—safety, security, and *peace of mind.* Her point was that she felt completely vulnerable

127

when she was out driving and something went wrong with her car. At that moment, her choices were few, and none of them were good. She could stop immediately and somehow or another try to summon help, but what time of the day was it? What was the weather like? Was she in a neighborhood she was familiar with or comfortable stopping in? If she ignored the problem and kept driving, it might be OK, but something really bad could happen. Maybe something really dangerous like the brakes might fail. So what to do? What you certainly weren't feeling during any of this was peace of mind, far from it, more like apprehension and panic.

But what if she could just push a button and ask a friendly, trained advisor to scan her car and tell her if everything was going to be OK? Just put the car into one of two categories; that's all she wanted. It's either too dangerous to drive and you need to wait for a tow truck (which OnStar could send), or it's more of a minor issue, so you can avoid the immediate disruption. Just keep driving, and take it to the dealership in the next day or so.

I loved this idea. I loved this framing. And, most of all, I loved the fact that it came from a subscriber. We could've been mad at ourselves for not figuring this out on our own, and over time, we'd need to get better at having those kinds of instincts ourselves, but we shouldn't be mad at all. We should celebrate that customers were having a real role in helping us invent the future of our business. How could we ever deny the value of listening to customers again when we had such a pie-in-the-face moment where we almost walked by something as incredibly important and significant as this? And to have been saved by the natural human instincts of our subscriber in Phoenix, someone who cared less about the technology or our internal GM process constraints, it was perfect! I didn't know whether what she was asking for was harder or easier to do than what the engineers had been arguing for, but it didn't matter. Her idea had just become item number two on the list of what the next generation of OnStar technology had to deliver, and that felt really good.

The "what's next" phase continued unabated at OnStar for the entire time that I was involved with the business, and I'm sure it continues in almost the same way today. It held the most challenges, was the most frustrating, and ultimately provided the most gratifying professional moments that any of us had experienced in our careers. We did develop a track record of discontinuous improvement and ended up being able to play chess more often than I would have expected. And the results were amazing: a team who could be humble and confident at the same time; a team who expected to encounter tough challenges and find ways over, around, or through them; and a team who could win using multiple scorecards, be they financial or be they accomplishing something that could change peoples' lives and maybe even a small part of the world—forever.

Walt and his team were able to deliver Gen 2, not exactly the way we'd conceived it, but very close, and that started the ball rolling on our vehicle technology roadmap. Since then, we launched Gens 3, 4, 5, 6, 7, and 8, with Gen 9 in final validation and Gen 10 on the drawing board as I was leaving. We knew we'd need to be able to do something like that if we were going to keep up with this business, but we had no idea whether we could actually pull it off. GM's vehicle engineers stepped up as well, turning an otherwise hostile vehicle integration lifecycle into more of a catcher's mitt, one that came to have growing confidence in Walt's team's ability to hit their target. It certainly wasn't without drama and acts of courage and heroism, but we collectively squeezed the life out of the learning curve and created a capability that was unmatched anywhere in the automotive industry. GM had stepped up to this challenge and done the right thing, and it would create massive value for the company.

And what about Fred? Well, this was Fred's coming-out party. Knowing very little about our technology or the cellular industry, he fearlessly jumped into the fray and delivered amazing results. What we ended up with was a new, non-geographic 500 area code approach that eliminated the need for individually tailored phone numbers depending on where a subscriber lived. That allowed us to simplify everything, taking a lot of the cost, hassle, and complexity out of the hands of our dealers and customers. This was the industry breakthrough we needed for factory installation, and it was masterfully accomplished through a well-orchestrated team effort, with Fred as the maestro. But as the next chapter illustrates, he was just warming up.

CHAPTER 10

Music from Outer Space

And now for something completely different. We were making progress on the OnStar business, and it seemed like a nice mural was taking shape on the ceiling of the chapel if you stood back far enough and squinted just right, but it was far from a masterpiece, and stuff continued to happen. Moles were poking their heads up and being whacked down, relationships within GM remained fluid, and there were some strange-looking clouds on the horizon moving pretty quickly in our direction—something called the Internet.

I wasn't really sure what any of that meant to us; it might be important or it might be nothing at all. Self-proclaimed experts were popping up all over the place, and that might've been helpful, except that you could literally find gurus who were evangelizing polar-opposite positions on almost every issue. They couldn't all be right, but that didn't prevent them from arrogantly asserting their "facts" and belittling anyone unenlightened enough to doubt their conclusions. If I had a dime for every one of these blowhards who were eventually proven wrong, I could've self-funded OnStar's start-up costs. Cars didn't turn into Java browsers on wheels, content wasn't always king, and if high-speed bandwidth is free, then what am I paying Comcast hundreds of dollars a month for? Oh, I get it, these were grand visions that were destined to be true "someday," and only small-thinking minds like mine needed more details than that.

The problem was that almost everybody at GM had his or her own opinion about the future, one that usually came from their favorite consultant, a consultant who may or may not have known what he or she was talking about. There were a lot of moving parts, but one thing they were all sure of was that all of these new technologies must have something to do with OnStar. And details of timing and laws of physics aside, they were equally sure they knew exactly what we should be doing with them. So we were getting an avalanche of unsolicited advice from every direction, and most of it had the potential to turn into big distractions that we really didn't need. Our newly developing "what's next" confidence was being tested.

One day I got a call from my old friend Vince Barabba who said he had a few of his people looking into something called satellite radio. It wasn't exactly an Internet idea, but these were confusing times, and to many people inside the company, all of these things seemed exotic and somehow related. Apparently, in 1997, the FCC had auctioned off two licenses for spectrum to deliver satellite broadcast radio content to customers across the United States. XM and CD Radio held those licenses and were in the process of putting together business plans to sell Wall Street on investing the billions of dollars necessary to launch their businesses. What the companies had were the licenses to use the airwaves and the technical confidence that they could make it all happen. What they didn't have were satellites, proven receivers, a viable high-volume distribution strategy, and a business model that made any financial sense. Oh, and by the way, Hughes was interested in selling some of their technology into this new category and had already established a relationship with one of the players, XM.

This was feeling vaguely like the War College conversation I'd had with John Jarrell years before, except without the free lunch. All right, Vince, interesting, but why are you calling me about this? Other than the fact that it involves unproven technology, an unfunded capital plan, and an unproven business model, what else did it have in common with us? We already had our hands full with enough of our own "uns" and probably didn't need to add any new ones. Vince had thought since we were already dealing with many of the generic issues that satellite radio would likely encounter, we might have some insights into what they'd be facing in trying to break into the automotive industry. He also wondered whether our experience would suggest that it made any sense for GM to look seriously at this opportunity. While we already had more than enough to work on, Vince did have a point. GM had already spent money and taken risks to start OnStar and deserved to get some payback on that experience. And we'd already seen what happened when ideas that overlapped with us were evaluated without our involvement, and it generally ended up badly. So, OK, as good team players (and also in self-defense), we'll take a look at this with your folks.

Vince assigned one of his best people, Nick Pudar, to manage the evaluation, and Nick had brought along a team of young, recently minted MBAs. These were very smart people, but their experience with funky stuff like this was extremely limited. They knew that and actually welcomed the chance to work with some grizzled OnStar veterans who could bring a more "earthy" perspective into their investigation. Fred was leading our new business development initiatives, so he became our point man. And if there was ever someone who fit the description of a crafty veteran who could bring boatloads of real-life experience to the table, forgetting for a moment that none of it had anything to do with satellites, it was Fred. Fred assigned one of his key people, Jim Smith, to the project, so it felt like this was starting off on a pretty good compass heading. Anyway, at the moment, it really didn't seem to be that significant of an issue, but since it had come from Vince, we needed to take it seriously.

A couple of weeks went by, and we got back together to review the group's progress. We now knew a lot more about satellite radio, but not enough to say we had it all figured out. A first pass through the issues identified that while technology was unproven, it was probably possible when given the time and resources to work on it. Hughes had already started DirecTV, but the difference here was they'd be broadcasting to vehicles that were moving at 60 mph and would routinely find themselves passing under bridges, through tunnels, and cruising down the building-lined streets of Chicago, New York, and San Francisco. The next obvious challenge was how much receiver hardware was going to cost, especially a version built to meet automotive electronics standards. Finally, there was the nagging question of whether this was really a consumer need that was aching to be satisfied or just something that satellite companies had gotten behind to create a new outlet for their technology. Who wanted over a hundred channels of radio, and more importantly, how much would they pay for them?

Hey, you could argue that there were no more unknowns in this than we'd originally faced at OnStar, and you'd have been right. But now we were a little smarter and knew just how hard it was to get something like this going. And we were already engaged in one risky battle with an uncertain outcome. Did we have the capacity to split our forces to start another? That's a terrible War College analogy, but it's the way it felt in my gut. This opportunity didn't seem compelling enough to jump on, especially if it was going to siphon off scarce resources from OnStar. So my strong recommendation was to back off. Who knows, maybe when they actually got something off the ground (no pun intended), it might be worth revisiting. But, at the moment, the whole thing was just a PowerPoint presentation, and I'd seen enough of those to be skeptical.

Surprisingly, nobody really argued with me. Many times people working on projects like these become personally vested during the study phase and will try almost anything to keep the dream alive. I'd seen that at OnStar; heck, I was even guilty of it more times than I'd like to admit. But, in this case, everyone seemed OK with the two-part conclusion: (1) This was something to keep an eye on, but it didn't need to be an immediate priority; (2) if you disagree with part one, don't attach it to OnStar since we already have more than enough on our plate. This felt good. We'd tied the evaluation up with a nice, tidy ribbon, and that hadn't happened very often—time to move on to the next issue on the pile.

Not so fast. When word of our conclusion was passed up the line to Harry Pearce, whose relationship with Hughes made him an interested party, he had a different thought. He didn't agree with part one, believing there could be an opportunity to be a first-mover in the category and create a real competitive advantage for GM vehicles. And he also didn't agree with part two, saying that he'd learned from the OnStar experience that this would need to be managed separately from the normal car business, and instead of starting a new organization, he'd rather add the necessary resources at OnStar so we could take it on. Oh well, another day in the snow globe. I needed a minute to let the flakes settle down, but we'd just inherited another thing to do. The good news was Harry understood we'd need more resources, but the bad news was that with all of the uncertainty surrounding this opportunity, it wasn't completely clear what they needed to be working on.

Harry also really wanted us to make something work with XM since they already had the beginnings of a relationship with Hughes. At this point, Fred grabbed me and said that if we were going to get dragged into this, we ought to position ourselves so that if it worked we ended up making a lot of money. He said our only chance to do that was to avoid pre-committing to XM and, instead, turn our partner selection into a high-stakes bakeoff between the two satellite companies. That sent me scurrying to set up a meeting with Harry to try to change his mind, which wasn't too scary since he was always very open-minded. I really liked Fred's positioning, but I couldn't be sure which way Harry would rule since he'd just tossed my recommendation to walk away from it altogether.

The meeting with Harry went fine. We explained to him that beyond the marketing claims of having satellite radio in our vehicles before anyone else did, there could be real value in brokering access to GM vehicles as a high-volume distribution outlet for their technology. Distribution was going to be critically important to these companies in order to attract the millions of paying subscribers who they'd need to make their massive up-front infrastructure investments pay off. And, even before that, they'd have to convince the capital markets to fund them in the first place, and having a tangible distribution commitment from the market's largest car company would make all the difference. So if we didn't force ourselves into a sole-source relationship with XM right out of the box, we had a chance to turn our willingness to be a first-mover into a strong negotiating position and potentially a great deal.

Harry wasn't completely sold on how great the results of the negotiations would actually be, but that was OK, neither were we. But he agreed it was worth a try and turned us loose so long as we checked with him before we made any deal, especially if it wasn't going to be with XM. That's all we needed to know. Now it was time to create a negotiating team, do a little pregame scheming, and see where it went. I'm pretty sure Fred appointed himself as captain of the negotiating team, but that was fine because, if he hadn't, I would've done it anyway. He decided to keep Vince's folks involved, as well as Jim Smith, and he craftily added Ken Enborg, our ex-Marine head lawyer at OnStar.

Ken and Fred had first met at OnStar, as their paths had never crossed in their prior GM experiences. But they were contemporaries in every sense of the word, and each had colorful stories with overlapping people in the company. These guys were made for each other, had complementary skills and experiences, and were cut from the same semi-insubordinate cloth. They were both schemers by nature, neither one had the slightest fear of taking a risk, and they genuinely respected and really enjoyed working with each other. They also really enjoyed spending time plotting at the whiteboard in their private conference room and intentionally locking me out until things were too far along for me to change. This negotiating team, and particularly these two characters, had the makings of something that was either going to end really well or really poorly. They'd decided to be extremely aggressive, completely violating the rules of "continuous improvement," by swinging for the fences with two men on each base. Hey, there aren't any rules that say you can do that—but that was kind of the point. These were all good, ethical people, with high morals and integrity, so I wasn't at all concerned that their scheming would turn into anything shady. But make no mistake, they'd suited up and fully intended to play their own version of major league hardball.

At this point, Fred pulled me aside and said he didn't want me anywhere near the actual negotiations. His sense was that they'd very likely be intense and highly emotional before it was over and that, if it worked just right, whoever won the deal would be wondering if they'd really won or not. In other words, he intended to push both parties to the limit, maybe even a little beyond their limit, and some feelings would undoubtedly get bruised. That'd be OK with the loser since, by definition, they'd be our competitor as soon as the dust settled, but the winner was going to be our partner. Somebody at a senior level at OnStar had to stay above the fray, show up for the photo op at the signing ceremony, and begin building the relationship necessary to make the business successful. While I wasn't completely comfortable backing away, especially with Harry looming in the background, Fred had a really good point. I'm still not sure whether he really meant what he said or if he was just trying to eliminate me looking over his shoulder, but I agreed, and he got down to business.

Fred scheduled numerous meetings with both companies and was very open with them on the process. There'd be separate, but parallel work streams with each company, with the objective of creating full, objective pictures of each potential partner. We'd be evaluating their technology plans, content plans, business models, financing plans, the talent they had in their key positions, and finally, the commercial terms of their proposed distribution agreement. This sounds a little intrusive, but not with what was at stake. What both of these companies wanted from us was a long-term, high-volume commitment to deploy their technology that they could use to raise the money necessary to launch their business. They then needed us to meet the volume commitment in order for them to add millions of subscribers so that their business models would actually work. For a thinking car company to do that and not have a death wish, you'd need to have a lot of confidence in the company you're doing business with. You'd be installing very unique equipment and selling it as part of your vehicles, and it could easily become obsolete if the company you'd chosen to work with screwed up or went out of business. This was a decision that had major, long-term consequences.

From the satellite radio companies' point of view, they seemed to understand, but I think they'd honestly believed getting a deal with the car companies was going to be a lot easier than it was turning out to be. They'd hoped that the "cool factor" of their technology, a hundred channels beamed from outer space to the dashboard of a new Cadillac, would've had the car companies tripping over each other to be the first kid on the block with this great new toy. And it might have actually worked out that way, except for two things. First, seriously off-template decisions like these are hard to make in car companies, as there aren't any natural owners or focal points to bring all of the various parties—engineering, manufacturing, purchasing, and marketing—together, at least not on an accelerated timetable. That all changes when they believe they're facing a competitive threat, but so far, nothing had happened, and nobody could tell if it ever would.

In GM's case, a juicy target because of our size, there was a focal point of sorts because we had already created OnStar. And since logic alone doesn't always prevail in big companies, Harry had further clarified the landscape by telling everyone inside the company, including us, that OnStar would be responsible to pull this all together—case closed. And that was the second problem the satellite radio companies had with their hope that the car guys would fall all over themselves to run with this new feature because, at least at GM, they weren't dealing with the car guys; they were dealing with us. And by us, I mean Fred, who wasn't looking at this from the perspective of what a car company wanted but from what XM and CD desperately needed, and that was distribution. Desperate needs trump wants and forms the basis for a pretty lopsided negotiation.

All of the work streams were finally completed, and Fred called an internal meeting around our now indispensible whiteboard, and what we'd hoped for had happened. There were differences in each of the companies' plans, but if you believed that either had a chance to be successful, then you had to conclude that both could be successful. Everybody was skeptical about anybody raising enough money to get started, but assuming they could, the bottom line was they were in a virtual tie. To Fred, this was perfect. It's extremely difficult to negotiate a great deal, even in a duopoly, if one company is materially better than the other. In this case, if either had been obviously superior, we would've had no choice but to pick them because of the outsized risk of doing anything else. They would've known that, and our negotiating position would've been greatly diminished. But a tie had all the makings of something really special—at least for us.

I don't remember if Fred cracked his knuckles to end the meeting or not, but it was time to turn him loose. We'd talked privately about what to shoot for, and he said fine, but that I should now step back and leave him and Ken alone with these guys. The negotiations started with the easy stuff, like how much they were going to pay us for each vehicle we built with their hardware and then how much more they'd pay when we activated the vehicle's trial subscription. Then it moved to the additional payments we'd get if the customer kept paying for the service after their trial subscription ended. That got divided into two buckets: (1) how much we'd get as a lump sum when they started paying and (2) how much of the monthly subscription we'd get thereafter. Looking at the future projections, this had the potential to turn into big money, especially in high volume. I'm not sure anyone completely believed the numbers we were conjuring up, but the point was that if even a fraction of this played out the way it might, we were talking about hundreds of millions of dollars, if not numbers that started with a B—real money, at least by OnStar standards.

Fred kept going, mainly because the dynamics of the negotiations were still squarely in his happy zone. OK, so all of the money up to this point was calculated on a variable, "per vehicle built and subscribed to" basis. What about an additional incentive for speed, for producing over a million vehicles in a relatively short period of time? Wasn't that even more valuable since it would likely force all of the other auto companies' hands and bring everyone into the game? Fred was playing chess. If we were the first-mover and moved with big volume, we would certainly create value by stimulating the entire market to come alive, and that would be worth a lot to companies that were desperate for scale.

Fred reviewed this idea with me, and there was no denying it was brilliant, but what about the risk of not hitting the big number? There wasn't a satellite in the air, and Fred was talking about guaranteeing a million-plus vehicles in what seemed like no time at all. Fred said that both companies were so desperate to get this deal that he believed the guarantee could be set up so that we'd get paid if we hit the number, but wouldn't lose anything except the added payment if we didn't. Wow, that was hard to imagine, but he was in the meetings and I wasn't, so we might as well go for it. How much were we talking about? He wasn't sure at that point, but he hoped a lot.

Rather than drag this out any longer, we ended up doing a deal with XM, so from a corporate standpoint, everybody was happy. But XM had gotten the business the old-fashioned way; they'd earned it—boy, had they earned it. Beyond all of the installation subsidies and revenue share numbers, Fred landed the guaranteed volume incentive—a separate additional payment of $435 million above and beyond everything else. He did have to agree that if we didn't hit the volume, we'd have to maintain ongoing penetration levels on GM vehicles equal to the average of the entire U.S. car industry, or the whole deal was off. But those were the sleeves from Fred's vest, because if this actually did take off, nobody in the car industry had more financial incentive than we did to put this stuff in our cars.

Oh, and one more thing. Fred said the deal he'd struck entitled us to 128 kilobytes of their satellite bandwidth, or the equivalent of five of their channels. It had some restrictions about not competing with them, and they asked us to let them keep using it until we figured out what we were going to do with it, but otherwise, we had that going for us, which was nice. I asked Fred why he did that. I knew he had no clue about the technology overlap with OnStar and no real ideas about how we'd actually use the channels. He just smiled and said that it was all equal up to that point, he needed a tiebreaker, and he didn't have the heart to ask either one of them for any more money. Unbelievable.

After the celebrating within OnStar subsided, we reviewed the deal with the rest of GM. They were amazed, but rightfully pointed out that all of those future cash flows were just a theory until XM's business got off the ground. And there was even a little concern that we may have driven too hard a bargain, which could cause them problems getting their business financed on Wall Street. And if they got the financing, they might run into cash flow problems down the line and need relief from our payments, and we could be stuck in a position where we'd need to agree to relief or watch them go under. Well that was a Debbie Downer way to look at all of this. Couldn't they just slap Fred on the back and say, "Great job!"? Harry and Rick actually had big smiles when we took them through the outcome, and so did Ron. But the more sober financial guys were justified in their caution; these were all still uncountable chickens whose eggs hadn't even been laid yet, much less hatched. The distribution agreement was phenomenal, but now it was on to the hard work of holding up our end of the bargain and helping to make XM successful.

Fred had been right. The day after the deal, the XM guys were feeling the hangover of what they'd agreed to, and he'd immediately become persona non grata. But aside from the difficulty of the numbers for XM, this was still a big win for them and something they really wanted to announce. GM had an interest in making a public announcement as well, as it was a claim of first-mover status in a cutting-edge, new category. So the PR machines went into gear, and on June 9, 1999, our plans were announced to the public. We said we had great confidence in the category and expected big things for the future of XM, and as a show of good faith, GM also announced a $50-million investment in the company. And Hughes put in another $50 million, which meant the entire family was now well represented.

So, all of a sudden, we were the undisputed leaders in a new category. It didn't have anything to do with the Internet, but the buzz surrounding digital signals from outer space created a fair amount of coverage. Sadly, our undisputed position didn't last very long, actually just twelve days. We knew that both radio companies had been talking to the other auto manufacturers; they'd told us as much to try to strengthen their positions during our negotiations. But, in the absence of a crisis, nothing was in any danger of happening very soon, but not surprisingly, our announcement had changed the dynamic, and now there was a crisis. Ford responded first, inking an agreement with CD Radio on June 21, followed a few weeks later by a CD deal with Chrysler. The details were sketchy, but we later learned that the financial incentives offered to both companies were far less than what we'd negotiated with XM. We'd made the deal they couldn't refuse, but also couldn't afford to give to anyone else. So that's where it stood in the summer of 1999. The first shots had been fired, the battle lines were being drawn, alliance networks were being formed, and it was time to mobilize the troops to get going. Now all we needed was a general.

It still wasn't completely clear what it was going to take to figure this all out and get it on a path toward production, but a few of the elements were coming into focus. XM was responsible for all of the technology and broadcast infrastructure, would develop all of the entertainment content and their brand materials, and manage their subscriber care and billing activities. And they also had to raise lots more money before we could chance putting anything into our vehicles.

On our side, we'd need to source the vehicle hardware and engineer a solution to integrate it into GM's various existing audio entertainment systems. In addition, we'd have to create the unique marketing materials to bring it to life at GM dealerships and invent an activation process. Finally, we'd need to ensure all of the pieces fit together and do a great job of creating loyal subscribers so that we could collect our share of the payments and stay motivated to put it into more vehicles. And while this was a little easier to smash into existing vehicle architectures than OnStar since it didn't need to mess with things like airbags, it was still way outside of normal process timing. If we intended to move as fast as we'd need to in order to collect the bonus for quickly getting to a million installations, more rules would need to be broken. Now that we understood the challenge a little bit better, we better make that at least a two-star general.

It occurred to me that there were a number of ways to approach this. We could take each functional piece and pile it on top of the groups already doing that same function for OnStar. The engineers could inherit the hardware issues. Why not, it was just another box, right? Similarly, the marketing guys could add this to their other OnStar chores in dealing with Chevy and Cadillac and their dealers. And I could somehow keep this all together in my head and bounce back and forth prioritizing initiatives between OnStar and XM. That approach sounded like what would've happened if pieces of OnStar had been spread across the traditional GM organizations at the beginning. It looks efficient on paper, but we weren't in the paper business.

The other extreme would be to build everything that was necessary to take on the XM business completely from scratch. That would mean dedicating all new resources with the singular focus of getting this business off the ground and humming. The problem with that, beyond its likely inefficiency, was that the interfaces we'd built between OnStar and GM for things like vehicle integration and marketing were already a pain in the neck, according to the vehicle guys. We were small, funky, and distracted them from their main car mission, but we'd lived through that and had now been grudgingly acknowledged as a part of the family—probably close to a third cousin twice removed. There was no way to double the funkiness in terms of interface points with the mother ship and not expect that to cause a riot. The stand-alone resource theory may have been theoretically right, but it had no chance of passing the political reality check.

So my thought was to form a separate, but very small team within OnStar who would focus exclusively on issues related to XM and have them function in the role of general contractor. They'd be responsible for laying out all of the plans and ensuring that each of the work streams were sufficiently resourced, either by having them done within the existing OnStar organization or, where absolutely necessary, adding newly dedicated people to the XM team. And since the XM business was different enough to easily pull out of the financial numbers, we'd set it up as a separate P&L, an XM business unit within OnStar, and use that to create unique objectives for the satellite radio business within GM.

You could tell that this was either going to turn into a really big deal or, for any number of unforeseeable reasons, evaporate and go away, and that outcome would ultimately depend on the quality of the leadership at both XM Corporation and at our little XM business unit within OnStar. We couldn't really influence how XM was managed other than indirectly through our seat on their board, but we certainly could make sure we had it under control on our end. I decided we needed a really special person to lead this initiative and that they should report directly to me to ensure access to the resources and the attention it would undoubtedly need. But the real key was going to be getting the right leader because, with so much going at OnStar, they'd likely be working without a lot of adult supervision.

Thankfully, another version of Fred and Walt magically emerged from the vastness of GM in the form of Rick Lee. Rick was tall and thin, about my age, and spoke with the clarity and common sense found in a University of Kansas graduate. Like Fred, he'd also earned his stripes in GM's Treasurer's Office, and at one point earlier in his career, he had actually worked for Fred. He somehow survived that and struck out for greener pastures, finally landing in GM's sales and marketing organization. There, he'd eventually risen to the position that was responsible for all of GM's fleet sales—nearly a million vehicles a year. He did that for a while, until the early rumblings of the Internet set a series of events in motion within GM designed to keep the company from being run over by this disruptive new force.

The problem with dealing with anything as different as the Internet inside a car company was that it appeared half commercial, half technical, and half insanely unpredictable—and three halves were only the start of the complexity. And there was no existing place to work the issue within the company, no natural owner. If you left it to the salespeople, they'd likely get wrapped up in short-term tactics and miss the nuance of the technology and where it was heading. If you assigned it to the IT people, you'd undoubtedly find a bunch of techies happily swapping jargon, but missing the fact that it needed to help sell twenty thousand additional Buicks—next week! So the company created yet another tweener and assigned Rick to a special assignment reporting to both the head of marketing and to the head of IT to try to figure it out.

The challenge of his role and the complexity of trying to sort out something like this inside a hundred-year-old car company were both daunting and instructive—and not completely unlike what was happening in the OnStar world at that moment. Unfortunately, the politics of the dual-reporting arrangement were just awful, which ultimately caused it to get set up another way. The other way that got invented came back to boomerang on OnStar, but that's for another chapter. The result of the change that was important to this chapter is that Rick was now a free agent and available for another assignment. And like Fred, Rick was a very senior executive in GM's structure, and there just weren't that many positions for someone at his level to land. Could there be another lucky red-circle in my future?

I honestly didn't know Rick at all at this point. I knew of him and had seen him in a couple meetings, but I had no idea what kind of person or leader he was. Fred loved Rick and told me I ought to talk to him about the XM opportunity. While Fred's Darth Vader reputation kept him from having anything to do with XM, he still really loved the concept of the business and wanted his masterful negotiation to turn into bushel baskets full of real cash. I sat down with Rick, explained where we were with the business, and told him how I thought it should be run. I half expected him to say he wasn't interested because most guys at his level (Fred aside) would've believed this was all beneath them. Too many people equated their number of direct reports and the size of their budget with their own self-worth, and it would take a real leap of faith, or at least a moment of severely bad judgment, to look at what we were doing and see the impact that you might be able to have.

For whatever reason, either his sense of humor or wanting a chance to be a cellmate with Fred again, Rick said he was interested in the job. At that point, I felt fairly comfortable pointing to the hundreds of millions of dollars that were at stake in order to justify Rick's move into the position, complete with the necessary red-circle. Thankfully, everybody whose support mattered bought in to the selection, and Rick joined the team. I'd just picked up another highly valuable veteran free agent, someone who could be trusted to get this XM opportunity organized and off the ground. And without knowing it, but of equal importance, I'd just added another key ingredient to OnStar's culture, someone who'd ultimately become a trusted friend and ally in keeping the good ship OnStar afloat during the rough seas that lied ahead. Life was good—for a minute.

What came next was almost a carbon copy of what we'd lived though with OnStar, except that Fred's great negotiation had made it worse. There was a well-defined and enormous pot of gold at stake if we could move fast enough to get it, but nobody, including us, was sure if that was possible. But we had to go for it, which meant sliding back out on the thin ice and hoping that global warming was a myth. And there was one added little wrinkle just to make things interesting. Our internal lead time to develop and validate vehicle hardware was just about the same as what XM needed to design, construct, and shoot up their satellites and get their studios ready to beam more than static toward Earth if a miracle happened and everything worked as planned. That meant we had two choices: (1) wait two years until we were sure that all of XM's stuff was going to work, which meant we'd get to market two years after that, or (2) begin our work now in parallel with all of XM's rocket science and run the risk of spending the money to have our vehicles ready to receive music from satellites that had never gotten off the ground.

This would've been much easier if there hadn't been so much money at stake, but the motivations of capitalism are good, at least if you were a fan of satellite radio. Rick laid out a very aggressive plan to have GM vehicles ready to deliver XM services as soon as the satellites were in orbit. That meant that you'd be able to buy a GM vehicle with factory-installed XM at the same time that a cobbled-in, aftermarket unit would be available at Best Buy. This had never been done before, as the car makers always lagged the consumer electronics industry by at least a couple of years. But Rick had gotten everyone together using his sales skills and our large financial upside to nudge all the reluctant parties within the company to get on board. There was a fall back plan if XM blew up, but it wouldn't have been pretty, so this was a big bet to make.

For the next twenty months, the place was littered with program management spreadsheets tracking the hundreds of things going on inside of Rick's XM team, while trying to keep them all from conflicting with the thousands of equivalent things going on inside of OnStar. XM needed to execute Gen 1 of their module, and during this period, OnStar would be launching our own separate versions of Gen 2 and Gen 3. Dealer training materials and process flowcharts were being reviewed, revised, re-revised, and then torn up and done again. We were determined not to duplicate the mistakes of the On-Star launch, particularly those that involved getting on the wrong side of the dealers.

By this point, we had a couple of things going for us in that regard. First, we'd established a dealer advisory committee where we worked with a handful of really good dealers from across the country to discuss our plans and issues. This had started as a purely defensive measure to avoid the dealer blowups we'd experienced during the OnStar launch, but had actually begun to morph into something much more valuable. I'd learned three things about dealers. First, they wanted to make money, and the more the better. This created the potential for conflict, as too many things immediately took on the character of a zero-sum negotiation, but as businesspeople, they were certainly entitled to jealously guard their own financial interests. Second, they always had opinions and wanted them to be heard and respected. Third, above all else, they wanted to be leveled with. They understood we wouldn't always agree with each other, but being honest and candid about why something was being done a certain way was really important to them because it meant we'd taken them seriously. These were smart folks, and drawing them into discussions about how we'd envisioned bringing XM to life in their dealerships was really helpful.

The second thing we had going for us with dealers was Rick. Rick was a seasoned sales guy, understood dealers, knew a lot of them, and respected how the channel needed to work. He wasn't a pushover with dealers, as he'd taken his share of tough issues into the lion's den over the years. But he knew how to pick his spots and not take on everything at once. If he'd been leading our initial OnStar sales efforts, things would have probably gone much smoother, but at least we had him now, and it was going to pay dividends.

It was literally countdown to launch in the late summer of 2001, and we were mostly ready, but our in-vehicle execution wasn't anything to write home about. Gen 1 XM was a separate box bolted into the trunk with some wires running to the radio, and its antenna was hilarious, unless you spent your life trying to produce beautiful vehicles. Since nobody had experience beaming signals from outer space to moving vehicles, the engineers' marching orders were to make sure it worked—period. That resulted in our first antenna costing $100 and physically resembling a small ski boot. And it got worse (or funnier) because, on some vehicles, it was mounted on the front of the roof near the windshield and next to a differently shaped OnStar antenna, vaguely conjuring up the appearance of a mildly deformed moose. All of the vehicle designers hated this, except the Hummer guys who thought the bigger and uglier, the better. But that's what happens when you have no experience and your only option is an over-engineered solution. The best thing you could say about the entire technical setup was that it worked, it accomplished getting to market on a crazy-fast timetable, and there had to be a Gen 1 before you could have a Gen 2, so you might as well get it over with.

As a footnote to history, XM's official launch of service at their studios in Washington, DC, was scheduled for Wednesday, September 12, 2001. No kidding, what a strange set of circumstances. And the national advertising campaign that was timed to coincide with the launch featured celebrities looking up as musical instruments—pianos, guitars, trumpets, violins, and so on—rained down out of the sky all around them. It was a clever way to introduce music from outer space, right? Sure, unless it's all supposed to happen the day after 9/11, and in Washington, no less.

I was stuck in Frankfort, Germany, on 9/11, about to head home from Europe's major annual auto show. I spent the next six days trying to catch a ride back to Detroit, while the small team we had in Washington for the XM press event watched the DC streets fill with military vehicles. Memories of that still seem surreal and immediately had me thinking about my former War College buddies and where they were at that moment—and how much more they had to worry about than I ever would.

Needless to say, the advertising campaign got scrapped, and the PR value of the launch got drowned out, but operationally, everything held together, and we were off to the races. The next few years were as crazy as you might expect in trying to get the category accepted by consumers and by the internal operating groups within General Motors. I eventually became a member of XM's board of directors and got to see how a stand-alone start-up looked from the inside. The board was initially over-weighted with financial types who had some funding relationship with the company. My hair would hurt during the majority of each meeting, as the focus was primarily on the "financial engineering" issues necessary to keep the business solvent. Everyone understood that it was going to require a massive investment—billions of dollars—before the company would have enough subscribers to generate a positive cash flow. That meant the continuous raising of money through stock issues, bond issues, convertible bond issues, preferred stock issues, sale-and-leasebacks of satellites and buildings—ugh! This was all necessary, of course, but I was always hoping to see more time devoted to discussing how well the business itself was actually doing—you know, like with real customers?

There were many similarities between our two businesses. Both were new entrants in new categories, were built on novel and rapidly changing technologies, and were dependent on acquiring subscribers through bundling services with new vehicles. Each of us ran large call centers, oversaw massive customer relationship management activities, and had immature brands that needed to be developed and nurtured. And we both faced the need to think carefully about our futures, as the strategic issues shaping our landscapes were complex and volatile. Being on their board allowed me to learn from their unique experiences and interact with some exceptional people. Two who I really came to appreciate and respect were Jack Shaw, the CEO of Hughes, and Tom Donohue, the president of the U.S. Chamber of Commerce. These guys were real characters, had amazing life experience that was considerably different than my own, and brought energy, wisdom, and common sense to every issue we discussed. I liked them both a lot, learned from our time together, and felt fortunate that our paths had crossed.

And while it wasn't without its share of drama and a few "agony of defeat" moments, our XM adventure ended up playing out much more like the "thrill of victory." The fact that Rick's aggressive launch plan had our vehicles ready to go in 2001 led us to blow by Fred's million vehicle commitment and triggered the additional $435 million bonus payment. Oh, and the GM guys had been right; XM did end up with a financing problem in 2002, which required us to let them defer $250 million in payments to help them through a liquidity crisis. But within three years, we'd gotten back the $250 million, with interest, and actually picked up a few million common equity warrants for our trouble, which we ended up cashing in for an additional $400 million that wasn't in the plan.

And remember the Ford and Chrysler deals with CD that were announced a couple weeks after we did? Well, Ford didn't get anything into factory production until 2004, and everybody else's programs were so low volume that, all the way through 2007, we'd built more vehicles with satellite radio than all of the other vehicle manufacturers combined! We'd more than held up our end of the deal with XM, and it played out just like Fred had predicted. While the other carmakers were slow, our contract had fired the first shot and caused them all to respond, which was the catalyst that helped create the industry. It all hadn't happened by accident, and it just went to show what a combination of great financial incentives (Fred's) and strong leadership (Rick's) could do, which was amazing.

Fred actually retired in 2002 after over a quarter of a century at GM, but I think he'd tell you his best six years were during his time at OnStar. The year after we officially earned the volume bonus from XM, I invited Fred to play in the Buick Open Pro Am event that OnStar sponsored in Michigan to recognize the milestone. We ended up being paired with Vijay Singh, and thankfully, for us, Tiger

Woods was also playing in the Pro Am that day. That meant the entire gallery was following Tiger not Vijay and that our errant shots were mostly falling harmlessly in the rough without harming any innocent spectators. While I'd intended the round of golf to be an official thank-you to Fred for the $435 million he'd earned GM, when it was over, he said playing those eighteen holes was more stress than anything he ever felt during the XM negotiation. Oh well, isn't it the thought that counts?

Rick Lee continued in the XM leadership role until he retired when I did on October 1, 2009. During that time, Rick ended up battling with serious health issues, but got through all of them successfully while exhibiting amazing courage, resolve, and good spirits. He was truly an inspiration to watch during those personal trials, but it wasn't surprising because those were the same traits that I'd come to admire in Rick for nearly a decade. As a testament to the never-ending insanity of bureaucracy, GM actually had been after me to un-red-circle Rick and reduce his level for a number of years prior to his retirement. With all he'd contributed by bringing the XM opportunity to life inside GM, literally billions of dollars, the system somehow still believed that since he didn't have a huge staff or a big expense budget, he must not have been doing anything that was really that important. How unbelievable and sad was that? Shouldn't producing the kinds of results Rick had and not needing an army to do it be celebrated and not penalized? Thankfully, I'd learned enough over the years to be creatively insubordinate on the important issues (with Fred and Ken's influence) and was able to stall long enough keep the company from doing something that would have been both misguided and wrong—at least this time.

CHAPTER 11

Excursions and Diversions

I wish our satellite radio adventure had been our only collision with the dot-com days because at least it was an interesting and profitable excursion. But, unfortunately, the technology storm raging during the late 1990s had engulfed nearly every business with the ferocity of a Category 5 hurricane. That meant everyone needed to batten down the hatches, and I hoped that our little boat was watertight enough to survive the passing swells. The forces that had pulled Rick Lee away from selling $15 billion a year in fleet vehicles and made him available to lead our XM initiative had spawned another organizational offspring within GM, and this one was headed right at us.

Rick's "How do we deal with the Internet?" assignment had fallen victim to a predictable turf-war outbreak within GM that made it impossible for him to get any real traction. The Internet had fallen smack-dab between two traditional organizations, sales and marketing and information technology. Both of these groups were led by strong (stubborn) individuals, and neither one was particularly interested in ceding their authority to the other, at least in the absence of a direct order from someone north of them on the org chart. I'm not sure how they got there, but at some point, the senior folks at GM decided that the Internet was unlikely to be a passing fad and was going to have serious implications for every business, even a hundred-year-old one that bent metal and made cars.

It also didn't hurt the buzz surrounding the phenomena that new companies were popping up out of nowhere to "harness" this force and were going public with astronomical valuations. The laws of economics seem to have been temporarily suspended, as market capitalizations of what turned out to be money-losing ideas were often orders of magnitude above many established, profitable companies. If you bought into all the hype, the old economy was already made up of the walking dead who just weren't smart enough to know it yet. It was a "get on board or get run over" stampede, and many companies were oddly stalled in the middle, not thoughtfully plotting their options, but frozen like deer caught in the headlights. The top guys at GM knew something needed to be done, and after their first approach hadn't gone too well, they accepted the fact that they were going to have to approach it from outside of the bounds of their normal structure.

So it was time for another new organization. This time, however, the decision had been made to announce it with great fanfare to signal to the world that not only did GM get it, but had embraced it and intended to lead the auto industry into this brave new world. GM didn't have a recent track record of leading with technology, so this would be our chance to put some PR points on the board and improve our corporate image as a progressive, hip, happening company. Hey, why not, if every stupid idea that turned into a company that ended its name with .com were suddenly worth a boatload of money, then surely a global enterprise that generated nearly $200 billion in annual revenue would get some credit for embarking on such a transformational journey.

A choice needed to be made regarding who should lead the effort, and rather than reach outside the company for some futurist with existing brand recognition, GM decided to put one of their own executives in the role. But it had to be someone at a high enough level within the corporate structure to bring immediate stature to the fledging new organization, and it would be helpful if the person was comfortable with change, maybe even somebody who embraced and enjoyed it.

I'd heard some vague rumblings through the grapevine, but assumed it was far enough removed from us not to worry about. Not.

The night before GM had scheduled a major press event at the corporate headquarters at the Renaissance Center, I got a call from my boss, Ron Zarrella, saying he had something he needed to tell me about. He confirmed that GM had indeed decided to form a new operating group, something called eGM, and that an existing GM Group vice president, Mark Hogan, had been selected to be its first president. He went on to say that OnStar would now be working for him and that I'd need to be at the press conference the next day, and not to worry, everything would be fine. He didn't have any more time to talk, but promised that there'd be more discussion over the next few days.

Now, that was a hit-and-run accident I never saw coming. It felt like Ron had just thrown me in a maze and set off a smoke bomb. What I knew for sure was I had a new boss, my third so far counting Ken Baker during Project Beacon and most recently Ron. But who did Hogan work for, was I still going to be the president of OnStar, and was Ron planning on maintaining any connection to us? And because that's what big companies do when a new sheriff comes to town, did this mean the company was planning on rethinking all of its technology strategies, including ours, and subjecting us to some kind of corporate group-grope process? Oh, and by the way, it was nice to say we'd have time for more discussion later, but that was technically a crock. At least if by "more" the implication was we'd had any discussion about this in the first place. There'd been no discussion, no asking what I thought, no opportunity to provide any perspective; it had been a set of marching orders, and unclear ones at that. Maybe I'd signed up for this when I was at the War College, but I didn't think so.

I put down the phone and sat stunned at my desk wondering what it all meant. Lorrie knew I'd just gotten off the phone with Ron and asked if I was all right. I said I honestly didn't know, but to clear my schedule for the next day because I'd be downtown at a press event to meet my new boss. Somehow Fred caught wind that something was up (probably Lorrie ratting me out), and he came into my office to see what was going on. I told him what I knew and what I didn't, and the "didn't know" list was longer. Fred got a big smile on his face and told me I was going to love Hogan. Apparently, Fred and Mark had also worked together back in the day in the Treasurer's Office; actually, Mark had worked for Fred at the same time Rick Lee was working for Fred. This was starting to get stranger than I could handle. Had everybody worked for Fred before? No matter, the good news was my new boss had, and Fred thought that I'd love him. He was right with Rick, so my instincts were to be comforted by his sense of Mark, but that didn't answer all of the other questions. The whole situation left me guessing, and I knew the next day would be quite interesting.

I arrived for the press event and found the room surprisingly full a half hour before showtime. There were rows of chairs for the media and tables full of computers in a U-shaped ring around all of the chairs. It was trying to look high-tech, but maybe just a little too hard to be credible. Someone from GM's communications pulled me aside and told me I'd be sitting with some other GM people in the front row of seats, and at some point in the presentation, I'd be introduced. Then yada, yada, yada, and I should be ready to answer whatever questions might be asked regarding OnStar. Questions about what? I'd be introduced as what? No time for any of that, they just assured me it would all be fine.

The event started, and the front row of chairs filled up with folks like Rick Wagoner, Ron Zarrella, Ralph Szgenda (GM Group vice president for IT), and of course, my new boss Mark Hogan. Rick made a few remarks confirming that we'd been closely following what was going on in the world of information technology and the Internet, understood that it had incredible implications for a global enterprise of the size and scope of General Motors, and had decided to lead the auto industry by creating an organization to bring it all together inside the company. Mark had been selected to lead the effort because of his deep industry experience and his proven track record of innovation and out-of-the-box thinking. Mark would work for Ron

Zarrella, but have a strong connection to Ralph and his team as well. He'd be responsible for all customer-facing initiatives in this area and would therefore assume responsibility for the OnStar business, with the president of OnStar (me) also reporting to Mark.

I think I was taking notes faster than most of the reporters in the room—all right, customer-facing initiatives, Mark works for Ron, and at least, for now, I'm still running OnStar. I wasn't completely clear about a few other details, like the rationale for putting us into this group in the first place, but it was better than it might have been. The press conference ended, I got no questions, and I had a chance to shake hands with Mark and tell him I looked forward to working with him. He said things were a little crazy at the moment, but he'd have his admin set up a meeting between the two of us so I could bring him up to speed on what was going on inside of OnStar. That sounded fair to me, although I was still a little nervous about what might be motivating our consolidation into eGM, but no sense being paranoid, at least not yet.

I went back to my office and was greeted by a number of folks who wondered what had happened. I told them what I'd learned and said that until we knew any better, we should stay optimistic and just keep doing what we were doing. I met with Ron a couple of days later, and in a very matter of fact way, he said there was no intention for any of this to change OnStar's mission or signal anything that should be interpreted as deemphasizing either GM's or his personal commitment to the business. We'd been thrown into the eGM organization at the very last minute, and that's why I hadn't heard about it until the night before. Someone had gotten concerned that there wasn't enough "e-ness" going on inside GM to credibly make this announcement, and they needed something that was real and tangible connected to it to improve the optics. Apparently, the real and tangible cupboard was bare except for us, so in we went. Ron said not to worry about it, that he still intended to stay involved with the business as part of the OnStar board of directors.

The OnStar board of directors was something that had been recently formed to satisfy the legal requirements that kicked in when we transitioned from being a division of GM to a wholly owned subsidiary. That happened because we'd become different enough from the car business, particularly the parts that dealt with telecommunications issues, that the legal staff needed to be able to draw some bright lines between where GM the car company stopped and we started. Up to this point, the board didn't need to be very complicated, as it was just Ron and me. But now it sounded like that was going to change. My boss would be Mark, but my old boss would be my new boss's boss, and the three of us would form the board. Not quite as simple as before, but the good news was Ron was planning on staying involved. I liked Ron, respected his business instincts, and more importantly, we'd been working pretty well together. It looked like this might end up being just fine.

I finally got my one-on-one time with Mark and found him to be very different than what I'd expected. Most GM Group vice presidents that I'd run into, aside from Ron, had large egos, practiced command and control leadership, and never shrank from the spotlight. My first impression of Mark was that he was warm, self-effacing, empathetic, fun loving, and empowering, maybe to a fault. I only learned later that he did maintain one GM Group VP trait, never shrinking from the spotlight, but that was probably a good fit for the role that he'd just been dropped into. He said he'd heard a lot of good things about what we were doing at OnStar and wanted to help in any way he could to make it even better. He also wanted to meet the key members of the OnStar team and said it was up to me if I wanted to attend his eGM staff meetings, as he knew we had a lot going on at OnStar and didn't want those to become an unnecessary distraction.

That first meeting went well, actually better than I'd expected, and when you combined that with Ron's pledge of staying involved, I felt my early coaching to my team to stay optimistic was turning out to be on target. So this wasn't feeling too bad at all. Heck, it might even end up being an advantage to have another highly placed executive in the company willing to help us with our issues; we sure seemed to have enough of them to go around. Oh well, at least it felt good for a while.

Mark quickly began assembling a team of people to take on whatever it was eGM was supposed to be doing, which wasn't all that clear. You could immediately see the difference when a GM Group VP tried to get resources to start something versus when an ex-locomotive salesman tried to start something, but unfortunately, it wasn't all good. Sure, Mark could get access to headcount allocations easier than we could; he wouldn't have taken the job if that weren't already a done deal. But that still didn't mean he was going to get GM's best and brightest to leave their auto-centric career paths and jump onboard eGM. So what Mark got was a really interesting combination of redeployables (at higher levels than we had access to), technology zealots, former cronies from past assignments in places like GM Brazil (where he'd been president), and relatively young rebels from inside the company looking for Mark to lead a techno-revolution that would transform GM. This wasn't a recipe for success, particularly when combined with an ill-defined mission and Mark's somewhat hands-off leadership style. This had all of the makings of an inmate-run asylum, which would've been fine with me except that somebody had signed our papers, and we'd been committed.

The trouble signs started early, as one by one my key team members started coming into my office complaining about how they'd been told they now functionally worked for their counterpart at eGM. Jon Hyde was told that he worked for Mark's finance guy, and our IT guy was being told he worked for his counterpart at eGM. Heck, even Fred and Ken were being told they had other bosses to deal with now. That really was a death wish for everybody involved, especially their other bosses. It was whack-a-mole time again; thankfully, we'd kept up our training on that, just a new set of rodents to deal with. But whacking moles is only fun when you're solving real problems or whacking competitors; when you have to swing at yourself, it's just tiring. We got through the worst of the nonsense unscathed, except that it cost us a few months of needless distraction and drained energy when we didn't have extra to spare.

Every time I'd ask Mark to reign in his subjects, he'd agree but insist that it was healthy to allow a little disorderly behavior from time to time; it kept everyone on their toes. I knew what he meant and that he didn't mean for it to be harmful. And I know how many of the people who worked for him took it, which was to use Mark's lax delegation skills to take license to grab whatever controls they could get their hands on. In the meantime, we were starting to see some of Mark's creative side come out, typically stimulated by the observations and comments made to him by numerous self-appointed experts.

With all of the emphasis that was being placed on web-based transactions at that point, it was only a matter of time before some of the deep thinkers moved into our territory. Wouldn't it be great to connect people while they were mobile and find ways to "monetize" them while they were out on the road? This was well before cell phones were really anything but cell phones, and the thought was that the relatively new concepts of website "stickiness" and "numbers of eyeballs on glass" could somehow be transferred into a vehicle. Never mind the fact that driving a car was challenging enough for most people and that 85 percent of the miles driven in the United States were in single-occupant vehicles where that occupant was supposed to be focused on driving, but somehow we could "own the dashboard." Instead of eyes on glass, we might be able to have "ears on speakers" or "tongues on microphones" (yuck!). This all sounded well beyond anything that made sense, even for those times, but Mark was listening to a number of people who thought it was exactly what we needed to be doing.

A term known as "mCommerce," or mobile commerce (transacting while mobile), was starting to gather momentum, and what better place to do that than when sitting comfortably in a GM vehicle connected to OnStar? Why, who knew what this might turn into. We could somehow find a way to help a subscriber pre-order their Happy Meal from Mickey D's and even electronically transfer the payment and keep a small portion for ourselves. Or we could set up in-vehicle stock trading, maybe charge hotel chains a "slotting fee" for referring our sleepy drivers into their cozy beds, or somehow facilitate gasoline purchases. Oh, and one of my personal favorites, maybe we could beam a virtual Grande Skim Latte coupon to the dashboard of the vehicle as it passed a Starbucks that was having a slow day. There were heads-up displays, so why not build an advertising platform featuring dancing holograms to broker our subscribers to any number of merchants ready to pay.

I didn't blame Mark for all of this, as it generally came in the form of well-meaning brainstorming, but too often, his eGM minions would decide that Mark really meant it, and if OnStar wouldn't step up and make it happen, they'd find a way to do it themselves. Never mind worrying about what was appropriate to do in a vehicle, how customers felt about being brokered and monetized, and what any of this might do to damage our increasingly valuable brand. Remember, these were heady times when technology evangelists painted the world as "for us or against us," and raising practical concerns was seen as surrendering to the narrow-minded thinking of the old economy.

Connectivity was getting a lot of attention, and a cottage industry of advisors was increasingly targeting the U.S. auto industry's fifteen million annual new vehicles as the net's next frontier. The number of gurus was multiplying faster than a herd of frisky rabbits, with a corresponding rise in the number of conferences, seminars, exhibits, and trade shows that all promised the answers to life, or at least an opportunity to network with people you might have seen on CNBC. Mark loved all of this stuff and hauled me along with him whenever he could to immerse me in all of the enlightenment. The bad news was that it was time-consuming, distracting, and usually ended with me getting into an argument with somebody because I couldn't help myself. The good news was I ate a lot of great meals in some pretty amazing places, and at least when I was traveling with Mark, I got to ditch my usual mode of transportation—seat 33E on Northwest airlines—for a much nicer seat on one of GM's corporate planes.

Actually, there was some good that came from of all of this. Out of necessity, I learned to become a reasonable judge of the people and hubris that were celebrated in the world of technology. The problem was that everyone spoke with such passion and conviction, and nobody's nose was obviously growing, that you had to just accept that being enthusiastic and full of confidence meant absolutely nothing. I also learned that you couldn't use traditional markers like job title, corporate logo affiliation, or educational pedigree as good sorting mechanisms because those were all over the map. And, finally, while I would've loved to find a positive correlation between high ego and being full of it, that didn't always work out either. So, on the surface, everybody either held the keys to the kingdom or should be given the keys to the outhouse, but it was going to take more than a little effort to find out which.

Thankfully, there were a few old economy clues that were actually helpful from time to time, things as pedestrian as "follow the money." When you'd hear rock-star CEOs talk about things like the car being a browser on wheels or that, in the near future, when you pulled into a Shell station, you'd be more interested in filling up with "content" than unleaded regular, it started to make sense when you understood they were running companies that made servers and routers. If they could evangelize a future (which someone else would fund creating) that hooked more things into the network, then they already had a part number on the shelf that you'd need to buy to manage that additional traffic. These were the arms merchants of technology, and they knew that if they could somehow stimulate industries to erupt into a competitive battle to imbed new technologies into their business models, they'd be able to sell their version of the bullets to everybody involved to help their side "win."

162

Then there were other people who were saying almost anything they could think of regarding the future and counting on the fact that almost nobody was keeping track. They'd invariably get a few things right, even if the timing was off by a couple of years, and it would be their correct Nostradamus proclamations that would be listed on their speaker's bio. The higher the percentage they got right, or the more recent that a big one had come through for them, the higher their status and consulting fees. Closely related to this group were people who'd already "done it," been successful in actually accomplishing something with technology, earned enough money from it to buy their own island, and were now content with either saving the world or indulging their personal passions.

There was no better example of that than a gathering that was held annually in Monterrey, California, called the TED conference. TED stood for Technology Entertainment and Design, and it was supposed to be a place where the real movers and shakers of technology and creativity gathered every year to stay connected, recharge their batteries, and inspire each other with the passions in their lives. It obviously wasn't only for real movers and shakers because they let GM guys attend, actually me for a few years. But there were enough of the real guys in attendance to keep the crowd coming back (at a few thousand dollars apiece). I have to admit that it was kind of cool to be in a relatively small group (a few hundred people in a small auditorium) and have the random morning's agenda include a former astronaut, a senator, Jim Fowler (Marlin Perkins's old side kick on Mutual of Omaha's Wild Kingdom), the former head of technology from a huge software company, and Yo-Yo Ma with his Silk Road Ensemble. And while you'd be watching those people, you'd look up and see Steve Case (back when AOL was still a big deal) sitting in the row in front of you.

It certainly wasn't a bad thing to see Yo-Yo Ma, actually a real thrill because he was engaging and amazing. And Jim was great, too; heck, he even brought a hawk into the auditorium and turned it loose, only to have it circle the audience and come back to land on his arm—Marlin would have been so proud. But the guys that had presumably done amazing things with technology came in and showed us their rare book collection, or lectured us on how everybody needed to give something back (excepting their multimillions, of course), or in one case, believe it or not, enlightened us with their theory of how dinosaurs had sex. What a crock. Just because you'd helped invent part of Windows or started a company that did graphics software, you weren't the smartest person in the world, and you certainly weren't the most interesting.

Anyway, all of this helped form my impression of this landscape, and while it wasn't perfect, it did help me stay somewhat sane through all of this zaniness. There were smart people, very smart people, who were bringing very creative and thoughtful ideas to the table, many of which had the potential to create a breakthrough in an area that nobody had ever heard of before. And maybe more than it had ever been in the past, there might be some crazy bank shot that came out of what they were doing in a far-off corner of landscape that could run right through the middle of your otherwise carefully laid plans. You had to be ready for any of that, whatever that meant, and try not to let it completely consume you with fear of the unknown, as it was, in fact, unknowable.

In parallel, and disguised in ways you couldn't decipher, were a range of posers, charlatans, and hard-minded capitalists who either had no clue what was likely to happen next or wanted to jawbone you into a position where they had just what you needed and were coincidentally ready to sell it to you. The fact that they had something to sell you didn't necessarily make them wrong, just worth being suspicious of. So there was no answer key, no secret decoder ring, and no crystal ball that could really help tell the future. But it was certain that the future was going to be way different than the present, it would come way faster than it had in the past, and its effects had little chance of being benign. You were either going to benefit from where things were headed, get run over by them, or more likely, have to become comfortably uncomfortable with the reality that it was going to be some of both.

We went to other events as well, with annual pilgrimages to COMDEX (Computer Dealers' Exposition) before it imploded and CES (Consumer Electronics Show). You always knew you'd end up with sore feet walking the halls of the Las Vegas Convention Center, but at least it was a convenient place to meet with a bunch of folks from all over the world and have dinner with the small number of them who you actually liked. We also learned very early on that it was crazy expensive to actually exhibit at any of these big shows, and more likely than not, our message would get lost on a floor full of glitz and tech-related eye candy. Safety and security wasn't exactly sexy enough to break through when the likelihood was that the booth on one side would have a juggling magician and an hourly performance of the Hooters Girls on the other. So we decided to behave like any other cash-strapped start-up and practice guerilla-warfare PR tactics. We'd get a room at the all-suites Venetian, cater it pretty well, make sure we'd made our bed, and invite battle-weary journalists to stop by for a bagel (a.m.) or drink (p.m.). Debbie Frakes, a wonderfully talented early PR executive at OnStar, invented this "stop by and rest your feet" approach, and it ended up working really well.

When it was a year that we thought we really had something special to show off, we'd either ask one of our suppliers who had a booth (folks like Delphi, XM, LG, or Qualcomm) to let us do something with them or we'd have a car on the roof of the Venetian's parking deck and take reporters up there for a private showing. We actually invented a service during the height of the dot-com hype that we thought was the best way to start our journey toward connectivity. We weren't sure where it would go or if customers really wanted it or not, but we felt that we at least needed to have an oar in these waters.

The service was named Virtual Advisor, or VA, and the idea was that we'd provide voice interactive connectivity to the kinds of things that you might want while you were driving. With VA, you could tell us ahead of time which sports teams you were interested in, which stocks you followed, and which route you drove to work and needed to know the traffic for. With the push of a button and a couple of voice commands, you could have that information delivered through the audio output of your car's stereo speakers. We'd also integrated an approach to use the vehicle's GPS location at the moment you pressed the button to get VA to look for traffic incidents within a preset number of miles of your current location or to automatically give you an on-demand, location-specific weather forecast. And just because we could, and not because it made any sense, we also offered daily horoscopes, lottery numbers, news stories—heck, we even provided daily soap opera updates recorded with voices that took great pleasure in delivering the fact that "Jessie slept with Greg" with just the right attitude. Because we weren't convinced that this was going anywhere, we worked with a small company in Silicon Valley, General Magic, to try to avoid distracting our technical team from their core mission.

This was one of the few times we strayed from our instincts of doing important things we believed our subscribers would really need, but at least we did it for a noble cause and with our eyes wide open. The noble cause was to keep people outside the business from having the excuse to mess with us because they were sure we were missing the cool part of what the technology could do. Apparently, saving lives was never really cool enough, but getting an on-demand Cubs score and knowing that this was a good day to stay inside if you were a Capricorn was. While this was also an opportunity to learn and test the edges of the technology and our brand, it was primarily meant to play defense, which it did very well. The eyes-wide-open part had to do with not going into this with high expectations and believing it was going to change the world, as that was highly unlikely. Hey, we'd been wrong before, and if this somehow took off, that would've been great. But my sense was that it would be better to stay sober and not behave like we were betting the business on this new category of service if we didn't have to. Saving lives might have been boring to the know-it-all techies, but it certainly wasn't boring to people buying cars. No matter what, we'd jumped into the connectivity game, and now it was time to see what we could learn about our customers and ourselves.

We'd run into the Microsoft guys from time to time, actually at some pretty senior levels, and they'd always take great delight in telling us that we were thinking about our business all wrong. Their model was that there were three domains—home, office and mobile—and that the automobile was only special to us because we made cars, but to the rest of the enlightened world, it was merely another place where you were mobile. Their approach was to create a version of their desktop model, shrunk in computing size and form factor, that you'd somehow have access to whenever you were away from the home and office markets, which they already dominated. And, by the way, if it somehow turned out that a car was special, which they weren't admitting, they were working on just the answer for that as well, something called the Auto PC. So better to leave all this technology stuff to the professionals, call it a day with OnStar, and just give them a purchase order and sit back and watch the magic happen

I've got to admit that we couldn't be sure they were wrong; nobody knew how all of this would play out. There was no arguing they had massive resources and a lot of clout in the technology world and were routinely renting Texas-sized floor space at the major trade shows to make sure nobody forgot it. There were some people inside GM who were inherently attracted to the thought of "partnering" with Microsoft as a way to simplify our approach and make the safe bet on the future. If we went with them, and they got it wrong, then who could blame us when even the mighty Microsoft couldn't figure it out. But if we went our own way with something as home-baked as OnStar, and we got it wrong, then we'd become a laughingstock and subjected to an avalanche of "I told you so."

While it sure didn't feel like the right time to surrender the field and concede that we couldn't lead in this category, we needed to be thoughtful and understand our limitations. We'd definitely need to create a strategy that allowed us to take full advantage of our automotive assets, without painting ourselves into an overly auto-centric corner. Was that possible? Was there a path through all of this that could keep us from becoming roadkill on the information superhighway? I certainly hoped so.

The other thing that came out of the technology churning was that it caused all of the other vehicle manufacturers to question whether they needed to be doing something in our space. Shortly after we'd gotten Gen 2 locked down and on a path to production, we started to sense the growing industry interest and wondered whether we should consider branching out to work with some of the other OEMs. This was a pretty interesting question, one deserving serious strategic thought, and one that we certainly weren't able to make on our own. The politics of this were predictably ugly, but rather than rolling over and leaving it alone, we thought we needed to at least bring it forward for a discussion.

The easy, natural answer to the question of whether we should work with other car companies would have been "No. Hell no. In fact, let me run you over for even thinking of it and then tell you hell no again. GM had made the investments and taken the risks to bring this to life, and you OnStar guys keep telling us what an important competitive advantage it is. So set aside for a moment that we're not behaving like it's a competitive advantage—why in the world would we want to share it with our enemies? I don't think you OnStar guys got the memo. Remember, we're a car company not a silly little service company, so get over yourselves and stop stirring up trouble."

The unfortunate part was that there was another side to this argument, and we felt compelled to make it. OnStar certainly was unique and valuable at this point, and that was only possible because of GM's willingness to spend the money, take the risks, and commit the unnatural acts that allowed it to come alive. And we did believe the research that said this type of service was a compelling vehicle differentiator, but there was another way you had to think about that research. First of all, anyone could field the same research and would certainly get the same results; these services are important. Second, the current focus on technology meant that all of the other car companies were now doing that research and would likely come to the conclusion that they would need to do something. So, logically, one way or another, sooner or later, everybody was going to have some version of what we were doing built into their cars. It wasn't going to be easy for them; in fact, they probably wouldn't want to do it themselves because of scale issues and it being so different from their core businesses. That meant that they'd probably look to partner with some service provider, and if they didn't like the small former home security company in Texas that claimed to be our competitor, then they'd just get somebody else interested in starting another company.

So our choices were to keep OnStar to ourselves and let the rest of the auto companies go their own way or try to get as many of them as we could to sign up to work on our platform. The problem with them going their own way was what if a significant number of them all chose the same other provider? We had access to roughly 30 percent of the U.S. market with GM vehicles, but wouldn't it be terrible if three or four car companies, whose combined market share would be much larger than ours, ended up turning our first-mover advantage into a scale disadvantage? And from what you could tell at this point, scale was going to matter, whether it was in developing and sourcing vehicle hardware, running call centers, setting standards with the 911 community, or in negotiating the most favorable terms with the wireless industry.

While this never got completely settled on firm, strategic grounds, we were reluctantly given approval to reach out to the other OEMs and see if they'd be interested in working with us. That didn't mean it didn't create hard feelings inside the company, particularly with the vehicle-marketing guys who resented what we were doing and really resented the fact that they couldn't stop it. But their objection was more emotional than rational. They really wanted it both ways. They wanted everyone to believe that this was so important that we shouldn't give it to our competitors, but not important enough that they should be held accountable to use it to help sell vehicles. So they wanted to keep their exclusive access to OnStar, but be free to hold back on promoting it until somebody else thought it was a big enough deal to copy, and then maybe they'd do something with it. There was no instinct for wanting to lead or for anything that had to do with understanding the perishable nature of a time-to-market advantage. From their perspective, the right thing to do was keep it in reserve, just in case they needed it someday. This would have only made sense if GM had been so overstocked with things that were already working that we didn't want to disturb our mojo. But our go-to play, our ace-in-the-hole, and the strategy we'd developed into a fine art was more rebate cash on the hood. And when that stopped working, we'd follow it with bigger helium balloons and the ever-popular slogan "Act now, and you get even more." Pathetic. Anyway, Rick and Ron understood why it made sense to try to expand the number of players committed to the OnStar platform and told us they were OK with the outreach. The only rule of engagement was that we couldn't go after the business through aggressive price-discounting that could disadvantage GM vehicles, which was an easy condition to satisfy because we had no intention of building our brand on low prices and rebates.

So we began traveling the world, starting in Southeast Michigan, but ultimately connecting with all of the Japanese players, most of the European manufacturers, and even the then small Koreans. This outreach effort fell under Fred's group and was led by Dennis Keith. Dennis was an interesting guy. He was smart and low key, spoke Japanese, and had spent time in prior GM assignments stationed in multiple locations in Asia. I always enjoyed traveling with Dennis and really appreciated his ability to navigate the tricky waters between the other OEMs and us.

We had a relatively simple presentation that tried to make a few key points. First, there was the market research that confirmed the strong value perception of safety and security services. Second, we showed that our current services and future plans were a really good fit with the market's needs. Third, we talked about what our experience had taught us and reinforced that that there were many more risks in the category than met the eye. Finally, we provided an overview of the talent we had at OnStar and a snapshot of our growing intellectual property portfolio, which then consisted of hundreds of patent filings and a new-patent-filing rate of one every six days. We really didn't spend much time in these early meetings talking about the brand, as it was just starting to gain traction. But, more importantly, we tried to stay clear of the brand discussion because GM still wasn't sure how they wanted us to deal with that issue.

Long story short, we flew around a lot, drank too much, and ate many questionable meals in far-off time zones. But we ultimately became familiar with the issues that were on everybody's minds and ended up landing deals with Lexus, Acura, VW, Audi, Subaru, and Isuzu. The Lexus deal was supposed to be a precursor to a higher-volume Toyota program, as was the Acura relationship supposed to lead to something with Honda. There were no contracts that said that, just inferences and the fact that it fit with their normal supplier selection approach. And we thought we almost had deals with a couple other manufacturers, until bigger players acquired them during the consolidation wave that was sweeping across the auto industry during the late 1990s. No matter, when you added up the share of the partners we'd landed and combined them with GM's, it totaled well over 50 percent of the market. That meant we'd accomplished our main objective, which was to create a reasonable hedge against losing our scale advantage, at least in the short term.

You couldn't see it at the time, but none of the other car companies really got behind the strategy with any energy or resolve. You just couldn't get around the fact that this was extremely hard to implement. I'm also sure it didn't help that despite our assurances to the contrary, many people within the other car companies assumed they were somehow being compromised by working with a supplier owned by GM, especially one that was in such a sensitive direct contact role with their customers. And because they weren't doing it all in-house, they didn't have the same economic incentives to push for more volume because they were typically only getting a percentage of the ongoing service fee in the form of a revenue-sharing arrangement.

As a point of fact, we always followed through on our commitments to maintain complete confidentiality regarding their programs and on our pledge to provide them access to our latest technology and services. When you looked at it from the outside, you could come to the conclusion that we always saved the good stuff for GM and that the other OEMs only got to pick from the day-old bread bin. But that was never the case. Actually, GM always seemed to end up with the newest stuff first, not because we held it back from the other players, but because their natural instincts as car manufacturers worked against them being able to grab the new technology and move fast with it. Their collective problem was that they hadn't been given a hall pass from their traditional vehicle development process timing. So if they wanted to go fast, they needed to take what they considered a safe, proven product that was already performing in the market and engineer it into their new cars.

That meant when one of the other vehicle manufacturers first launched a private-label version of OnStar service, they were using our older Gen 2 technology at the same time that new Cadillacs had already moved to Gen 4. And contrary to normal automotive thinking, rather than Gen 2 being the "safe" choice, it was actually just the opposite. It was much more expensive, was lacking a number of new service features like hands-free calling, was built using an older and less-capable voice recognition engine, and was missing the experience-based reliability improvements that we'd baked into Gens 3 and 4. Worse yet, two years later, when new Cadillacs had moved on to Gen 5, their new vehicles were still being built with Gen 2 because their rules didn't allow them to make any changes until the next major re-design of the entire vehicle. So we were offering the best we had, but because they weren't able to deal with the rapidly changing nature of the consumer electronics industry, they couldn't take advantage of it.

Our little excursion into the world of the other OEMs didn't last all that long. The cellular industry's conversion from a common analog signal to whatever digital protocol each carrier wanted to implement meant keeping up with technology cycle changes was going to get a lot harder and a lot riskier. And with everything else going on in the automotive industry, from changes in government-required safety and fuel economy standards to the expanding range of hybrid-propulsion alternatives that everyone was chasing, they just didn't think it was worth the engineering distraction, especially at such low volumes.

We did learn a lot from these relationships and confirmed that Toyota, Honda, and VW customers behaved consistently with what our research had predicted. And while we made money on the programs, once GM made the decision to make OnStar standard equipment on all of their retail vehicles in 2003, it was less clear that we should push hard to keep the other companies on board. The OnStar brand issue never settled down, until a decision was made to stop allowing Acura and VW/Audi to use it on new programs after they'd already been installing our little blue button in their vehicles for a number of years. Not surprisingly, that didn't make us too many friends. The confusion and indecisiveness on our side exposed just how fragile the support was for doing this inside the other companies, and without our constant pushing, the programs just died of their own weight.

A sidebar to all of this was the formation of a new competitive entry that was supposed to be the answer to OnStar. Actually, it was merchandised as being much better than OnStar and was formed as a joint venture between Ford and Qualcomm. Ford was not about to be outdone by GM in this category and had already shown that they didn't intend to get left behind on any of these new technologies when they jumped through the hoops necessary to sign their deal with CD Radio two weeks after we'd signed ours with XM in 1999. But as the vehicle connectivity drum kept beating louder, and they didn't have anything they could point to as evidence of their superior vision in this space, they felt like they needed to do something splashy.

We'd been in discussions with Qualcomm for a few years, and when the wireless industry announced their plans to transition to digital, we'd actually chosen their CDMA digital protocol for our system. We'd worked well together and liked their guys a lot. They were happy when they learned we were going to pursue the other car companies since we'd obviously be bringing our commitment to CDMA into whatever relationships we might establish. But we both knew that we wouldn't be able to land OnStar deals with all of the other car companies, particularly Ford. So Qualcomm decided they'd enter into an agreement with Ford to create a new joint-venture company to service their vehicles (and get them committed to CDMA) and possibly bring other manufacturers on board as well.

In July 2000, with great fanfare, the two companies announced the formation of Wingcast, a San Diego–based company that was going to revolutionize in-vehicle connectivity and services. They'd hired a recently departed Microsoft vice president to lead the effort and were immediately declared to be in the lead by the automotive and technology press that were covering the story. Sure, they'd do the easy and boring stuff like safety and security; why, that was almost too trivial to mention. But what they were really going to be all about was creating a rich range of data- and content-heavy connectivity solutions that would revolutionize driving forever. They didn't actually say they could make vehicles levitate or that that you could go in the backseat and take a nap on the way to work, but I think those were both planned for Gen 2.

Anyway, we took a beating—I mean, a real beating from many people within General Motors who wondered how we could have let this happen. We'd been outflanked (cooler promises), outgunned (Microsoft VP vs. locomotive salesman), and outmaneuvered (they had a partner paying some of the bills). Why couldn't we grow up to be like them? In fact, why don't we just dump OnStar and source our stuff with them? While that thankfully wasn't the position of the people at GM that counted, it was, no kidding, some of the sentiment that was bouncing around with some of the working-level folks. When Wingcast announced they had signed up Nissan as a distribution partner, you could almost sense the inevitability that this juggernaut was building. We kept trying to learn everything we could about what they were planning, how well things were going, and what we might be able to do about it, but most of what we were hearing back didn't make sense. Things weren't adding up, but these were times when things didn't always add up. Then, all of a sudden, a company would make a surprise announcement, execute their initial public offering, and everybody would end up rich. You could just never tell.

By the middle of May 2002, it was starting to look more and more like their planned Nissan launch in August was in trouble. A rumble here, an equivocation there, all little signs, but something was up. I got a call out of nowhere from a woman who had worked for GM in the past and was now a VP at Ford in charge of all things Wingcast asking if I had any interest in acquiring their share of the business. She said they loved it and would hate to part with it, but we were probably in a better position than Ford was to take full advantage of the "amazing technology and team" that they had assembled. I told her I didn't think we'd be interested, but I'd kick it around a little bit and get back to her. She said she needed an answer within a day or, otherwise, not to bother—so I didn't.

Less than a week later, on June 3, 2002, twenty-three months after their high-powered launch announcement, Wingcast quietly slipped below the surface and confirmed that they were out of business. Nothing had been delivered, two hundred people had lost their jobs, countless suppliers were not going to get paid, Nissan was being left at the altar, and somewhere in the neighborhood of $150 million had gone up in smoke. Hey, this stuff was hard to do, and that, but by the grace of God, could have been us on any number of occasions. We decided not to allow ourselves the luxury of gloating in public, but we were competitive enough, and these guys had gone out of their way a few times to highlight how "cute" we were with our little safety focus, that we needed to do something. I'd read an article about the closure that mentioned something about an auction of property to raise money to pay some of their creditors. I asked Ken Enborg if we could participate; I wanted to buy a big conference table from their San Diego headquarters, mount an appropriately inscribed brass plaque on it, and haul it back to Michigan. I don't know why, but it felt like a Viking-conquest moment, and I thought it would be good for morale. Ken, being of good Swedish stock, said, sure, we could do that and registered for the phone auction, which entitled us to get a detailed list of the property to be sold. Unfortunately, most of the furniture had been leased, and what hadn't been was being bundled together in a big group. Fun was fun, but I sure didn't need anybody from GM's audit staff wondering why I was buying file cabinets and coatracks from California, so we couldn't land our spoils of victory. But there was intellectual property on the list, and I thought that maybe I'd accidentally stumbled onto a gold mine.

We had Walt and Ken's guys pour over the materials, and by their judgment, it was less than worthless. What? Their view was what Wingcast was claiming they had was so thin and weak that if someone with money (like us at the time) acquired their stuff, there was enough potential for counterclaims from people that had better stuff that it might actually cost real money in future lawsuits to defend it. Hey, I certainly wasn't an expert in this area, and since Walt said he wasn't interested in it anyway, we decided to pass. But we did call in to the auction just to see what happened. When all was said and done, the entire intellectual property portfolio that had been created in nearly two years of effort, consuming over a $100 million dollars, had sold for less than the price of a used Ford Taurus. Justice was served, even if we didn't have our table to show for it.

The final irony of these tumultuous times came as an unexpected chance to reconnect with an old friend, and one of my alma maters. We'd hired a very talented young man by the name of Erik Roth from outside of GM to work in our marketing group. Erik was smart, had a lot of energy, and was articulate and extremely personable. He was the kind of guy you liked to work with and knew had a bright future ahead of him. After a couple of years with us, Erik decided to go back to school to get his MBA, and before you knew it, he'd been accepted at the Harvard Business School. While we certainly didn't want to lose Erik, this was a really good move for him. So, when the time came, we bid our farewells, I wished him luck, and told him that we wanted him to stay in touch.

I'm not sure of the timing, but I think Erik met Professor Clay Christensen when he took his second-year elective course on innovation. Professor Christensen was a rising rock star at Harvard at the time, having just published his groundbreaking book *The Innovator's Dilemma*. I'd actually seen a picture of him on the cover of *Forbes* magazine in early 1999 towering over the CEO of Intel, with the caption "Andy Grove's Secret Weapon." I knew I'd seen him, not because I pay that much attention to *Forbes*, and not because I randomly follow the careers of Harvard faculty members, but because I knew Clay, at least I'd known him back in the day. We'd been at HBS getting our MBAs at the same time, actually in the same year. Better yet, we were in the same section, C, and we'd played side by side (his six feet nine inches and my five feet ten inches) on Section C's highly decorated intramural basketball team. I really loved thinking I knew famous people, and in his world, Clay certainly fit that description. Just like so many things in life, we'd all gone our separate ways after school, and I'd lost touch with most of my old classmates. Now, what in the world was ever going to give me a reason to reconnect with anyone as accomplished and famous as Clay? Was that another snicker from above?

It seems Erik told Clay he was interested in working for him to help develop a case that might fit into his innovation course. When Erik explained to Clay that he'd been working at OnStar before school and what that was all about, Clay was intrigued. His sense was that big companies typically have a very difficult time spawning new innovations, and if you had to pick a big company that you'd think would have a particularly tough time with it, General Motors would be the one to come to mind. So if GM was doing this, then there must be something that could be learned from it. Remember, you just don't learn from success; many times, the most important learning comes from watching failure. You know, like what happens when you put together the pieces from the plane crash to try to make sure it doesn't happen again? So win or lose for OnStar, there was the potential for a teachable moment for a class on innovation.

This all led to a call from Clay, which was one part catching up after twenty years and one part asking if we would be willing to let them write a case study about what we were up to at OnStar. The catching-up part was fun, but the offer of a case study was a little scary. Every case study I remembered that involved GM over the two years that I was in Boston ended up with us looking like Laurel, Hardy, or Graucho. We were always the "before" to Toyota's "after," and since I was there on GM's dime, I always felt compelled to defend the mother ship to the death, which meant I died a lot. The OnStar story, at this point, was anything but complete; heck, nobody knew what the ending might look like. I understood the fact that it didn't matter for Clay's purposes how it ended; there'd be something to learn from the case one way or another. But did I really want to be the potential source of humiliation for future generations of GMers at the school?

I knew Clay was aware that Rick Wagoner was an HBS alum, and I told him I'd have to run this by Rick to see if he was comfortable with the idea. A couple of weeks later, I was in a meeting with him and got around to asking what he wanted to do. He said he didn't know and asked what I thought. I said nobody could guarantee anything out of this, but if we couldn't get a fair shake out of Clay, a Rhodes Scholar, former White House Fellow, and a section-mate who I'd generously fed with bounce passes in the low post more times than he deserved, then we'd probably never get a fair shake. The one thing we didn't know, actually couldn't know at that point, was how this adventure was going to end. It could be the case that ends up showing GM did something amazing when all was said and done, or it might end up looking like we were the last guys to invest in an eight-track tape factory. Rick thought about it for a second, got a smile on his face, and said to go for it and that we'd just better make sure, for both of our sakes, that it ended well.

So Erik and Clay wrote the cases. There was an A and B version of "OnStar – Not Your Father's General Motors." They ended up presenting a pretty fair and balanced view of the things that were going on in the business, which meant that there were plenty of places that you'd have to wince because everything certainly hadn't been done perfectly—far from it. But it did seem to illustrate a few interesting points, and amazingly, Clay ended up liking it enough to use it as one of the final cases in the course right before the final exam.

When I first heard that, I was flattered. How cool was that to be put in the anchor position? We'd be one of the final lessons on innovation that these impressionable, aspiring captains of industry and commerce would be taught by the pied piper of innovation himself. My wife tells me that it's important to stay humble, and part of her role as a good partner is to make sure I constantly understand that. Well, in this case, she didn't have to raise a finger. In a wonderfully candid discussion, Clay explained to me in his usual calm and understated way that he really loved the OnStar case because we had broken or offended almost every rule and model that he was teaching about innovation over the entire semester, and it was his sense as an academic that there's always something important to be learned by studying the outliers. Now, I knew he wasn't really complimenting us by basically saying that it was a miracle that we were still alive, but somehow the way he said it made it sound just fine.

Clay had enough of a sense of humor to occasionally invite me into his class on the day the OnStar case would be reviewed. In the early years, when it was completely up in the air what would happen next, he'd let me sit anonymously in the back row while he led the discussion about this strange business called OnStar. He'd continue until he got to the point of talking about leadership, where he would ask the reasonable question of "Who in the world, other than General Motors, would start something like this and put someone as ill-equipped and unprepared to lead it as this locomotive salesman?" Before anyone could answer, he'd say, "Let's take a vote. How many of you guys would fire this Huber character?" When all of the hands were predictably in the air, he'd pause and say, "Now, I have someone that's joined us today that would like to talk to you a little bit about OnStar—my old friend Chet." Those classes got a lot more fun to attend as the years went by and we were still alive, but it didn't necessarily mean those early students' votes had been wrong.

So there's a lot of craziness that takes place inside a technology-based start-up, and in our case, it got compounded by an interesting change of bosses, an auto industry full of unpredictable gyrations, and the coincidental arrival of the mother of all disruptive forces—the Internet. I think my favorite memory of this entire period, and something that summed it up for me better than anything else, happened at about forty thousand feet onboard one of GM's company planes while heading home from a meeting with Microsoft's big boys in Redmond. There were four or five of us on the plane, but the moment took place between Rick Wagoner and GM's guru of information technology, Ralph Szgenda. Somewhere eastbound over North Dakota, with the sun setting at his back, Rick took a deep breath, looked at Ralph, and said, "eGM—what were we thinking?" What indeed.

CHAPTER 12

An Amazing Two-Sided Brand Compass

When you do an online search for the term "brand," it returns half a billion results. If you plug the same word into Amazon's book section, it gives you over seventeen thousand options to choose from. With so much written on the topic, the truth must be out there somewhere—at least if you're an *X-Files* believer. Like it or not, branding is one of those topics in business that too often ends up overlooked and marginalized or conversely overthought, overprocessed, and overblown. That's not to say that there aren't companies, many very prominent ones, that haven't gotten it just right. And that's also not to say that getting it just right looks the same in every situation; it certainly doesn't. But there are few serious people who think about this topic today, especially in a world crammed full of too many choices to indulge too many impulses, who would say that a brand isn't an important asset that deserves to be thoughtfully conceived and carefully nurtured.

My good friend Professor Christensen has devoted a fair amount of thought to branding—how consumers relate to products and brands, and therefore, how enlightened companies ought to think about the subject. It's led him to create a model where he believes people "hire" products or services to do "jobs" for them and that companies need to understand this dynamic when they approach segmenting markets to introduce and position new products. It goes on to describe a branding corollary where if the product has been well conceived and performs the unique job it's being hired for very well, then it can be represented by a "purpose brand." A purpose brand then can serve as a very powerful and effective two-sided compass, with one side pointing prospective customers toward a well-understood and satisfying product experience and the other guiding the company itself toward operating policies and future product executions reinforcing the purpose brand's position.

While I only became exposed to these concepts years after our launch, I have to say that Clay, as usual, was right. The fact that we'd only come to understand it the old-fashioned way, through the hard knocks school of trial and error, didn't diminish the power of the insight; in some ways, it magnified it. Our wanderings through the branding wilderness with a disjointed and too-broad set of services before we settled on the singularly focused "provide me peace of mind while driving" cost us time, money, and a lot of frustration. With so many seemingly unrelated services competing for airtime, customers had little chance of understanding what OnStar was really all about. Additionally, without the focus that a strong "purpose" provides, our product planning and business development efforts were scattered and confusing. We were missing the second side of the compass's benefit, one that would provide context and guidance to all our future roadmaps. And, in our case, it might have actually been a little worse. The open-ended and immature nature of our technology, combined with the uncertainty created by the early-stage implications of the Internet, gave too many people the license to freelance in almost any direction without being declared out of bounds.

But many of those frustrations and lessons were still ahead of us because, at this point, all we really understood was that we needed a brand. Now, we may not have been the least well-equipped organization in the world to take this on, but with my nonexistent background in consumer goods and GM's historic brand challenges, we didn't have a pedigree that would guarantee success. To us, or at least to me, once Rick Wagoner had agreed to stand in front of the audience at the 1996 Chicago Auto Show and announce our launch, what we really needed was a name. Choosing a name became another line item on the enterprise program management timing chart, right between "find office space" and "develop vehicle hardware." In the case of naming, the process seemed pretty simple. Just plug and crank the agency and legal machines and out would pop the right answer—in our case, OnStar. Then we ran the name through the world of graphic artists, actually twice since my initial homemade version wasn't very inspiring, and voila, we had a logo. To a locomotive-selling mechanical engineer, this seemed like a rational way to approach the issue and probably all the effort that it deserved at this point. Sure, we can call it a brand instead of a name if that makes it sound more sophisticated—that doesn't cost any extra, does it?

I wish I could say that we'd given it more thought than that, but at that moment, we really hadn't. We were still working on what we wanted our little business to be when it grew up— what services would we deliver and how we wanted to think about ourselves. But we didn't honestly sense any profound connection between those issues and our name. Was there a mechanical connection? Sure. You'd stamp this logo on a brochure of services and that would be us. But was there something real or alive about that connection? What, are you going to start burning incense and chanting mantras? Come on, this wasn't that deep. Wrong again.

Maybe if we'd been conceived at Procter and Gamble, or if I'd been the former brand manager for Snapple, or if our first couple heads of marketing had any real game, things might have been different. But, as it was, the concept was to Velcro whatever we somehow decided we'd deliver as services to whoever our customers would end up being and manage it all under the name (er...brand) OnStar. Actually, one of the early PowerPoint presentations from our first agency had a cute picture of an umbrella with our logo on it, and underneath, sheltered from all of the harsh realities of the world, all of our available services were listed. That seemed good to me—a nice graphic and a little jargon. Hey, this branding stuff wasn't all that hard after all.

There was a sense that we needed a vision statement, or was that a mission statement? I could never keep those straight. I'd been in meetings back in the locomotive business where we tried to do that, and they were always the most frustrating wastes of time and effort that you could ever imagine. Typically, you'd have the top people in the company sweat bullets and arm wrestle over the most meaningless choices of individual words or the placement of punctuation marks. If we all didn't know what we were doing at Electro-Motive, a *locomotive company*, heaven help us all. But it was supposed to be empowering, team-aligning, and a way to solicit personal buy-in to what was always coming after the mission/vision. In our case, at EMD, that generally meant how we were going to cut more people and further reduce our budgets.

But, who knows, maybe this Kabuki Theater really was necessary when you're starting something from scratch. Besides, how much could it hurt to get our team together, grab some facilitator, and start thinking deep thoughts about what our future might hold? Maybe we'd kill a few trees filling the walls with chart paper, and maybe it'd get a little awkward when we dimmed the lights and immersed ourselves in all of the OnStarness, but getting a little alignment and a measure of everybody's buy-in to what was coming next had a certain practical appeal. So vision/mission or mission/vision didn't matter. It was time to dive in.

It didn't take long before the general sense of our focus on safety and security started to take shape and began to produce a series of words that the facilitator said would begin to represent our "brand character." Helpful, personal, innovative, professional—hey, I think if you added thrifty and obedient, we'd already have had uniforms and a new name, the Boy Scouts. Who wouldn't want his or her company to be all of those things? Hmmm... Wasn't a company that was useless, offensive, backward, and amateurish actually *out of business*? I did my best to stay calm through all of this and was still naively hoping that our marketing guy would bring some structure to the discussion, but no such luck. We finished the exercise, and amazingly, most of the people who'd participated thought it'd been very worthwhile. Looking back, I think that must've been because these were mostly mid-level GM folks who hadn't participated in a process like this before and actually liked the fact that they were finally "in charge" of something. That wasn't all bad, but what it really meant was that we all had a lot to learn.

So we gathered up our growing list of services, slapped them all together in an OnStar wrapper, and the journey began. The problem wasn't that we had an overwhelming number of services; the problem was more of how diverse our initial offering turned out to be. We started out with crash response and a closely aligned set of other emergency services, but we were also trying to stretch the brand to cover things as seemingly unrelated as finding hotels and helping to plan parties—concierge services. I don't know if you've ever noticed those racks of brochures that are typically near the door at small motels or restaurants in tourist areas, but they probably hold fifty or so four-by-ten-inch cards with big colorful print on the front that scream at you to take a ride in their hot air balloons, fish in their trout pond, or explore the ancient nearby caves and see the stalactites. To me, that's what our brand message was starting to look like. Our brand was the rack, and it felt like our services made about as much sense together as the pirate mini golf and the outlet mall. Oh, and how is it again that you feel about that rack? Do you hold it in high esteem for organizing all of those amazing choices for you, or are you more likely to be overwhelmed, confused, and resent the rack's predictable effect on your kids, which is to start a fight about whether you should spend your hard-earned money at Indy Karts or Din-o-Rama.

Unfortunately, we actually had some people in the company, ones who were supposed to know what they were doing, who thought the rack analogy was correct and was actually good for us. Hey, this was all new stuff, and not everyone would be equally drawn to everything we could do. So what better approach than throw everything we had against the wall and see what stuck. Better yet, different things might stick to different people, so this would be the way to get the maximum positive impact from what we had to offer. We'd let the customers stare at our rack and figure out our brand, kind of like a Rorschach test. That would make it personal for them, and wasn't that one of our brand character elements?

Wait, it got worse. While we were arm wrestling among ourselves, we forgot for a moment that there were other interested parties circling overhead. Actually, those parties—the car brands like Cadillac, Chevy, and Buick—thought they were the only brands that should matter. They were the adults in this equation, and they had the organizational size, operating inertia, and advertising budgets to prove it. They'd be calling the real shots if there were any real shots to call, and they had no shortage of ideas that they intended to use to assert their control. There was an early attempt to un-name us OnStar and create a separate name for what we'd be doing for each car brand. We might be called "Golden Touch" at Cadillac and "Save Me" at Chevy. That would follow tradition by respecting what they felt were the profound differences in the only brands that really mattered, the ones that sold cars. "We should consider ourselves an 'ingredient brand,' " someone said, "You know, like MSG in Chinese food." I actually only saw an early full-page Cadillac print ad for OnStar on the first day it ran in newspapers across the country and not before it was sent to print. It was a picture of a very sinister-looking satellite hovering in the darkness of outer space aiming what looked like two ray guns at a black Cadillac DeVille. I don't even remember the words, but it was apparently supposed to leave you with the impression that we were very high-tech and constantly had our eye on you.

When I saw the ad, I blew up at our marketing guy, who'd been assigned to OnStar from Cadillac, for heaven's sake. I never knew for sure whether he'd been told about it ahead of time, because once he saw my reaction, he swore they'd done it without his knowledge. But their version of our brand couldn't have been more wrong, at least if we believed what the research was telling us. It was way better to have our story be about human beings helping you when you were in trouble, and under no circumstances did the customers want to feel like they were under surveillance. So an ad featuring a stalking Death Star, with no carbon-based life forms in sight, was probably more than a little off target, probably more like about 179 degrees off target.

Thankfully, when things felt like they had a serious chance of coming off the rails, like just before someone started printing the Save Me brochures, we'd be able to get the attention of the real adult supervision, generally Ron Zarrella, and he'd impose martial law and get it stopped. But while keeping people, including ourselves, from hurting this new brand was good, it was far from the standard that we needed to hold ourselves to. This was a once-in-a-lifetime chance to do something like this and get it right, to build something from scratch that we could all be proud of, and to turn our brand into a significant competitive advantage for GM vehicles. I honestly didn't fully appreciate the scope of that at the time—none of us did because our early instincts were that branding was more about advertising than anything else. But the more we got into it and the more experiences we lived through, the clearer it became that building our brand wasn't a marketing responsibility at all. Sure, we'd need to be able to communicate our brand effectively through our marketing efforts, but that was only a small part of what our brand was all about. The brand was alive, or at least it wanted to be alive, and if we had half a brain, we'd make sure it stayed that way. Actually, for our business, I think the organ that needed the greatest involvement wasn't the brain, but the heart. And I think the term "brand character" turned out to be backward as well. This brand reminded me time and time again that what OnStar really demanded of us was that *our* character needed to be strong enough to faithfully shepherd it toward its very special purpose.

So we got into business without suffering any fatal self-inflicted wounds and rapidly began to live and learn. The subscriber's letter about his wife's heart attack while driving through Atlanta had made a profound impact on me and brought flesh-and-blood reality to what had only really been an artist's concept up to that point. But far from being the one iconic event that forever defined our business, the hour-by-hour growing flow of OnStar interactions meant that the next iconic event would probably happen in the next half hour, or maybe it had already happened an hour ago and we just hadn't heard about it yet. This brand was exercising itself 24/7, and all it asked was that we respected it enough to stay engaged with what was going on and act on what we were learning.

From Gen 2 OnStar forward, we've always been about the "three buttons." There was no magic in the initial choice of three buttons; it was more about practical necessity. We thought we needed a button to contact OnStar and another button to end the interaction (which eventually also allowed you to start interactions with Virtual Advisor or make personal phone calls). And then there was the part when you didn't need a button at all because the car itself called us when it had been in a crash. People loved the "automatic" nature of that, but since we were using airbag-system logic to make it work, what happened in the case of a crash that didn't trigger an airbag deployment? Back in the late 1990s, most vehicles only had front airbags, so a side crash, or one from behind, or a rollover might not trigger an automatic call. Didn't we need a button for someone to press when that happened? So the third button's intended purpose wasn't about trying to find a florist; it was to let us know that you'd been in a crash that didn't involve the airbag.

Saying we didn't completely understand what we were getting into when we put that third button in was an understatement. We immediately got a faceful of events like the Atlanta heart attack, followed by infants having bad reactions to medications they'd just taken, drivers having strokes, customers witnessing horrific crashes that happened around them, and people seeing road hazards like downed power lines. What we quickly understood was that the emergency button wasn't for non-airbag crashes at all, at least not very often; it was really the "life happens while you're driving" button. Americans spend five hundred million hours a week in their cars, which leads to a lot of life's experiences playing out while you're on the road. What we'd become, not because we'd planned it, was everyone's copilot. You were always an index finger button press away from your posse, your backup. In the words of my old War College Tomcat pilot buddy, we were your wingman and had your six, and in many cases, we had the six of a whole bunch of other people that weren't driving GM cars, but were lucky enough to get help from someone who was. We'd created a new role beyond protector of our own; we'd empowered a growing band of high-tech good Samaritans, and it felt great.

This is where we began to see the early edges of our mission of "being there for our subscribers" expanding to also include being there for others, creating societal benefits. It's funny how trickles turn into tributaries if you're not careful, but we didn't want to be careful with this if careful meant sticking to the original script. Our brand was telling us that it hadn't read the script, and besides, there was a higher calling that wasn't all that hard to understand— just do the right thing. And before you had a chance to take a breath and figure out what that meant, the river took off in another direction.

Bill Ball, our incredibly talented head of public policy, had a really good sense for the places where our objectives might be aligned with other groups, either inside or outside of government, that were involved in supporting the public good. His instincts were to try to build bridges with these organizations and attempt to find common ground where our individual efforts could be supportive of one another's mission. It was a wonderful orientation to establish, and far from being distracting, it actually helped bring focus and clarity to many situations. We were wading into space that intersected with many other interested parties, and respecting that landscape and looking for places that we could be helpful set just the right tone.

I was routinely traveling to Washington, DC, to attend XM board meetings, and on one of the trips, someone arranged for me to have din-

ner with Ernie Allen. Ernie was the head and cofounder of an organization called the National Center for Missing & Exploited Children, or
NCMEC, the people behind the AMBER Alert program. The genesis
of AMBER alerts went back to the tragic kidnapping and murder of
Amber Haggerman in Texas in 1996. In 2001, NCMEC, under Ernie's
leadership, led a campaign to have AMBER Alert systems established
nationwide, and Ernie and his team had been tirelessly working on
that important mission ever since.

Over dinner, I found Ernie to be a wonderful, passionate, deeply
committed leader who I knew, as a parent of two children, was on the
side of the angels. Before the meal was over, I either wanted to adopt
Ernie or have him adopt me; I wasn't sure, but either would do. Without ever really having to acknowledge it, the discussion completely
skipped the topic of whether we should be doing something together
and immediately jumped to *what* we were going to do together. This
was one of the biggest no-brainers of my life, right behind asking
Barb to marry me. How could it not make sense? Ernie had one of the
most important missions in the world, recovering missing children,
and we had a growing group of OnStar-technology-equipped good
Samaritans just itching to use their index fingers to help. Our living
and increasingly assertive brand would have taken me out back and
given me a wedgie if we failed to step up to the plate on this. So, OK,
we were going to do this. Now all I had to do was go back to Detroit,
grab a few people, and prioritize "reverse-geocoded AMBER Alerts"
as a new service. I knew everybody already had a full plate, but come
on, just one more Thin Mint?

Since the very beginning of OnStar, we'd established a tradition
of bringing the entire organization together on a monthly basis for a
family meeting. It was actually easy at first, getting the ten or so of us
together, pulling up our chairs in a circle, and making sure everyone
knew what was going on. I'd like to think this was some kind of enlightened leadership gene that I'd inherited from somewhere, but it
was honestly a very practical response to things moving so fast that we

basically needed a place to "re-sync" the team on a monthly schedule to make sure everyone knew what was going on. It also had the effect of reeling in many activities that had somehow gotten off course because we just didn't have the resources to handle the distractions. As the business grew, we decided to maintain the tradition. It became a little less tactical and a lot more logistically complicated as the group got larger, but the value of keeping everyone more or less aligned with the compass heading of the business remained very high.

I'd seen what happened inside the big GM when things got too specialized and too compartmentalized; each department saw its role as an end unto itself and became increasingly less clearly connected to the mission of the overall business. It was tough if not impossible to run anything as massive and broadly distributed as GM and not allow that mentality creep in. Sales had a mission, engineering had a mission, IT had a mission, manufacturing had a mission, finance had a mission, design had a mission, and marketing had a mission. It was a well-intended attempt to create focus and clarity around the contributions of each functional department when they might have otherwise been lost inside the much larger corporate structure. But it just ended up creating too many moving parts for the whole thing to hang together in a highly cohesive way and, intentionally or not, fostered the development of mini-cultures and dysfunctional esprit de corps. Too often, that led to strangely compartmentalized objectives that had lost touch with the overall enterprise's mission.

My sense was that if all of the OnStar functional teams didn't see that there was really only one mission for our business and somehow didn't understand that they were all responsible to apply their efforts to the care and feeding of our constantly evolving brand, then we'd have no chance to be as good as we would need to be. We couldn't allow ourselves to substitute departmentally focused success metrics for the real essence of why we were all there and working so hard in the first place, and that was to generate life-improving benefits for our subscribers. Sure, it's important for an enterprise to be functionally excellent in everything it does and to take pride in being great designers or marketers or service delivery experts, but everyone needed to understand and accept that the only success and team spirit that really mattered was connected to OnStar's overall mission and our commitment to our customers. And while it got more complicated to pull off a monthly all-employee meeting as we progressively outgrew the places we had to hold them, like a resale dress shop we'd once rented (no kidding), we were determined to stubbornly hold on to this family-meeting tradition no matter what because it just helped ensure that everyone's heart was in the same game.

What all that meant was when I came back from DC and got the folks together, they all instinctively understood why this obviously needed to be a priority and just dug in to make it happen. It was in how we responded to issues like these that you could see how our brand had insidiously invaded everyone's conscience. Walt and the engineering guys looked at what they might be able to do, but in this case, the real challenges were going to be in the changes necessary to support our advisors handling this service extremely well. A natural, predictable reaction from operating guys is to push back whenever they are told they have to add something to their plate, particularly if they need to do it fast. Certainly, everyone should understand and accept that they're already busy with everything else they're already doing—go away and come back tomorrow, or better yet, next year; maybe even bring back the witch's broom if you really want to be taken seriously. But, thankfully, our business began to attract more people like Walt over the years, folks who had deadly serious operating capabilities, but who the brand had turned into pushovers when it came to doing whatever was necessary to do the right thing. In this case, that person was Scott Kubicki.

Scott had joined OnStar from GM and was initially distinguishable by his drive to get things done, his energy and enthusiasm, and his willingness to stretch and take risks. These were all laudable traits and ones that fit the circumstances at OnStar very well. I liked what I saw in Scott a lot and eventually entrusted him with a huge responsibility: managing our service delivery and subscriber retention efforts. He jumped into those tasks with the energy and optimism that I knew he would, but what I couldn't tell was how long it would take for his natural business instincts to be tempered with a heart-driven passion for what we were all about.

Call centers and CRM activities can be very sterile, numbers-driven, almost clinical exercises in a big company. You'd actually often find people with functional expertise in these areas who bounced around between companies that sold insurance, processed warranty claims, solicited for religious institutions, or fronted for the Book of the Month Club. It didn't matter really; average call-handling time, speed to answer, and the yield on direct mail marketing solicitations were all relatively similar metrics in this world no matter what you were trying to do. But we needed something different. Sure, those activities would need to be run professionally and efficiently, but what our brand was telling us, actually demanding of us, was that we'd better bring more game than that. And that game better center on the "P" word—passion.

It was so gratifying to watch Scott jump into this role with both feet and create an amazing team who really made the magic happen. Very quickly, these guys stopped needing any coaching or lectures from me on what business we were in; they were inventing it themselves and asking me if I would please try to keep up. They could certainly take on the AMBER Alert challenge; actually, it would have been impossible to stop them once they heard about it because they were all parents themselves. But there was going to be more, much more, that we'd need them staying on top of, and some of it was right around the corner.

In 2004, we had our first serious intersection with what we came to regard as regional crisis events when a number of hurricanes hit Florida. We'd probably intersected with broad-scale acts of nature events before, but we'd been small enough that our individual subscriber interactions hadn't formed any discernable patterns. But, by this point, our subscriber volume had gotten large enough that we could actually see a spike in call volume because of the storms, and Scott and his guys quickly began to learn what that meant to our business.

One thing they spotted early on was a noticeable upturn in the number of our subscribers who were upgrading from our base Safe & Sound package to Directions & Connections while literally right in the middle of the hurricanes. They needed directions to hurricane evacuation routes and sometimes around the routes if they were already congested. And they wanted to have us help them get reservations at hotels that were to the north of their location and out of harm's way. They also had questions about things like the location of nearby evacuation shelters and whether they had room or were full.

Scott brought this information into a meeting that we'd called to try to stay on top of the storms, and we all immediately came to the same conclusion: There was no way we could feel good about accepting money from our subscribers to upgrade their service with us just because they were staring down the barrel of a monster storm. Sure, it was an effective "call to action" in marketing terms (it would have been hard to imagine anything more compelling than being trapped by Mother Nature), but this wasn't something that anybody at On-Star could be knowingly complicit with, much less condone. We didn't know exactly how we'd accomplish it, but right in the middle of hurricane number two that year, we said we were inventing a new policy. We would automatically upgrade all of our customers in any area affected by the hurricane and give them access to anything we had without charging them for it. There was nothing hard about that decision. We didn't ask anybody at GM; heck, even our finance guy at OnStar, Jon Hyde, went native and said it was the only reasonable thing to do. So now we'd mastered hurricanes, which left us feeling pretty good.

It felt pretty good until the following year when Katrina and Rita infamously visited the Gulf Coast within a couple of weeks of each other. By then, Scott and our IT team had developed an amazing new set of technologies that we could use to manage any crisis. They allowed us to draw geographic boundaries around any area we thought should be declared part of the regional crisis and would upgrade (at no charge) any customer calling from those areas during the crisis so they would automatically be entitled to all of our services. Scott also decided that we'd be better able to manage these events if we could route the calls from the affected area to a dedicated group of advisors who could be briefed on the hurricane as it unfolded rather than let the calls be randomly distributed to the entire group of advisors on duty. Finally, we'd learned to do some outreach to the local emergency service agencies before the storms hit so we could confirm we had the right evacuation routes in our database and make sure if something changed mid-crisis that we'd be able to quickly get our hands on the updates. We were buttoned up and ready to go—or so we thought.

All of our pregame preparations kicked in once Katrina hit, and thankfully we'd put so much effort into it because, even with the added preparation, this was unlike anything we'd experienced. Katrina covered a massive area and had her own strange set of unique edges. Upgrading customers to get directions and access to reservations services was working great, but then another "problem" showed up: We were selling too many personal calling minutes.

In addition to being able to use the OnStar system to contact us, it was also an incredibly capable, very powerful, voice-interactive, hands-free personal calling system from Gen 3 on. It worked by allowing you to purchase minutes from us, typically a hundred at a time, and then they were stored in an electronic bank in your car. The main reason people liked this service—and, at that point, we were actually selling roughly thirty million minutes a month—was that it provided a backup connection beyond your normal cell phone. It worked great if you were in tough driving circumstances and didn't want to use a handheld device or if your portable phone's battery had died and you were in a remote area with spotty cellular coverage, where our more powerful system was much better at connecting. The storms were causing all those problems, and as a result, people with OnStar needed to use our system more often to stay in touch with loved ones and were therefore buying more minutes.

Again, our sense was that bad things like hurricanes shouldn't necessarily equal more sales for us. So we made the easy decision to give away thirty free minutes to everybody who contacted us from within the crisis area so that they'd have the confidence that they could be reached by family members or friends while they were battling their way through the chaos of the storm. It took a little duct tape and rubber band MacGyvering, but we pulled it off mid-Katrina and had it ready to go for what we knew was coming right behind— Rita. You have no idea how great it felt to have the complete freedom and authority to do the right thing, for all the right reasons. This brand had infected all of us and was smiling about it.

I actually received a call from the attorney general of one of the affected states while all of this was going on. He'd read an article about an OnStar subscriber who got help because our system was able to connect during the storm and was wondering if we would make some vehicles available to the local law enforcement agencies because their communications had been so disrupted. He was sure OnStar must use satellite phones, but explained to him it was just a more powerful cell phone. I did say we'd still try to get them access to some vehicles if he thought that might useful, and he was appreciative but wondered what else we might be able to do to help the citizens of his state.

I told him about our policy of opening up all of our services to our subscribers in the area and that we were also downloading free minutes. He said that was great, and he wanted us to issue a press release to make a big deal out of that. I think he wanted a few public examples of that kind of behavior in order to stimulate more of it from other companies. I apologized and told him that we weren't going to put out a press release because we didn't want to look like a company that was doing these things just to get attention. He said that if we wouldn't do it, we needed to get him the facts because he was going to issue his own press release to draw attention to us and a couple of other companies he thought would be examples of the right kind of behaviors. We got him the info, because the alternative was avoiding all travel through his state for the rest of my life. I'm not sure if he ever did anything with what we sent him, because with everything else going on, there wasn't much time to worry about press clippings.

Katrina finally dissipated, and Rita began. I went down to visit the OnStar Command Center early in the morning the day before Rita was scheduled to make landfall. I'd been down there a lot during Katrina, and at the peak of the storm, the place looked like a frat house with pizza boxes stacked all over the place and chart paper taped all over the walls. I just wanted to make sure everybody had what they needed and were pumped up and ready for round two.

When I arrived, there was a digital map of Houston occupying one of the six-by-eight-foot screens on the command center's wall. It was the same screen that we'd used only a few days before to keep track of what was going on in New Orleans, but now the trouble had moved west. The screen was filled with little blue electronic dots that represented the locations of the calls that we'd taken since midnight. They formed an amazing pattern that basically showed how our subscribers were evacuating from the city—an incredibly powerful visual. I asked our command center supervisor, Dan, if he could capture that image and send me a copy. He said he thought so, and within thirty minutes, he'd sent it to me attached to an email.

I thought for a second about what I should do with that incredible picture and finally decided that there was someone outside of OnStar who deserved to see it—and that person was Rick Wagoner. Rick had been with us from the beginning and had always come through when it would have been easier to call it a day, and I was hopeful he'd get the significance of what we were in the middle of. I typed a quick note and hit the send button. The note said, "Rick, I'm not sure we've got it all figured out, and there's still more we're learning every hour, but you're the only person running a car company who's there for your customers in Houston this morning, and here's what it looks like." Rick was always good about personally responding to messages, and in about twenty minutes, I got one back from him that just said "WOW." I saw him a couple of weeks later and asked him what "WOW" had meant. He said it meant, "WOW, that's great," and "WOW, don't screw it up." I guess there's always a coaching moment, but he was right, as usual.

Actually, the hurricanes gave our brand one more chance to do a little coaching of its own. By this point, we were fairly sophisticated at tracking our subscriber retention and were able to very quickly spot trends in the data. Within a couple of weeks of the hurricanes, we started to see retention dip in some of the coastal counties that had been involved in the worst of the storms' effects. How could that be? How could we be worth less to these people after an event like this? It made no sense. Maybe there were financial issues because of the property damage, who knew. We poked around and quickly found out that the Postal Service had actually suspended service to certain zip codes because they'd been so disrupted by the aftermath of the crisis. Subscribers weren't getting their mail and probably didn't even know, in many cases, that their OnStar subscription was about to expire.

In our world, no response to the mail basically meant the subscriber wanted to cancel their subscription, unless, of course, it really meant that they just hadn't gotten their mail. Scott knew that, even in normal times, not everyone subscribed, but felt that, in this case, it would be much better to just continue the service for free for three months for everyone who we couldn't contact in order to give everything a chance to settle down. It would cost us money, but the alternative was that we'd likely be canceling the subscriptions of some people who were really counting on us being there for them, and that just wasn't acceptable. In another moment of obvious decision-making, it took all of about five seconds to have Scott explain what was going on and approve what he planned on doing. I loved this brand. In many ways, it really made this an easy business to run.

Well, it might have been easy to run (not really), but it certainly wasn't easy to market, at least not in the early years. The brochure-rack approach ran its course, mainly because it had become painfully obvious that it wasn't working. We surveyed people who'd decided not to keep the service after their factory-included year to ask them why. Was it the cost, or some concern about their privacy, or maybe they'd had a bad service experience? Sure, there was some of all of those reasons, along with others, but the biggest problem by far was they didn't understand what services they actually had. These were our own customers, they'd had OnStar service for a year, and they'd invariably say things like, "I don't need concierge service," or "I never go anyplace where I might get lost." But what about the part that responds to a crash and *might save your life*? When we asked that, we too often got back a response like, "Oh, it does that, *too*?" Ay, caramba! And if our own subscribers were this confused, you just knew that we weren't reaching all of the new vehicle shoppers who we were hoping would be drawn to GM vehicles because of OnStar.

We had a problem, and it was one big one, but we had no real money for advertising early on because the vehicle marketing divisions were mostly controlling it. We managed our PR messaging, but our news pickup was relatively small in the beginning, particularly compared with what could be accomplished with advertising. I was never sure why, but the car guys never really exploited the undisputed leadership position that OnStar's unique lifesaving technology brought to GM vehicles. Sadly, they either completely ignored the opportunity to use OnStar to help them sell cars or would occasionally delight in asserting their independence and presenting us in nonsensical ways. There were examples like Cadillac's original "Satellite Death Star" ad and, later, when everything we'd learned about the power of the brand should have made them know better, hiring celebrities like Jimmy Kimmel to help tell our story. The approach was sadly distracting and completely ineffective.

And it wasn't rational either if you took the time to look at the research on new-car buyers. The conquest and loyalty impacts that came back from customer studies consistently confirmed that OnStar was the single-biggest feature GM had to differentiate its vehicles. There was even an analysis that subdivided people who were intending on buying a new vehicle in the next two years into nine different segments, depending upon whether they already owned GM vehicles or were considering GM for their next purchase. In the worst possible box for General Motors, 25 percent of shoppers who didn't own a GM vehicle and said they wouldn't even consider one for their next purchase said they would prefer to have OnStar on their next new vehicle. Did that mean we'd win with those folks no matter what? Absolutely not. These were research findings in a research setting. It still meant that they'd need to know about OnStar and what vehicles it was available on and that GM vehicles in their preferred segment would have to be otherwise competitive with the other brands they were considering. But in an extremely cluttered market where you'd fight like a dog for a small change in consideration for your vehicles, this gave GM something to talk about that customers had said really mattered. And it was something absolutely unique, not the screaming $5,000-cash-back drug that we'd fallen so in love with and that was not only easy to copy, but ultimately so corrosive to the perception of our vehicles' value.

If you can say insane politics are rational, then maybe there was something rational about how this all played out. In the early days, when it was understandable to be skeptical regarding OnStar's potential to impact vehicle sales, GM's marketing guys held back on aggressively promoting the service, probably wanting to get a little more real-world experience about how it was going to be embraced by car buyers. In addition, it would have been completely reasonable to also be a little concerned about whether the service would work the way we said it would. If they'd prematurely bet the marketing ranch on our brand's promise, and we'd found ourselves unable to reliably deliver services like crash response, it would have been a disaster. So an early wait-and-see attitude, while frustrating to some of us at OnStar, might have actually been a fair place to start.

But as time went on, like months turning into nearly a decade, there was a mountain of evidence that the technology was on target and well executed and data that said a significant percentage of folks shopping for cars would want to find OnStar on their next new vehicle. Unfortunately, during that same time, a series of circumstances had driven GM toward a one-size-fits-all marketing strategy that was all about price. The competition, particularly the Japanese manufacturers, had seized the high ground on reliability and was using it to slowly, but surely erode our market share. Due to the high-fixed-cost nature of the auto industry caused by the self-inflicted constraints of severely outdated UAW contracts, there was a lot of internal pressure to keep the volume as artificially high as possible. Compounding that was a regime change in the marketing organization that resulted in an obsessive short-term orientation to "move the metal," and after an extremely positive reaction to GM's massive "Keep America Rolling" across-the-board rebates following the September 11 terrorist attacks, they now knew just how to do it. Price discounting became the strategic instinct of the marketing team and was staggering in its size and scope. It also typically lacked careful or nuanced execution and was more like carpet-bombing, including examples like Corvettes and Cadillacs being leased to employees at under $250 per month. I only know those because I had one of each in my garage, which was amazing for me, but not so great for either vehicles' brand health or residual value.

So why, with all of that going on, wasn't OnStar the perfect antidote to the profit-poisoning effects of chronic rebate syndrome? And if not the cure (because OnStar was too small to work everywhere), why wouldn't it at least be embraced on the margin as a part of the solution to start weaning the company from its dependence on customer cash on the hood? Well, all I can say is that it didn't fit with the tribal customs embraced by the vehicle marketing group at the time. Despite the research data, they'd made their judgement early on that OnStar couldn't help them sell cars, and reversing their position on that years later risked criticism for their missing the boat in the meantime. Besides, OnStar actually *added* price to the vehicle, and if someone started to expect the marketing team to be able to sell value and unique features instead of the lowest monthly payment, it could potentially set a dangerous precedent. Selling value and unique features was just too risky; it was better to stick with what they knew worked, except that it wasn't working anymore. These were some of the same guys who thought they were living the essence of the Cadillac brand if they wore work black shirts to work every day. Hey, I'll admit to my share of frustration and cynicism on this, and it doesn't make me right, but I honestly used every ounce of my average IQ to try to understand how to reconcile their behavior with the facts and could come up with nothing other than arrogance or a fundamental lack of marketing competence— undoubtedly, it was some of both.

And I wasn't just frustrated with them. Our own marketing team at OnStar was proving equally incapable of breaking out of neutral and shifting into high gear, and things were starting to get ugly. We actually went through four separate marketing leaders in the span of about six years, and all we had to show for it was a reasonably nice-looking logo and a deal with Warner Bros. to use Batman as our spokesman. We were awful, awful, awful in this area, and I certainly wasn't showing myself capable of providing much help, except in churning one guy after another out of the job, only to be replaced with someone else who wasn't much better. They were all different and all washed-out for different reasons. The first guy should've never been put in the job in the first place. He was sent to the OnStar colony as a redeployable asset from Cadillac and was severely ill-equipped to build the marketing foundation for a new business. It wasn't his fault. He was trying, but he just didn't have either the leadership strengths or functional skills to handle the role. The other three guys were all pretty different, but looking back, they all had one common characteristic: Before the ink had dried on their OnStar business cards, they were already positioning themselves for their next job.

I guess that's more common than I would've thought in the world of marketing and branding. You move from one product like dental floss to another like shaving cream until you finally move up to something big and important like Oldsmobile—oh, sorry, that's not in business anymore. These positions weren't places to make a profound difference; they were auditions until their next "real" job came along. And in GM, the next real job for a serious marketing person was back doing something with cars. Was there any conflict of interest with that? Not necessarily, unless, of course, the car guys think OnStar is annoying and would prefer OnStar's marketing leader didn't make waves if they knew what might be good for their future career. Unfortunately, this wasn't irrational paranoia; it was reasoned paranoia, and pretty simple to understand. The godfathers had spoken, so if there was a tough issue where we needed to push back on GM or bang heads a little in order to advocate for positions important to OnStar, we were going into those meetings unarmed. We'd roll over faster than a cocker spaniel in a room full of Dobermans. When you're bobbing and weaving to try to live through meetings, you don't tend to sweat the critical details that might make all the difference in the way your brand is communicated. Anyway, as I said, I was batting zero for four, and my star free agent was Batman. Could this get any worse?

My fifth choice for the job, a GM veteran by the name of Tony DiSalle, would've by all external views looked remarkably similar to most of his fallen predecessors. Someone steeped in GM experience (most recently as the brand manager for the GMC Envoy), he also had an obvious career track back in the car business and ambitions to someday run one of the big nameplates, like Buick. While I was concerned about him being such an insider, one of my earlier failures had been an outside hire from a big-name corporation, so it wasn't clear to me that just because someone hadn't worked at GM that they'd somehow be above the politics and a better leader, as number two obviously hadn't been. Honestly, if the stars ever aligned on this role, having GM marketing experience could be a big plus. You'd understand the process, know the people, and be familiar with the tribal rituals at the big house. The trick would be finding somebody who wasn't a slave to the process, a lap dog to the people, and religiously committed to the rituals—a trifecta that I hadn't pulled off yet.

I tried to use every bit of painful experience that I'd gathered working with the earlier marketing guys in my interview with Tony and could feel myself pushing on him so hard that I was sure I was talking him out of being interested in the job. I hadn't seen any flaws to want to scare him away, but I really had to know that he'd be up for this position. I'd already failed the OnStar team too many times by not landing a great person for this incredibly important role, and I owed it to all of them to finally get it right. Tony was so calm and professional during the questioning that I almost hated myself for swinging at him again and again. Was he sure he could stand up to the higher-level folks at GM if that were necessary to get the job done? How would he handle it when he saw them do really stupid things that would harm OnStar if left unchallenged? It was like punching that inflatable figure with sand in the bottom, and Tony thankfully ignored my abrasive approach and kept popping up for more. He said he really wanted this job and had actually wanted it when it'd been given to one of the previous guys. He thought the challenge of working with a new brand would be great and claimed to have a real strong attraction to working on something like OnStar because of the profound impact we were having on our subscribers' lives.

All right, he had me. He seemed to get and appreciate the unique challenge of bringing something as new and different as OnStar to life. Even more importantly, he expressed what felt like sincere, personal empathy for the mission. While delivering improved marketing results was going to be important, accountability at OnStar wasn't just about putting numbers on the board. The real consequences of not getting this right were that people, either current subscribers or new vehicle shoppers, wouldn't comprehend what this amazing technology could do for them or their families. To me, it was a problem, but not a tragedy if people understood what our services were all about and made an informed choice that OnStar wasn't for them. We wouldn't like it, and we'd try to find ways to change their mind, but that was just business and was bound to happen. Not everybody liked ice cream or puppies, either. But if people missed what we were all about because our marketing approach remained flawed, and they thought OnStar was about hotel reservations and stock quotes instead of safety and security, then that was the tragedy because we'd done them a serious disservice.

I offered Tony the job, he accepted, and I left the meeting feeling very optimistic. I found myself using optimism a lot because, back then, the alternative usually made my head hurt worse than it did already. But at least I'd learned "optimistic but verify," and this was one role that the verification process would be out in the open for all to see. I really, really, really hoped I'd gotten this right, because if I hadn't, I was sure I'd get a faceful of attitude from my OnStar teammates and a very cranky living brand.

As it turned out, Tony was a wonderful addition to the team and just the right person to lead the marketing efforts that brought the real meaning of OnStar to life. He was warm, sincere, collaborative, and tenacious, which were perfect fits for the current situation. And did I mention fearless? He did it in his own way, which meant he didn't turn all red and shake like I was prone to do, but I don't remember one time where he backed down from a serious or difficult issue. Compromise, sure. A lot of times it made sense to work around some problems instead of plowing right through them, but never once did the compromises seriously affect the business or give anyone at OnStar reason to wonder whether Tony was rolling over to feather his future career nest. The brand really approved of Tony, as it already had Walt, Scott, Jon, Fred, Ken, and many, many others.

Tony would be the first to tell you that despite all we had going for us, the road to fully realizing the power and value of OnStar was still filled with more potholes than unrestricted-speed zones. Batman was serving his purpose by helping the OnStar name break through and allowing us to highlight some important services like crash response without being too scary. Video of a real crash is hard to watch, but when the cute Bat-shaped airbag deployed on camera, and it was clear that Batman couldn't be hurt by a mere crash, it seemed like a pretty clever way to finesse the issue. The problem was the brand's name was becoming reasonably well known, but the brand's meaning wasn't doing so well. So more work needed to be done, and more arch-villains needed to be paraded out to highlight other important services—or so we thought.

Then one day I got a letter in the mail from a subscriber, actually a mom, who'd been involved in a crash where we'd been able to get help to the scene fast enough that her daughter's life had been saved. It was a love/hate letter, but all with loving intent. The love part was obvious, particularly if you were a parent. The hate part came out of left field; she hated Batman, at least as a spokesman for OnStar. She said that having a cartoon character represent our business really trivialized what we were doing, and instead of that, we should be telling the world about the reality of the lives we were already helping to save. She wasn't angling for a job at all, but generically, she was saying, no, imploring, "Tell *my* story."

Wow, that was a bucket of cold water in the face. We'd completely ruled out turning this into "reality TV" for a number of reasons. First, there thankfully weren't cameras at these crash scenes, at least not at the moment they occurred. And even if there had been, the footage wouldn't have been anything that you would've wanted to see. Second, the whole idea of reliving some of our subscribers' worst moments didn't feel right; it felt exploitive. But here was a woman with very sincere motives after experiencing a horrific crash who wanted other people to understand the importance of what we could do. To her, it wasn't exploitive; it was being clear regarding what OnStar was really all about.

I loved our subscribers, I really did. I loved them when they appreciated what we did, loved them when they told us what we were doing wrong, and really loved them when they got our attention and adjusted our course. The woman in the Phoenix focus group who "invented" OnStar diagnostics had been one in a growing list of examples where interested parties, our subscribers, helped bring voice to our brand. I'm sure we missed opportunities to always hear the whispers, but this letter wasn't a whisper—it was an important wake-up call.

I called Tony in, showed him the letter, and said we really needed to think this through. There was no denying the power of her suggestion, but also, there was no denying the implications to the business if we changed paths and got it wrong. This is where Tony and his team, particularly Andy Young and Chris Hamer, really earned their stripes. Chris had worked at Priceline.com before he came to OnStar and had been part of the team there who had come up with their then famous radio ads featuring William Shatner. Back then, not many companies were using radio for national campaigns; the medium was thought to be more about local or regional advertising. And as far as the car guys were concerned, radio was the domain of the dealer where the neighborhood Buick store could scream $249 monthly lease payments for a new Regal. But radio wasn't for Buick themselves. How were you going to show stock footage of a Regal driving on the same curve outside of Denver that every other car company uses if it's on the radio? But we didn't exactly have stock in anything at that point, so we were pretty much free to give anything a try.

Andy knew that we didn't have video of any of our real interactions, but remembered we had audiotapes of the actual service events, which we kept on file for quality-monitoring purposes. In fact, Fritz

Beiermeister, who was then handling our relationships with large-fleet vehicle owners, had actually taken his own initiative and put together a very powerful four-minute video infomercial for a fleet show using some of those recordings to recreate a pretty dramatic crash story, and it had been very well received. Fritz was definitely on to something, but would it be possible to retain the impact using only sixty seconds of audio? While our recordings would periodically get erased, there was an inexhaustible supply of new interactions because they were happening by the thousands every day. Long story short, the tapes were an amazingly rich and incredibly poignant source of the reality of OnStar. Everything from serious crashes, to people who were lost, to pets that had locked their owners out of their cars, to people caught in hurricanes. They hadn't been recorded to produce high-quality commercials and sounded more like the audio equivalent of the "shaky-cam" video technique. Andy worked with our agency, cut a few of the pieces together, and added some narration, and within a couple of weeks, he was reviewing the results with Tony.

A few days later, Tony grabbed me and said they had something they wanted me to hear. He asked me to keep an open mind, but that he'd never personally experienced anything as potentially impactful as this in his career. We filled the conference room with the senior staff of the business, and Andy hit the play button on his boom box. Andy had put together a couple examples of crashes, and I think a non-crash emergency call. He played them back to back, and when they ended, you could've heard a pin drop. These were powerful, highly emotional, and advertising strategy aside, meant a lot to everybody in that room. I'm sure Walt was thinking about all that had been done to get the hardware ready, and Greg Payne was probably proud of how the advisor in each case had handled the call and a little concerned about how the power of the event might have affected them. Ken would have been reflecting back on all of the arm wrestling that had been necessary to clear the legal hurdles before we could take our first call, and I was more than a little blurry-eyed with emotion to have these events served up in a way that defied you to conclude that something amazing hadn't happened. Did this somehow surprise us? Hadn't all of us been involved in every piece, every detail of making this happen? Hadn't we all sat side by side with advisors taking emergency calls so that we all knew exactly what this business was all about? Sure we had, but somehow those amazing sixty-second recordings had packaged the incredible complexity and palpable emotion of OnStar into bite-sized summaries of what we meant to our subscribers. Tony was right; this was powerful. But was it too powerful?

We ended the meeting in agreement that the approach we'd just heard, what Tony and Andy eventually named the "Real Stories" campaign, had the potential to be the breakthrough we'd been looking for. But we needed to think carefully about this and not just knee-jerk it into production. While it certainly didn't feel exploitive to us, the last thing we wanted to do was inadvertently come across that way to the rest of the world. Tony commissioned a fast, but important round of research with both subscribers and new vehicle buyers to see what they thought, and more importantly, felt, about this approach. We decided to go out of our way to be less than neutral in probing for whether we'd be seen as trying to take advantage of our subscribers' distress and literally invited criticism in the way we asked the questions. Incredibly, the negative perceptions of the ads were almost nonexistent and were actually even lower than the Batman campaign. And radio, as it turned out, was the perfect medium for this approach. It was all audio-based anyway, took sixty seconds to completely tell an individual story, and the audience would almost always be listening to the message when they were sitting behind the wheel of their car.

We approved the strategy and began production. These were relatively easy ads to produce since there were so many actual new events taking place every day. We asked each subscriber involved for permission to use his or her experience and had an amazingly high percentage of customers who were not only willing, but also anxious, in many cases, to have their stories told. We ended up making hundreds of individual commercials, and the approach just seemed to feed on itself. Early on, I saw a few checks come across my desk that had gotten flagged because they were in a new category of expense—residual payments. I asked what that was all about and was told that GM had a standing agreement with the actors' union that if we ever used any of our own people in ads, we'd make them members of the union and pay them to scale. I guess that was supposed to eliminate any incentive we might otherwise have to avoid hiring actors to try to save money.

Anyway, the checks I was seeing were part of the residuals our OnStar advisors were earning for their radio commercials. This was too good to pass up, so I asked our guys if it would be all right if we turned the delivery of those checks into a ceremony to honor the advisors involved. It was a perfect way to recognize their amazing work and to show all of the advisors how much we appreciated what they were doing to bring OnStar to life every day. We eventually settled into a cadence where we'd go to each OnStar center on a quarterly basis, gather as many advisors as we could into a big room to serve as the audience, and honor the handful of their peers who had been featured in the most recent round of commercials. We'd call them up one at a time, play their spot for everyone to hear, and then present them with a CD with their commercial. I also awarded them each an Academy Award statue with their name on it and gave them their residual check.

These eventually turned into wonderful celebrations and generated a little good-natured competition between our two biggest locations—Charlotte, North Carolina, and Oshawa, Canada. The advisors would get dressed up, there'd be big cakes for everybody, and we'd take pictures of them receiving their award. I absolutely treasured these ceremonies, maybe even more than the advisors did. When we played the commercial where the pet monkey had locked its owner out of his or her Chevy, everybody laughed. But when we played the ones where someone had just gotten help in a crash or for a medical emergency, there weren't many dry eyes in the house, including mine. This was marketing, but it really wasn't. This was our brand, alive and well and not too bashful to pull at the heartstrings of the very people who actually delivered on its promise every day. Our advisors were incredibly proud of what they did and would've been the first ones to call us out if we'd disingenuously tried to turn their work into some slick marketing sizzle. No, this really did have meaning, and if it also worked as advertising, then that was all right, too. I'd always get a chance to make a few remarks at the end of each ceremony, but never had any lectures to deliver, no rah-rah motivational speeches up my sleeve. My words would invariably start and stop in the same place about how thankful and appreciative I was of what they were all doing to bring OnStar to life every day and how much I knew that meant to our subscribers. I always ended up hugging more people than the father of the bride at a huge wedding, but that was OK because we were just one big family.

The Real Stories campaign continues, at least it has up until now. I wish I could say that the power of that campaign magically aligned the cosmic tumblers inside GM, but sadly, it didn't. Unbelievably, even into my last year in the business, I had a meeting with GM's head of vehicle marketing who said what we really needed to concentrate our efforts on was making OnStar cool. According to him, we needed to make it real by inventing a "thing" that somebody could carry around in his or her pocket to make OnStar tangible, and then they'd be able to advertise it. Unless there was something physical, a dongle of some sort, then there really wasn't anything they could sell. Heaven help this company. I wish I thought this was just another convenient way to rationalize why they didn't want to advertise OnStar, but the tragic part was I think he really meant it. Hey, maybe you're not the sharpest marketing mind on the planet, but you can't be that naive about business, can you? Ever hear of a little company called Google? It's called a *services company*, and I'm not sure I've ever seen their dongle. And the last time I checked, its market cap was somewhere north of $150 billion. This lack of business substance was unconscionable, but, sadly, not unbelievable. Clay might say that it was a good example of what happens when there is no brand compass to point them in the right direction. One-size-fits-all product positioning, over-trained on how to creatively package price discounts, unfortunately missed the marketing nuance that could've otherwise been extremely valuable to the struggling car business.

But missed opportunities aside, the OnStar brand was alive and kicking. More importantly, it had infected all of us as surely as you'd catch a runny nose at a day care center. Tony and his team were bringing it to life in advertising, and everybody else working in the business was busy bringing their part of it to life every day. This brand had an attitude and wasn't at all shy about telling us how it wanted to be managed. Sometimes it screamed at us, sometimes it just whispered, but once you got on its frequency, it was hard to miss its message. And, thankfully, it just kept on transmitting.

CHAPTER 13

People and Progress W.W.O.D.

Time passed, people came and went, and the business continued to grow and evolve. Thankfully, eGM ran its course, and Gary Cowger stepped in, replacing Mark Hogan as my fourth supervisor since I'd been at OnStar. Gary had mostly been an operations guy, with experience in manufacturing and labor relations roles, until he was named president of GM's North American business, replacing Ron Zarella. Ron was returning to Bausch + Lomb, the company he'd worked for prior to his move to GM, as chairman and CEO. I'm not really sure how Ron would describe his time at GM. He'd pushed the marketing folks in the company far beyond their comfort zone and had made some meaningful progress, but too many people had never stopped resenting an "outsider" being given such a prominent role in the company. I'd miss him, and the company would sorely miss his talent, but there weren't many other people at GM expressing that sentiment, at least not openly. I couldn't tell if that's how people really felt or if it was just the usual "the king is dead, long live the king" mentality, which works about as well in big companies as it did in medieval monarchies.

Gary wasn't a bad guy; in some ways, he was actually a nice, stable change from Mark. But that wasn't all Mark's fault. He and eGM were just destined to create the perfect storm of distractions, and I had to admit to being happy that it had passed. Our boat had survived, but we'd taken on water. No, you wouldn't mistake Gary for Mark. Gary liked being in charge, had strong opinions on almost any topic, and spoke with a cut-through-the-bullshit style that you'd recognize in a minute came from his experience in the plants. I had an interesting relationship with Gary, and I'm still not particularly sure how to describe it.

At first, I didn't much like him at all. He came in with guns blazing, telling me that he'd heard a lot of grumbling from engineering and manufacturing about what a pain in the ass OnStar was, but that was mild in comparison to the complaints he was getting from marketing. As far as Gary was concerned, we were guilty until we proved ourselves innocent. But, in fairness, for all I knew he was telling the marketing and engineering guys they were full of it as well. That was just part of Gary's style; he'd come at you hard and see how you reacted. I'd been around long enough that I'd seen that approach many times before, so it wasn't particularly intimidating. But it did feel like more drama and theater than was necessary, especially at that level in the organization. There was real work to do, hard work, and I didn't know too many people who did their best stuff with somebody sitting on their chest. Oh well, once again nobody asked me to vote on who I thought I should be working for, and I knew I could've done much worse.

Actually, Gary and I came to have a pretty good relationship over the years. With a little bit of time, he seemed to appreciate the complexity of what we were trying to accomplish and came to really embrace and support our mission. For my part, I got to know the Gary who was right beneath the operations-hardened exterior, and he was a genuinely good man—smart, good instincts, and someone I could learn from and trust. He got behind making OnStar standard on all GM vehicles and was actually the guy who decided to take on the challenge of getting me promoted to the vice president level. To a GM lifer like me, that meant a lot, even if it didn't come with any extra money. In some ways, the distinction meant more to the business than it did to me personally since it meant I'd now be officially included in

GM's quarterly officer meetings. It wasn't that the contents of those meetings were so important, but being there meant there was one less way OnStar could get messed with. Before I was promoted, some officers would take great delight in telling me how OnStar had been criticized at the last "Grand Poobah" meeting as a way to bully me into better behavior. But now, since I was in those meetings, the mystery was gone and, magically, so was a lot of the drama.

One thing that had changed over the years, and actually helped the situation quite a bit, was the expansion of the OnStar board of directors. Besides Gary and I, Rick Wagoner had also joined the board, as had GM's then CFO, John Devine. And even though Mark had moved to another job in GM and was no longer my boss, he stayed on the board because he was still interested in what we were doing. Over the years until my retirement, more people came and went. We eventually had GM's North American head of marketing join (at Rick's request) as well as Fritz Henderson, Tom Stephens, Troy Clarke, and automotive industry legend-in-residence Bob Lutz. For the most part, these guys were all supportive of what we were doing, even if they didn't always carry that support around with them when they were outside of our meetings. We met quarterly, usually for two to three hours, and it turned into a really important place to keep the venture on track and force alignment within the company when a tiebreaker needed to be settled.

Thinking back, this was a pretty good way to finesse the natural buck-passing tendency that takes place inside of big companies and was certainly taking place within GM. Too many times, you'd be in meetings with rooms full of people, and when it came time for the tough call, invariably, you'd look around and see that one of the key decision-makers wasn't there. So you'd gotten all worked up and arm wrestled until you were exhausted, only to see the issue fall victim to the dreaded "tabling" maneuver. I'm sure some people counted on that as a defense against making tough decisions, especially when the issue to be decided looked like there'd be "winners" and "losers." Unfortunately, there were too many people who thought that a "punt" was the same as doing real work. Hey, we talked about doing something, doesn't that count? No, it actually doesn't.

So our board was a place where, every three months, we knew we'd have everybody necessary to make any decision that needed to be made. Need an answer on whether we can violate a corporate policy on in-sourcing some IT function or whether we should do business with other OEMs? Those would've required crazy contortions without this board. And taking on XM, particularly the way that it developed through the negotiations, would never have happened if we'd been forced to string all of the pieces of the company together separately. Better yet, since everybody eventually understood our quarterly board process, most of the time we got issues resolved outside of the meeting because nobody wanted to explain to Rick why we couldn't reach an agreement on our own.

Rick really understood this dynamic and was committed to helping the process be as productive as possible. One example involved remote diagnostics. We felt that there was an opportunity to use our growing experience with remote diagnostics to actually help the design and validation phase of new vehicles. If the vehicle engineers could use OnStar's remote diagnostic capability to find problems they might not otherwise find until production, that would be worth real money in terms of lower warranty expense. Fewer warranty claims also meant happier customers and a chance to improve the perception of GM vehicle quality. But nobody expected the engineers to grab hold of this concept without a little encouragement; their plates were already full, and they were under the same pressure to reduce headcount that everybody else had. Since there was nothing obvious they could stop doing to take this harebrained OnStar idea on, inertia was against it gaining traction on its own.

But Rick thought this might be a big deal and decided to use the OnStar board process to get at it. He asked the head of vehicle quality to come to our next board meeting and give a report on how he intended to evaluate this opportunity. If there was nothing there, fine. It'd a shame, but as long as it'd been taken seriously, everyone could just move on. The approach worked. There was a lot of scurrying around in the two weeks before the meeting, and it confirmed that this could be a big deal. How big? Well, the process that was eventually spawned by that evaluation ended up saving hundreds of millions of dollars a year in warranty costs. And there were a lot of other opportunities like that, side benefits that cropped up by the company keeping its mind open to the possibilities that the new technology was creating. They weren't all worth hundreds of millions of dollars, but you never knew until you got into them and figured it out.

And there were other board-worthy issues that were just as important. But the challenge wasn't to make something new happen; it was to make sure something new (and possibly stupid) didn't happen. The potential for mischief lurked around every corner. Let's partner with Microsoft and turn everything over to them. No, let's connect the Internet to the backseat. No, let's get out of the car altogether (because it's a pain to execute), and let's sell connectivity into hotel lobbies (that actually happened in Europe). No, let's turn the roof of the car into a phased-array antenna and sell DirecTV to our customers. Our board became the place to rein most of that in because, thankfully, it included all of GM's chief deciders.

Beyond all of the "help" we were getting from people within GM, there was a small group of people from outside the company who were actually important in keeping OnStar on track—and me from jumping off the roof. They were made up of emotionally kindred spirits like Ernie Allen, who was fighting to recover missing children, and intellectually stimulating and challenging folks like Professor Clay Christenson from Harvard. They were great-sounding boards, especially Clay, and kept our little OnStar team from suffering the corporate equivalent of the Stockholm syndrome. No, the world didn't actually begin and end in Southeast Michigan, and it honestly wasn't always about the torque.

Clay was always fun to visit. Once the OnStar cases were published, I'd look forward to my next semester's invitation to come spend a day in his class at Harvard. Being with the students was great, and their curiosity and fresh perspectives would invariably lead me to develop alternative ways to look at our issues. It also gave me a chance to poke at their preconceived notions of GM always being the slow kid on the block, because in the literal case of OnStar, it certainly hadn't been.

But what I treasured most was the early-morning time I'd spend with Clay before the day began. He'd invite me to his office for coffee about an hour before class, and I'd sit on his couch while he'd explain the new theories he was working on. It was fascinating stuff, and while not all of it applied to us, a lot of it was spot on. He'd ask questions about what was going on back in Detroit, and when I'd tell him, he'd think about it for a second, then start sketching a diagram that explained the dynamic that we were experiencing. I saved a few of those pieces of paper, hoping to someday auction them off on eBay for enough money to buy a new car (just kidding, Clay). But it was uncanny how insightful he was about us from six hundred miles away.

I also really loved talking to Clay because we always sounded smarter after I'd listen to him describe us. I learned that we were a classic case of an "emergent strategy." When I first heard that, it wasn't immediately clear to me that it was a good thing. An emergent strategy was supposed to be one of two possible choices, with the other being a "deliberate strategy." Wait a second, wasn't the opposite of deliberate closer to accidental? Was this another left-handed compliment from Clay, like getting a trophy in third grade soccer because we'd "tried hard"? Apparently not. It seems that when you're in a completely new space, where the cause-and-effect dynamics of a particular business sector aren't mature, then "emergent" is the enlightened way to go. It's not an accident; it's on purpose. I guess that kind of makes sense, in a too-deep-for-me-to-appreciate sort of way. Anyway, it sounded much better than how I'd been describing our approach, which was "making it up as you go."

He also had evolving theories on marketing, talking about the "jobs" that customers hire companies to perform for them. He thought OnStar was a really good example of us handling the "job" of "protect me and my family." He also thought we were a well-focused "purpose brand" and that our Real Stories ad campaign was the perfect way to bring our brand to life. He said that every commercial was actually a rehearsal of our service, something that he felt would connect extremely well with our intended audience. Again, I'm not sure how we'd done it, because we honestly hadn't tried to fit his theories. But the fact that, by his estimation, we were on the right path really helped strengthen our confidence and resolve to stay the course, even if the forces within our own company were too often trying to steer us off in another direction.

There was an additional concept that we talked about at one of my more recent morning sessions, one that I wish we hadn't been a good example of. It was right around the time that I'd been told that I was getting my sixth supervisor change. I'd lived through Gary, actually ended up working directly for Rick Wagoner for a couple of years, and was then shuffled off to the most recent inhabitant of GM's top North American job, Troy Clarke. Clay sensed my frustration with all of the bouncing around and said he wasn't completely surprised. While he'd been amazed how OnStar had successfully found its way through the minefield of starting up inside of GM, he said what I was now experiencing in terms of OnStar's revolving-door connection to GM's org structure was symptomatic of the next thing companies tended to get wrong.

Apparently, when big companies try to start something completely outside of their core business, there were a number of fairly predictable ways they could screw it up, and most of them mercifully happened early. The fact that we'd survived that stage, particularly inside of GM, was close to a corporate miracle. Now the miracle was behind us, and it was time to get on with the rest of our life, but it was generally during this "rest of your life" stage that the next business killer would usually show up. This was where top management at the parent company would suddenly forget what it took to make the new venture work in the first place, allowing it the freedom and flexibility to tailor its strategy and execution to its unique mission. No, the "need to be different" stage had passed, and they'd naively think that it was now time to "fold it back into" the real company where it belonged.

Clay described this in unusually blunt terms for him, which must have meant that it was a relatively emergent insight. (Do you like the way I used "emergent" in a sentence?) He said the problem the top guys had at this transition stage between childhood and adolescence was "where to stick it." He seemed genuinely interested in my impression of how this was playing out at OnStar, so we were probably about to become another data element in his newly forming theory. When we first talked about this, my frustration was with rotating through too many supervisors, none of whom had any experience with our kind of business. But, as time went on, my concern deepened, as there'd been an escalating trend toward imposing rules of engagement on OnStar that were far more appropriate for a struggling, hundred-year-old car company than they were for a still early-stage growth company.

Increasingly, there'd been talk of becoming "efficient," "zero basing versus Toyota," and "aligning with the GM North America team." Hey, there was nothing wrong with efficiency; we'd been routinely generating double-digit annual productivity improvements on every meaningful cost element of our business for years. That wasn't because we were so smart or worked so hard, it was that way because it should've been that way. We were a young company, our processes were still immature, and we fully expected to find ways to completely reinvent ourselves and improve everything we were doing. We hadn't been at this for a hundred years like the car guys had, so it was easier for us to find things with a big upside. And we'd been using those improvements for two important purposes: (1) to generate better financial performance so GM would stay committed to the opportunity and (2) to create the headroom necessary to bring in the additional resources that were required to aggressively pursue OnStar's open-ended growth prospects.

In GM's core vehicle business, the definition of efficiency was cutting overhead, what they called "structural costs." GM North America wasn't a growth business; it was a "shrink slower" business. And, unfortunately, what had shrunk the slowest over the years wasn't the revenue, but the overhead. So there was always pressure to cut headcount, and marketing expenditures, and IT investments, and whatever. And for us to "align" with their approach to that, we were under increasing pressure to be looked at as a cost center; get in line, and get on the team. We'd been "stuck" somewhere all right, stuck in neutral with a reasonable risk of shifting into reverse.

This made no sense for a company at our stage of development, but that was the point of Clay's theory. The predictable inertia and politics were playing out and, if unchecked, would likely cause us to do absolutely inappropriate things. It wasn't because our mission had changed or the dynamics of our business had suddenly and coincidentally morphed into those of a car manufacturer, but rather, because we were beginning to be absorbed by the mother ship. This was the teenage disease that would wipe out a fair number of the start-ups that survived birth in a big company, and what I was describing to Clay sounded like we were showing its symptoms. Oh well, maybe knowing that would be helpful someday, but it wasn't about to change anything for us in the short term.

There were actually many other people who helped shape the future of OnStar over the years. Sorting through all of the other consultants who GM would routinely send our way, there was at least one who was really helpful—Adrian Slywotzky. Adrian was a partner in his own strategy consulting firm and had authored numerous books on optimizing enterprise value. Adrian was scary smart, very quick, and had strong opinions about how effective business strategy should be formulated. These were all good characteristics, but wouldn't have distinguished him from many other consultants who GM had sent over to "help us," yet added no value to our business. Adrian was different because he didn't behave as if GM was his client and we were his project, but that we were his client, and more precisely, I was his project. That subtle difference meant that he took the time to fully understand the issues through our eyes and further made the effort to think through the additional challenges that we had in running OnStar inside of GM. It was along the lines of Clay's insights; actually, their support was very complimentary. But Adrian helped me think through more of the detailed issues that were important to understand in trying to survive while stuck between the worlds of a technology start-up and a mature and challenged auto company.

I can't point to any one example of Adrian's coaching; it was more along the lines of him being an encouraging, patient, thoughtful family friend. He was optimistic about the potential of OnStar, but realistic about the various give-and-takes that were confounding our progress at any point in time. If Adrian thought that there was a way through the woods on our issues, then how could I not believe it? I was never really a big fan of consultants, and I'm still not, but there are exceptions that prove every rule. Adrian was one of those exceptions, and he helped me, and OnStar, in more ways than he will ever know.

So there were a lot of cooks in the kitchen who were involved in making the OnStar broth. We had the team at OnStar, our subscribers, kindred spirits like Ernie Allen, a range of luminaries from inside GM, a famous Harvard professor, and an accomplished strategist. Oh, and we had the brand itself—increasingly assertive, demanding, loveable, and unpredictable. And much like my sister, Sharon, had done many years before, the brand had its own desire to be a matchmaker. It set me up on a few more "blind dates," and I hoped they'd be as special as Barb.

DIGITAL CRASH SIGNATURES

From the very first day of the business, automatically getting help in response to a crash was an important part of OnStar. It was one of those things that we were pretty sure was the right thing to do when we started and immediately began to appreciate how critically important it was once we began to get some experience. The emergency medical community describes the time immediately following a crash as the "Golden Hour," a well-accepted concept that says that it's extremely important to begin the medical response to any serious injuries, like those from a vehicle crash, within the first sixty minutes of the event. Slow response time was the enemy of good outcomes, and anything that shortened the time from crash to help arriving would not only save lives, but also lessen the consequences of other injuries.

We'd gotten into business by believing that concept and with the admonition from Harry to live up to the standard of always doing it the best way we could. But what did that standard mean? Who set the bar for this category? Well, as onerous as it sounded, we did. There wasn't anyone else trying to do this when we started, so our first airbag response was, by definition, state of the art at that particular moment. It'd all come out of nowhere so fast that I remember a briefing we gave to a woman from the U.S. Department of Transportation about six months after we'd launched our service. She was in Detroit for discussions with all of the domestic automakers on other subjects, and someone from GM thought it would be good to show her what we were up to at OnStar.

We went through a few PowerPoint slides that described our technology and our services, and she seemed really engaged. At one point, she stopped the presentation and asked when we were planning on doing all of these new things—three years from now or four? Maybe this was a concept overview, which was fine, because it was an area that she had a great deal of interest in. I stopped for a second and was a little surprised and confused by her question. When were we planning on doing what? We hadn't reviewed any of our future stuff; I was talking about what we had in the market right now and what we'd been doing for the past six months. When I told her that, she seemed stunned. Crash response now? Already deployed? She was aware of a demonstration project sponsored by DOT where a small number of vehicles somewhere in Pennsylvania had been equipped with crash-response technology, but as far as she knew, none of them had run into anything yet.

I was a little nervous that she might be embarrassed and wondered for a moment whether she was going to say we'd crossed over into their jurisdiction without appropriate authorization. Thankfully, she really was a believer in the concept and was genuinely excited that we'd taken the leap of faith and deployed the capability for real. Production vehicles and real customers driving the highways and byways of the entire nation, and not just in rural Pennsylvania—she was amazed. We knew this was important, but at that moment, it became clearer to me that it was going to be important to many other people as well.

So we got down to business learning and improving. We had cars crashing into trees and bridge abutments or driving through guardrails and down into gullies; one actually ended up in a lake. There were car-to-car crashes, including head-on collisions, T-bone wrecks, and rear-end accidents, and they were coming to rest right side up, on their side, or upside down. There were single-occupant vehicles, cars full of people, and sometimes pedestrians involved. The crashes were taking place on expressways, at crowded downtown intersections, and out on otherwise deserted stretches of rural roads. They happened at night, during the day, when it was 110 degrees, and during blizzards. And they occurred in jurisdictions that had well-funded, sophisticated 911 centers and in other jurisdictions where the 911 center at midnight consisted of the local sheriff's phone next to his bed. The permutations just seemed to multiply, and each one provided another small glimpse into the complexity of what had previously seemed like such a straightforward objective of getting help to a crash. They also reinforced, in very dramatic ways, the human importance of making sure that we always got it right.

There were lists of things that we were learning, and we worked through them one by one. I didn't know there were over six thousand separate 911 jurisdictional boundaries in the United States and that at the time we started there was no accurate national geocoded database that showed precisely where one stopped and the next started. We found that out early and also determined that the only way to reliably maintain up-to-date information on that was to do it ourselves. We also worked to take advantage of improvements that were happening with technologies like GPS so we'd be more accurate in pinpointing the locations of crash scenes. We learned to adopt the training standards from government-run 911 centers to use with our emergency advisors, and we continuously worked to refine and harden our vehicle-imbedded technology. We added signals from side airbags when they became available and continuously sought to bolster our vehicle packaging strategies to improve the crash survivability of our hardware. This was fertile ground, and it was clear that the effort was important. You couldn't be halfway into this; you either needed to be into it with both feet or stay out of it altogether.

And you had to become comfortable with the fact that most of the ongoing effort was never going to result in any additional marketing claims. It was hard enough to get people to understand that an OnStar-equipped car was smart enough to automatically get you help in a crash; nobody was really going to care that you were now using a twelve-channel GPS receiver augmented by ABS dead reckoning. A lot of the effort was going into behind-the-wall plumbing, which is necessary to have the bathroom work well, but otherwise not really all that interesting. We learned that we needed to push ourselves to develop unique, in-house expertise in all of the subtleties of this category. And we also needed to supplement that by hiring real experts, people who'd spent their lives before OnStar working in the world of 911 response centers.

Then one day, while attending an emergency response conference, someone came up and introduced himself to me. His name was Dr. Rick Hunt, president of the National Association of EMS Physicians and the department chair of Emergency Medicine at the State

University of New York Upstate Medical University at Syracuse. Dr. Hunt asked if I was the "OnStar guy," which, back in those days, didn't always lead to a great conversation. I said I was, half expecting him to tell me that we weren't able to find an Italian restaurant for him on his last trip to Buffalo. No, Dr. Hunt wasn't a subscriber, but as an emergency physician, and one who had spent a great deal of his career dealing with the aftereffects of thousands of car crashes, he said he wanted to thank me, and General Motors, for what we were doing with OnStar. He said he'd been involved with auto crash trauma care for a long time and was just waiting for someone to step up and bring automatic crash response to life. He said he knew it must be hard and risky, and he wanted to personally confirm for me that it would make a difference and save lives.

Wow. That was the best response I'd ever gotten to saying yes to the question "Are you the OnStar guy?" I simultaneously felt a strange sense of pride and humility in response to Dr. Hunt's words. Pride because I was proud of GM for what they'd stepped up to do. It certainly hadn't turned out to be easy, but that hadn't caused the company to back down. Humility because I wasn't sure we were completely worthy of Dr. Hunt's kind words. As I saw it, it was folks like the paramedics and the doctors who saved the lives; we were just a piece of the circuit that got help there a little quicker. But that was Dr. Hunt's point. The Golden Hour was real, and we'd just made a contribution in that area that had the potential to make all the difference in the world to many future crash victims.

So I have to say I went from being a little nervous meeting Dr. Hunt to really liking this guy. That was until he took a breath after his kind words and kept going. He said it was great what we'd done *so far*, but that he really needed us to do one more thing. He said, "Tell me something *about* the crash. Tell me the forces involved in the crash, tell me the angles of the forces, whether the vehicle had rolled over or not—those were all really important pieces of information." I didn't understand, so he backed up a little and explained. He said that all of the car companies had done such a good job padding the inside of vehicles over the years, with front airbags, side airbags, energy-absorbing steering wheels, and padded dashboards, that the superficial injuries that used to be very common in crash victims had been greatly reduced—fewer cuts, bruises, broken bones, and missing teeth. Basically, you could be in a pretty bad crash and come out of it looking and feeling better than you should. He said that old trauma docs like him (he wasn't that old) used to be able to use those non-life-threatening injuries as indicators of how bad the crash was and what kinds of forces your body had experienced. If the forces were high and of a certain type, you could look fine but might die a day later from internal bleeding.

He said if he was lucky, there might be a paramedic at the crash scene who would take a Polaroid picture of the bent metal of the car and bring it back to him at the emergency room. That way he could see how bad the crash was and what type of crash it was, and he could use his experience and judgment to help diagnose the potential internal injuries. But not all paramedics took pictures, and the pictures would be subjective at best. It was time for science and engineering to step up. He said that a human body was far more susceptible to a serious internal injury if it was accelerated laterally instead of from front to back. Apparently, your internal organs and all of your plumbing runs into itself in worse ways if you're violently shaken from the side, which is the equivalent of a T-bone crash. So that's basically why he wanted the new information—to understand the amount of the internal organ shake and its direction to determine what probably ran into what. It actually did make some sense to a mechanical engineer, in a creepy sort of way.

What could you do if you knew all of these things? Well, Dr. Hunt said three things could change. If you knew it was a certain type of serious crash, you might choose to send an air ambulance to the scene instead of a ground vehicle, and as air assets were scarce, this information would help prioritize their dispatch. Second, if the information indicated the likelihood of a severe injury of a certain type, you might choose to bypass the nearest emergency room and go directly to a Level One Trauma Center. If you got that right, the statistics said you'd have a 25 percent higher likelihood of surviving. Finally, if the technology really became advanced, the information might actually begin to form the basis for a pre–ER arrival triage capability. That might allow for preparation of confirmatory tests and the reservation of an operating room with the proper specialists for your expected injuries.

My head was spinning after the part about a side crash causing your spleen to run into your liver, or was it the kidney? Boy, was I glad that there were people who were experts in all of this and equally glad I wasn't one of them. But this guy, this Dr. Hunt, the person who three minutes ago I really liked, had just given me a huge headache and a stomachache, too. Yea, I was coming down with Harry Pearce syndrome. Harry's words were playing in one ear while the good doctor's were coming in the other: When you're in the crash-response business, you had to maintain constant vigilance and evaluate every practical way to get better. If doing that meant the costs would rise so high that nobody could afford OnStar, then that wasn't the right answer. But if something came across your radar screen with this kind of potential, it had to be run to ground. This sure seemed like it would be bizarrely expensive to accomplish, but how could you be sure unless you rolled up your sleeves and figured it out?

I think I said something like, "Thanks a lot, Dr. Hunt," meaning that his professional insights had been interesting and helpful, and also meaning thanks for the headache. If he'd only stopped with the part about being proud of GM, but no, he had to get the rest of it off his chest. When I got back to OnStar, I pulled Walt aside and dropped this on him. I said I had no idea what might be possible, but that we had to take a look at it and see what we could come up with. My sense was that it would be a long shot, but one way or another, I owed Dr. Hunt a response.

I can't remember exactly how long it took Walt to get into the details and figure it out, but he came back with an unexpected answer. Walt really liked this idea, and as a result, he had put a lot of great scheming in motion between our engineers and the technical folks at GM. After looking at it, they thought something might be possible, and it might not even require any new sensors. If one of the scenarios they'd identified could work, there wouldn't need to be any additional hardware costs at all. With an investment of a few hundred thousand dollars in software changes to the airbag and OnStar modules, he thought the accelerometers already in the vehicles to fire the airbags could do double-duty for this objective as well. It would require everyone to work outside of normal process timing if we didn't want to wait five years to get something into production, but what else was new. The good news was that everybody who'd heard about this idea from inside GM appreciated how important it might be and were up for giving it a chance.

Long story short, soon after Dr. Hunt's suggestion, we invested in creating the software, validated it, and found the first available vehicle architecture to put it in—the 2004-model-year Malibu Maxx. The Maxx was a really interesting car for GM; it was a four-door hatchback Malibu that looked a little bit like a small station wagon. I never understood why GM hadn't promoted the Maxx, as it was a nice size, the styling of the hatchback looked like an early version of a small crossover, and the utility of the interior was amazing. Well, not that it would matter to the vehicle marketing guys, but this otherwise under-marketed vehicle was now about to have yet another amazing distinction that probably wouldn't be marketed, either. The first vehicle in the universe that was going to be capable of wirelessly transmitting a "digital crash signature" from an accident scene wasn't going to be an $80,000 Mercedes, or a BMW, or a Volvo, or even a Cadillac. It was going to be a $21,600 MSRP Chevy. What an incredible claim, which unfortunately never got made, at least by Chevy. Too bad, but this idea hadn't been about marketing anyway; it'd been about taking our commitment to develop cutting-edge crash response technology literally and making something really special happen.

This was the beginning of an important relationship with Dr. Hunt and something that turned into a wonderful personal friendship as well. What a gift it was to intersect with someone so accomplished and experienced and someone who was as passionate about his mission as we were about ours. Rick was subsequently asked to become a section head at the CDC's Center for Injury Prevention and Control in Atlanta. At one point, he actually got me involved with the CDC, serving on a Federal Advisory Committee for the Injury Prevention Center. It was really an honor and something I certainly would've never seen coming my way before OnStar. Our head of public policy, Bill Ball, did some great work coordinating an effort with Rick where we provided funding to the CDC Foundation to study ways for the 911 community to fully exploit our newly deployed digital crash signature technology. By that time, we'd rolled it out across almost all of GM's new vehicles. What an amazing thing it was to help bring to life, and what an amazing blind date it was that had brought it into existence. Dr. Hunt had every reason to be personally proud of making this happen, but he wasn't interested in credit, only progress.

Crash response isn't completely mature yet, as there will undoubtedly be new breakthroughs and important next steps. Our learning curve approach really helped, but in this case, it was turbocharged by listening to someone as accomplished and driven as Rick. In November 2008, OnStar marked an incredible milestone for this amazing service line when we responded to our 100,000th-crash event. No, we didn't respond; the nation's real heroes, the 911 community, responded. We were the "pre–first responder" for the 100,000th time, in many cases being inside the vehicle with our subscribers before they'd actually come to a stop. Dr. Jeff Runge was with us to mark the event, as was Chief James Harmes. Jeff was also an emergency physician, the former NHTSA administrator, and had most recently been the first chief medical officer of the U.S. Department of Homeland Security.

Jeff had been a consistent and vocal proponent of bringing lifesaving technologies like OnStar to life and was someone who I was extremely proud had wanted to join us for the announcement.

Chief Harmes was the former head of the National Association of Fire Chiefs, an interested party since it was local fire departments across the country that responded to 75 percent of vehicle crash sites. He was convinced that we were helping fire departments get to accident scenes faster, which was saving lives. When I thanked the chief for joining us, he said that while he'd appreciated what we'd done, he was actually there for another reason. He said he was hoping the event would get a lot of attention and stimulate all of the other car manufacturers to step up and do something like this themselves since he knew what that could mean for everyone on the road. I couldn't argue with that sentiment; competitive juices or not, it was just the right thing to do.

At one point, we did see another high-volume manufacturer start to talk about getting into the crash response category, but what they were saying didn't really make any sense, at least considering our experience. They said they planned to accomplish it by having the crash calls routed through your own portable cell phone, a device that had a fair probability of becoming a high-speed projectile inside your car during a crash. For it to work, the phone would need to be with you, have a charged battery, survive the crash, and be wirelessly "paired" with a Bluetooth connection into their vehicle's electrical system— and that was only the beginning. There was no GPS, no external antennas, and obviously no imbedded connection. When you got into the engineering details of what could go wrong, a FMEA (failure modes and effects analysis), the no's continued. The biggest no was that you could have no real confidence that it would consistently and reliably work. Hey, I'm sure their lawyers had looked at it, and I'm also sure the fine print would have been enough to fill more than a few pages of the owner's manual, but our experience had taught us that there was a right way to do this, and it wasn't to try to cut corners to make an easy marketing claim. People's parents, or their spouses, or their daughters, or their sons might rely on that claim, and it would be terrible beyond legal consequences if they got it wrong.

No, this hit much closer to home for me. For my daughter, Taylor, I chose the Malibu Maxx as the car that would be her wingman for her first two years at Gonzaga University. It had a very special feature that you couldn't get on a car that cost twice as much, and my sense was she deserved it. Besides, I even knew the very special doctor at the CDC who'd invented it.

YOU'VE GOT MAIL

If I've said it once, I've said it a hundred times, thank God for that woman in the Phoenix focus group, because without her, we might've walked right by one of our more interesting services— remote diagnostics. Diagnostics had actually turned out to be perfect for our business and a wonderful extension to our peace-of-mind promise. It was also something that built on the special relationship between a vehicle and its owner, the fact that your car occupied a very special place in your life. It wasn't as important as crash response, but thankfully, crashes didn't happen all that often. But, at some point, you'd undoubtedly experience a vehicle problem while on the road, and in those cases, OnStar's unique ability to remotely read your car's diagnostic system could be really helpful.

I'd actually experienced it myself one Sunday afternoon driving through downtown Detroit on I-94 when coming home from Metro Airport. It was amazing how fast that "check engine soon" light caused a mechanical engineer and GM employee to immediately start worrying about what I was supposed to do next. Thankfully, I remembered that OnStar had remote diagnostics, hit the blue button, and was told that the vehicle was showing a minor fault that would probably clear itself in two or three ignition cycles. The advisor asked if I'd recently driven through a puddle, and I actually thought I had, but wasn't sure. Anyway, just knowing that I could keep driving until I got home was an amazing feeling of relief. The problem did clear itself in three ignition cycles. So that's what peace of mind feels like—excellent.

But this was just too juicy a target for the engineers to leave alone, so they jumped back into it to see what they could do next. Sure, the Phoenix woman had saved their pet project, but they were determined to reassert control over this platform and make some magic happen. From time to time, we'd find that Walt's guys had quietly slipped some software into the next-generation module without telling anybody. It wasn't being insubordinate, or at least I'd convinced myself it wasn't, because I liked them too much to want to be mad at them. It was always well intended, came from their deep passion for the business, and invariably ended up being the right thing to do. No, they weren't trying to start a revolt; they just secretly fancied themselves "junior marketing experts." It just looked like so much fun that they couldn't help themselves. And it was lucky for us that they behaved this way because there'd been numerous occasions when we'd found ourselves in a tough situation wondering what we could do about it, only to discover a piece of non-merchandised code available to magically do just what needed to be done. Don't ask where it came from, and don't ask what else was in there, just be grateful and step away from the controls. And now these guys thought they'd done it again.

A number of engineers were sure that the next big thing we should do with diagnostics was to have the car automatically scan itself, probably at night, and call us if it found a problem. It would be like a doctor's house call for your sick car, except that the doctor was a wirelessly connected computer, and it would happen in your garage or driveway. Walt told me what they were thinking, and as usual, it was after they'd already done it. He wanted to know if I thought it was something that made any sense? I said it sounded interesting and told them to go back to the lab and see what they could make out of it.

A couple of weeks later, Walt came into my office with some bad news. The idea of a car checking itself at night and letting us know if there was a problem wouldn't really work. It seemed that for the OnStar module to have access to the car's diagnostic system, the engine had to be running. And since it wasn't going to be running in the garage, we couldn't check the vehicle the way they'd envisioned. Maybe we could have the car automatically call in if it found a problem while someone was driving, but that had enough other potential problems that we probably needed to save it for another day. Wow, what a shame. It really did feel like it would be great to take advantage of this wireless telemetry capability; in many ways, it was as sophisticated as the monitoring that went on during the race at the Indy 500. Guess it will have to wait, unless...

A couple of days later, I asked Walt a question. Could we set the vehicle up to check itself out while it was running and call us one way or another to let us know what was wrong or *right* in the vehicle? I mean, you couldn't be sure, but wasn't there some potential value in our customers knowing everything was OK, at least everything we could check electronically, as opposed to no news is good news? And could it be set up to do the check and automatically send the results to its owner, maybe in an email? Walt thought about it for a minute, got a smile on his face, and said yea, maybe that was possible. But would anybody really care? I said who knows, but let's at least see what it feels like. So Walt went off to cobble something together in a test vehicle. He came back and said it was possible, but we'd need Gen 5 hardware, which wasn't yet released for production. But I knew where there was a Gen 5 vehicle running around Michigan. It was the Corvette I'd purchased a couple of months before that had a prototype Gen 5 unit in it because it had technology that was supposed to help with voice recognition in convertibles with the top down. I'd volunteered my then company car for the testing, and when I bought it, it was still part of the car.

I don't think Walt liked this idea one bit. Who knew how many car batteries this unproven software routine might eat while they were working out the bugs? And who needed me as their development partner? I was designated as the "bad luck kid"; everything I touched seemed to break, so why would this be any different? Besides, the Phoenix woman had already hijacked the fun diagnostic category before, and the engineers wanted it back. If I got involved, who knew how silly the ideas might get. At some point in the discussion, he understood that I probably wasn't going to be easily discouraged, so he reluctantly agreed to include my Corvette in the test. That meant I got a call from Chris Osterling, one of our highest volume patent holders and a really bright guy, and he got me all set up.

I talked to Chris, we discussed what I was looking for, and he went back to the lab and "provisioned" my Corvette to be part of the pilot. We weren't sure how often we'd really want to do this diagnostic probe with real customers, but for the test, we needed to get a reasonable volume of interactions, so he set it up to report on every ignition cycle. So every time my car's engine was started, it would review its diagnostic condition and send me an email with the results. Nobody had really talked about what the email should look like at that point; we were just more interested to see if the plumbing would work.

My first email came a few days later. It was nothing fancy, just black-and-white text. It showed my odometer reading, how many gallons of fuel I had left, and what percent of oil life was remaining from GM's oil life monitoring system. It also included diagnostic code information for three categories—the OnStar system, the power train system, and the dashboard integration module. If there was a problem with any of the systems, there'd be a list of numbers, something like "A2 06 55," for each fault detected. If everything was OK, it would simply say "none." Like everything else that ever happened with new things at OnStar, my first reaction was to be amazed that it was actually possible, and I was immediately sure we could do it better. Celebrate for about a minute and then start grinding on a list of ways it could be improved—at least I was predictable.

It was at about this time that I reviewed the concept with my old friend, Phil Samper. I'd been introduced to Phil by Vince Barabba back in the late 1990s during the early stages of dot-com mania. Vince thought Phil might be a good guy for me to know. He was someone who didn't work for GM, and therefore a politically "safe" person to have candid conversations with. Phil had been vice chairman and chief marketing officer at Kodak, retired from that job at fifty-five, and had gone on to do things like run the supercomputer company Cray, serve a stint as COO of Sun Microsystems, and sit on numerous other corporate boards. Now Phil was a partner in a new venture capital firm called Gabriel Venture Partners based in Silicon Valley. Phil loved the fact that I thought he looked like Sean Connery (no, Phil, not Bond, more like Indy's dad), but his role at OnStar was much more along the lines of Yoda.

From my vantage point, Phil had seen it all, done it all, and could have had the T-shirts to prove it, except that he preferred turtlenecks. He'd worked inside big companies, small companies, and high-tech companies and was involved in newly forming start-ups. He had wickedly quick marketing instincts, knew the politics of big organizations inside and out, and had the character and integrity of someone you admired and wanted to emulate. I don't exactly know why, but Phil took an interest in OnStar before there was really anything to be interested in. And, more importantly, he took pity on me. He became my father confessor, psychiatrist, bartender, cheerleader, and strategic consultant, all wrapped up into one loveable package. He'd administer a kick in the butt when I was too slow to step up to tough personnel issues and roll his eyes and give me a hug when I finally caught on to something he'd been trying to teach me. And one thing that he was always extremely good at was helping me think through new ideas.

When Phil first heard of our original version of vehicle diagnostics, he thought it was a really big idea, something we should do more with. And when the OnStar Vehicle Diagnostics email (OVD) concept surfaced, he was sure we were on the brink of another breakthrough for the business. He'd been amazed at how GM had consistently fumbled the marketing leadership claims they had with OnStar, and while he shared my frustration and would periodically indulge me with a couple of "ain't life awful" moments, more often than not he would yank me out of my pity party, and say, "All right, now what are we going to do about it?" Once he got radar lock on the OVD opportunity, whether I thought it was a big deal or not, he wasn't about to let it go. Thank God we were thinking about this one the same way because he would have been a royal (but loving) pain if we hadn't—a role he would have relished. So bolstered yet again by Phil's size 10 D, I mean his helpful encouragement, let the games begin.

The initial reaction to the email from our engineering guys was "Ho hum, so what?" Most vehicles wouldn't have fault codes displayed anyway, as most vehicles were going to be fine most of the time. The fault codes I was seeing on my Corvette had to do with the fact that we'd cobbled Gen 5 into my vehicle as a prototype, and the normal system was just reacting to the unexpected probing that was going on. Otherwise, this looked boring to our engineers, nothing very interesting going on.

It got worse when we reviewed the idea with the rest of GM. The vehicle quality and manufacturing folks both said there was no way we should do anything like this. It would likely confuse customers, would draw attention to problems, and could drive more warranty expense. The vehicle marketing guys didn't like it either, but for different reasons. They said we had no business getting into the vehicle serviceability category; that was the domain of the dealers. Keeping customers informed about the operation of their car and performing routine maintenance was their job, not ours.

When we reviewed the concept with a few dealers, they echoed the marketing group's concerns, and a number of them jumped on the fact that they didn't like the oil life information being displayed.

Even though GM had invented this system, and on most vehicles customers could already see the oil life reading if they knew how to cycle through the car's information system, many dealers had never really liked the concept. What it basically confirmed was that you didn't need to change your oil every three months or three thousand miles, the rule of thumb that had been part of American motoring lore for decades. No, the mileage interval was more like seven thousand miles or twelve months, depending on how you actually drove the car. That's what the oil life system was supposed to monitor, and it was meant to help customers save the money and hassle of more frequent and unnecessary oil changes. But many dealers had built a "customer reminder" system, with postcard mailings around the three-month intervals, and were sure that we'd cost them a lot of business if we shoved the actual readings in front of a customer in an email.

This was silly for a couple of reasons. First, dealerships did very little oil change business since most of it had been lost to the quick-change artists like Jiffy Lube years before. Second, GM had already decided to do the right thing for customers, and the environment, years before by inventing the oil life monitoring system in the first place. Even if most customers didn't know it, the data was already in the car; it just hadn't been properly explained to them. And, anyway, was marketing something unnecessary for customers, like more frequent oil changes, honestly going to be the way to build customer trust and loyalty? Apparently, that was none of our business. Had we forgotten "who owned the customer," at least in the service bay?

While we were engaged with all of these internal gymnastics, Tony and his guys took the concept out to research with our subscribers. After they absorbed the fact that it was legitimate, which took a little coaxing, they loved it, loved it, loved it. The concerns about being legitimate centered on two themes. First, was this really possible? I mean, come on, airbags are one thing, but my car sending me an email? That sounded a little fishy. The second theme was a concern regarding our motives. Why were we doing this again? There must be a catch; you're going to try to get us to buy something, right? I get it, when you're having a slow month in your service bay, I'll mysteriously need an oil change, or my muffler bearing will need changing. But if subscribers could be convinced it was real and under their control only, then the love part flowed through; however, if it turned into some shady way that they'd be marketed to, then they clearly weren't interested.

OK, our customers being inherently suspicious of GM's motives was a tough message to deliver back to the company, but the good news was that the service itself looked great. It was the perfect extension of "peace of mind," because for most people, their car wasn't their hobby. It was a complicated piece of machinery that they counted on, didn't completely understand, and always felt vulnerable about when it came to maintenance. So if we could demystify and simplify their relationship with their car and its maintenance needs and add a much-desired component of trust, then they were all in. But they'd be watching and waiting for us to cross the line and violate that trust, because as much as they'd come to have confidence in OnStar, they were sure, at some point, we wouldn't be able to avoid the temptation to shift our focus from helping them to helping ourselves (to their wallet).

So we'd learned what we needed to. Subscribers really liked this email idea; as usual, we had a set of challenges to solve to deliver it; and predictably, many of them were going to be internal. Our ad agency, Campbell Ewald, took a stab at producing a few creative treatments for the email's look and feel, and the version with the systems we were monitoring prominently featured on the left side of the report, with a simple red, yellow, or green icon next to each one indicating whether everything was OK or had a problem, was clearly the best. It organized a lot of otherwise messy details into an easy-to-understand format, which was a wonderful fit with OnStar's overall brand promise. The initial content included the four systems—OnStar, power train, airbag, and antilock brake—that we could monitor at that point, and within those categories, we were actually able to review over 1,600 separate diagnostic codes. We also decided to show the odometer reading (to remove any doubt that we were actually connecting to their vehicle) and the percent of oil life remaining.

We reviewed that version with the OnStar board, together with a recommendation that we test pricing it as a separate feature at between $2.95 and $4.95 per month. We said the alternative was to just include it as part of the base OnStar package and use it to add more value to our subscription. Depending on which research you believed, the predicted customer penetration rates of the priced version could be as high as 25 to 40 percent, so this wasn't a trivial decision. Rick liked the idea of the diagnostic email and also liked the creative approach that we'd finally settled on. He said this seemed like something that should be a part of OnStar, and rather than fight to get more money for it, he suggested getting it out there to see how people would react to it. If we decided later that there were parts of it that made sense to price separately, fine, but at that point, it was a matter of getting it into the hands of as many subscribers as possible. Excellent—that orientation was just right. And if it was included in OnStar's base package, it could be yet another unique and customer-valued feature GM could claim for their vehicles. And, who knows, at some point maybe they'd actually start to use some of them.

So we launched the service and tried to stay out of harm's way with the internal GM organizations and dealers that still weren't all that happy with what we were doing. Then, about two months later, the strangest thing happened. Tony and I were at a dealer meeting in Philadelphia and were being predictably chewed on by a guy with an attitude about the emails when a dealer interrupted him and said she thought he was all wrong. She said her service manager had just told her that he'd seen a couple customers coming into the shop with print-outs of their OnStar Vehicle Diagnostic email, saying that their car had told them it needed some work done. She said her service manager had been blown away and that if we could get more people reading and reacting to their emails, it could be really good for everyone.

Tony sensed an opportunity to reshape this debate and came up with an idea to include the selling dealer's name and contact information on the bottom of each email. It wasn't going to cross the line in terms of turning this into a screaming marketing tool, which would have been its death knell; you could honestly think of it as a service to the customer. The customer would still be in control of their information, but this would simplify their life when they needed to make a call to set up an appointment for a service visit. Talk about a game changer! With one fairly easy change to our email template and no additional cost to anyone, the dealer just inherited twelve monthly touches with their customer a year. Brilliant! And, better yet, it really worked to change the dynamic from "Leave our customers alone" to "How can we get more people enrolled in this?"

As time went on, this service platform just kept getting more interesting and more fun. This was one of my favorite service lines to personally mess with, and I'm sure my incessant "coaching" drove everyone nuts. We decided to add a category for open recall campaigns, meaning if you missed the postcard that GM sent informing you that your vehicle was involved in a recall, our OVD email would help you remember to get the work done. We'd pop a red message on your monthly OVD email as a reminder until you got it taken care of, and then it would go away automatically the month following the repair. Subscribers loved that, as did NHTSA, because it really helped accelerate important repairs to the affected vehicles. We also added tire pressure monitoring where the underlying sensors were built into the vehicle. It was no longer necessary to get out in the mud or the snow and fumble around with the "silver stick," which most people didn't do anyway. We'd tell you which tire needed air, and we'd explain to you that if you filled them up properly, you'd be driving a safer-handling car that would get better gas mileage. We also considered adding more diagnostic categories, but which ones would make sense?

One of the potential additions we considered was the vehicle's emissions system. Customers were becoming increasingly interested in environmental issues, and many wanted to make sure that their car was leaving as small a carbon footprint as possible. There were actually over twenty states that required cars to undergo periodic emissions testing and certification, usually on an annual basis. How perfect would it be if OnStar could do that for them, eliminating the hassle of taking it in for a physical test? We couldn't do a tailpipe sniff, but we could read all of the diagnostic codes that would tell if the emissions were within spec. Unfortunately, after a little more research, we determined that the state regulations were all so different and were set up to deal with all makes of vehicles that getting an exception for OnStar vehicles wouldn't be possible for years. So if we tackled emissions, it might leave us in the awkward position of having to explain why we couldn't meet the state testing requirements, and an otherwise good idea would end up sounding really lame.

Whenever we'd get in front of media folks, they'd always ask one predictable question: "What are you going to do next?" In a way, it was a compliment because it generally meant they thought we were a highly innovative company. But it was also frustrating because most of the reporters who were asking about the future had very little idea about what we were already doing. So if you answered them literally, their audience would only hear about things we might do *someday*, and they'd miss the more important information about what we already had available *today*.

Anyway, on one particular day, our head of PR, Jocelyn Allen, had arranged a radio interview with a small station outside of Atlanta. Jocelyn was a terrific PR executive, had great instincts, a lot of creativity, and had brought her heart with her to the business. We had an agreement that she would "spread the wealth" of media encounters by developing as many qualified OnStar spokespeople as possible. I understood that many times it would have to be me, but it certainly didn't *always* have to be me. So we'd settled into a cadence where I'd do about 30 percent of the interviews, and other members of the OnStar team would do the rest. You could tell that meant a lot to the folks involved, not because they had oversized egos, but they were just so proud to have a chance to represent the business. I was a little surprised that Jocelyn had assigned this particular one to me, a call-in show on a five-thousand-watt station with a name that was something like "Joe's Garage," and on Saturday morning at 8 a.m. no less. But I'd learned over time that it would just be easier for everyone to shut up and do what Jocelyn said.

So I was sitting at my kitchen table in my pajamas with a cup of coffee in my hand when I called in to talk to "Joe." It's a live show with maybe fifty people listening, so not something that would cause a lot of stress. We talked for a couple of minutes about OnStar, some of the statistics about us responding to two thousand crashes per month, and a little bit about our OVD platform. Then he got to the question that I knew was coming: "What are you guys planning on doing next?" We'd just been talking about the emissions issue the week before, and I thought, "Why not try it out here? Nobody was listening anyway." So I said we'd been thinking about adding an emissions test to our OVD email service. Before I could complete the thought, Joe jumped in and said, "Great—we have an emissions test requirement here in Georgia." I thought, "Oh no, now I've stepped in it. When I tell him we can't run the test for him, he'll probably get irritated and think we're useless." But before I could start apologizing, he said, "You know, I always feel like I'm going to get ripped off when I get my vehicle tested, and if I had OnStar, I'd know ahead of time if I was OK or not. That would be fantastic." I got a big smile on my face (which he couldn't see over the phone) and told Joe he was right, and that was a big reason why we were thinking of doing it. Well, it was a big reason now that he'd told me it was a big reason. It made all the sense in the world. Joe had just invented a new service, or at least the reason for doing a new service.

We talked about Joe's insight at work the next week, and both Tony and Walt immediately got it and liked the framing. A couple of weeks later, I was doing another radio interview, this time on a much bigger station in Chicago. Thankfully, we finally got around to the "What's next?" question, and I said we were thinking about emissions testing, because "you know, you always feel like you're going to get ripped off when you have to get the state test, and we can help that from happening." The host said, "Yea, you're exactly right." No, technically Joe had been exactly right.

More happened with this platform, and I'm sure will continue to happen into the future. Unfortunately, while we were able to get internal alignment fairly early in this case, it didn't mean that everyone was happy. We were collecting email addresses for nearly 70 percent of new GM vehicle buyers, and our open rates for the OVD emails were off-the-charts high. Our subscribers really came to appreciate the value of the format and content and the fact that it wasn't full of extraneous, self-serving messages. They also seemed to trust our motives because we'd done what we said we would—give them control over their information. OVD was about peace of mind, not trying to sell them something.

But both of these newfound assets—getting a 70-percent email-capture rate from our new vehicle buyers and having people actually look forward to opening their OVD reports rather than treating them like spam—were just too tempting for the vehicle marketing guys not to mess with. Without OVD, email-capture rates for new vehicle buyers across the entire industry were single digits at best. There simply wasn't a compelling reason for a customer to give up their email to the manufacturers since they knew it would probably only get used to send them marketing materials that they didn't really want. OVD had dramatically changed that dynamic, and now it was time to move over and let the real professionals do their jobs.

There were many "suggestions" that came in from the vehicle guys, things that they were sure would improve the value-capture of this platform for GM. First, take the email address that we'd just collected and give it to everyone else in the food chain. Give it to the vehicle marketing divisions, the dealers, GMAC, anyone who might be able to use it to communicate with the customer. All of our subscriber feedback told us sharing their email address would be a problem, and we wouldn't get a high sign-up rate if we brokered them to others, especially dealers. So to eliminate that concern, we specifically committed that their email address wouldn't be shared outside of General Motors Corporation. That left room for some use by the vehicle marketing divisions if someone came up with a good, brand-consistent use case, but there was nothing specific in mind when we started.

But the world was increasingly adopting a wide range of eCommerce strategies, and GM was no different. They'd been fed the most recent agency jargon on CRM, or customer relationship management, and had deployed a wide array of tactics to reach out to prospective vehicle buyers when they thought they might be shopping for a new car. The triggers would be things like the number of years since their last purchase or a lease that was about to expire. Most of the communications involved physical mailings, a lot of times expensive pieces like multipage, multicolor brochures. But if they only had email addresses, then that would change everything. Costs would go way down, and the richness of the content could go way up. It was a win-win situation from their standpoint.

I was a little nervous about the negative reaction we might get from our OVD subscribers if their email addresses became overused by the company, but I honestly had no legitimate way to stand in the way of "progress." We'd already said no to giving email addresses to dealers without a separate customer opt-in, but technically, Cadillac was a part of GM Corporation and one with a lot more stature in the company than we had. And you'd have to assume that these guys would behave responsibly since they wouldn't want to spoil this amazing and unique enabler to their CRM strategy. If they used it thoughtfully, with a nuanced sensitivity to our customer's concerns, then this could turn into something really special.

We had enough other things on our plate that I'd lost track of this issue and was actually surprised a few months later when I received a personal email from Cadillac. I'd recently purchased a CTS, which

I absolutely loved, but hadn't remembered giving them my email address. Oh yea, they must have gotten it from OnStar because I'd signed up for OVD. Cool, I could experience Cadillac's new CRM strategy for myself, just like a real customer. If they'd checked their other databases, they would've known I was a first-time Caddy buyer. So for all they knew, I'd just left a BMW 5 Series for my new love, a CTS, and I was being welcomed into their family.

My first impression was that the email was hard to read. It had small print, and most of it had a black background. Somebody had sold these guys that black was cool and a key ingredient of their brand character. That meant everybody at Cadillac who wanted to be cool wore black shirts, and black was the ad nauseam color treatment for everything they did. But for their typical fifty-plus-year-old Cadillac owners (and that was kind), what they'd actually created was something that was nearly too cool to read. It bothered me for a second, until I fought through the blurry images only to wish I hadn't. The first sentence worked; it said thank you for your recent purchase of a CTS. Then, I think maybe in the same paragraph, it went on to try to sell me a new Escalade. *Say what?* Where did that come from? And it actually was using price as a call to action. So here I was, and for all they knew, someone really proud of joining the Cadillac family and someone who'd just bought their entry-level luxury car, and what was their message to me? Well, the CTS is OK, but if you really want to be cool, how about spending another $50,000, less a $2,000 rebate, for a blinged-out, blot-out-the-sun-sized 'Slade. This was insanity.

This wasn't CRM; this was ATM, or accelerated transaction management (which also fit with treating your customer like a cash machine). Unfortunately, it was another example of the vehicle guys not being able to help themselves. They were always thinking about how to get the customer to buy more or buy faster. This email hadn't been used to draw them closer to their customer in a wonderful and mutually beneficial "relationship." What this email made clear to me was the only relationship Cadillac was interested in was with my wallet and the sooner the better. I'm sure somebody had done the analytics, and the calculation confirmed this was a great idea. An email costs a couple of cents to send, and if they sent a hundred thousand, and only one person bit and ended up with a new Escalade, it would've been a "profitable" campaign. What they missed was the effect the message would predictably have on the other 99,999 "non-conversions." The cost wasn't fractions of cents; it was the absolute clarity of the message Cadillac was callously sending to its new buyers. It screamed that what Cadillac really wanted from the relationship was more of their money. Come on, this wasn't that hard to understand and get right, or maybe it was.

I hit the forward button and sent the email to Tony. It wasn't his fault; he couldn't control Cadillac. Tony knew better. He was a thoughtful, professional marketer; he got what brands were all about. But this, well, it was just another pathetic example of a short-term, opportunistic approach that was way more huckster than cool, even if it was done in black. They just couldn't help themselves, and at this point, there really wasn't anything we could do about it. Our concerns had been well founded, but it didn't matter. We were hopeful that we'd be able to keep this orientation from spinning completely out of control and blowing up OVD by turning it into a garish brochure rack like the ones in the hotel lobbies—buy this, come in for that, act now or you'll miss out, unless, of course, you wait for the better offer that will come next week. This principle was worth trying to defend the fort on, because decisions like these truly define what your brand stands for. OVD was an amazing platform, destined to be loved by subscribers and to accomplish great things, I only hoped we could keep it that way.

STOP THIEF – I REALLY MEAN IT!

Another service that went back to the early days of OnStar was automatic stolen vehicle assistance, which was an example of where we'd gotten a little ahead of ourselves; we'd sold this wine before its time.

Automatically sensing that a vehicle was stolen didn't turn out to be as easy as we'd thought, and that was confirmed by a small, but growing number of our own subscribers who we'd inadvertently helped audition for a *Cops* episode. No, our customers weren't "bad boys, bad boys," so we turned off the automatic part of the service and just concentrated on finding vehicles our customers knew had been stolen.

But even without it being automatic, locating stolen vehicles turned into a relatively high-volume and high-visibility part of OnStar. And, for once, we had something that was pretty easy to understand, thanks to a pre-existing frame of reference that LoJack had already brought to the market. It was great doing completely new stuff, and we had more of that coming out of our ears than you could imagine. It made for extremely unique marketing claims, but the flip side was that it was really hard to create awareness and comprehension for something people had never heard of before, no matter how compelling it looked. Every now and then it was nice to just add a "me too" claim for something people already understood.

There are over one million vehicles stolen in the United States annually, and for years, there'd been aftermarket companies that sold all kinds of car alarm systems. LoJack had taken the category to the next level, developing a product that specialized in recovering a stolen vehicle and doing it using a national brand strategy. Because of the nature of their service, which required local police cars to be specially equipped with their "locating technology," it wasn't really nationally available. But it had fairly broad national awareness, and more importantly, it had already established that using technology to locate a stolen vehicle was possible.

Once we figured out that our service needed to rely on our subscribers telling us their vehicle had been stolen, we set up a solid process and got down to business. The actual numbers of stolen vehicle location requests grew quickly over time, happening nearly seven hundred times a month. Our experience taught us how to do this better and better, and we also learned to listen carefully to the real professionals in this area—the police. In order to make sure we protected everyone's privacy, we required our subscribers to involve the police any time they thought their vehicle had been stolen. So they'd either call us first or they'd call the police, and we'd confirm that a stolen vehicle case had been opened. At that point, we'd try to locate the vehicle and relay the location to the police so they could handle the recovery. The alternative of trying to do it any other way had too many places where something could go wrong. We didn't want this turning into vigilante justice where an upset subscriber would try to get his or her own truck back, as that had the potential to end very badly. And worse yet, what if the vehicle hadn't been stolen at all, but party A just wanted to know where party B was at that moment, like maybe at a nearby motel? No, that wasn't what OnStar was all about and never would be. This was about stolen vehicles where we'd be working with the professionals, the police, and they'd handle it from there.

This eventually turned into a really interesting service domain, one with an amazingly rich range of stories that would often get picked up by the media. There were normal property crimes—bad guy takes car, and we help get it back. One time that happened to a subscriber who was picking up carryout ribs during halftime of a Super Bowl game, and we helped the police get the car back before the ribs got cold. There was another time when I got a letter from a subscriber who thanked us for recovering his Jaguar. All right, fun is fun, but didn't this guy know what kind of car he drove? We weren't available on Jaguar, but OK, thanks for thinking of us, I guess. I kept reading the letter and learned that he'd heard a noise in the middle of the night and saw someone driving off with his Jag. That was the bad news. The good news was they'd also stolen his OnStar-equipped Chevy Tahoe. Within a few hours, we'd located the Tahoe at a nearby chop shop, parked side by side with its little brother the Jag. I couldn't resist sending the subscriber back a note thanking him for telling us the story, including a brochure for Cadillac's two-seat sports car, the XLR. I said he couldn't always count on big brother

Tahoe being there to help out, and he probably needed a car that could take care of itself.

There were many more examples—like I said, seven hundred a month. There was a GM dealer in Florida who was kidnapped by an employee, duct-taped, and stuffed in the trunk of his (OnStar-equipped) car. We found the car and the dealer locked in a storage garage before anything really bad happened. We learned that most vehicle theft wasn't the work of professional thieves; it was committed by amateurs, and knuckleheads at that. We also found you had the highest chance of getting your vehicle stolen at a self-service gas station because, many times, you were distracted and left your keys in the car. And while "stupid" and "car thief" was a common combination, it wasn't a good one. Sadly, more times than you'd like to believe, the crook wasn't even smart enough to notice the baby seat in the backseat of the car. So it wasn't about recovering the family minivan; it was about recovering Emily, who'd been inadvertently abducted as part of the crime.

I once received a VHS tape from an assistant county prosecutor from somewhere in Mississippi, along with a note that said, "Thanks for the help, I thought your team might enjoy seeing this." It was a local TV segment on a stolen vehicle case that we'd been involved in, and the story was priceless. It seems this genius stole an OnStar-equipped vehicle, which we helped the police recover a couple of hours later. But, wanting more than just the car, they staked it out, and what do you know, the crook came back. When they grabbed him, he said he hadn't done anything and was just an innocent bystander. The best part was that the real owner had left a duffel bag in the backseat with a change of clothes because he'd planned to go to the gym. The perp had looked in the bag and liked what he saw so much that he'd ditched his own clothes and was wearing the shirt and pants of our subscriber. The story ended with a cutaway shot of the thief (handcuffed and in an orange prison jumpsuit) walking in front of the local courthouse, shaking his head, and saying, "OnStar...don't mess with OnStar." That tape got played to roaring laughter applause at more dealer meetings than you can possibly imagine.

So sometimes it was funny, but most times it wasn't. There was a case in Florida where a woman in her mid-twenties was abducted at gunpoint as she was getting money out of an ATM. She'd been on her portable cell phone talking to her mom at the time it happened, and all her mom heard was, "Don't hurt me! Don't hurt me! Mama, help!" No parent could possibly imagine what that would feel like, but thankfully, her mom quickly called 911 and told them what had happened. We later got a copy of that 911 call, and the mom and the 911 operator were amazing. The mom described the situation, and the 911 operator kept asking questions to get more and more details. The mom's emotional state varied from calm to hysterical, but she hung in there. Finally, the operator asked what kind of car her daughter was driving, and the mom said it was Cadillac CTS. The operator asked if it had OnStar, which the mom, in her distressed state, hadn't even thought to mention. She confirmed that it had OnStar, but she wasn't sure if her daughter knew how to use it. The 911 operator just said, "That's OK, we know how to use it." This was one time where high brand awareness didn't sell a car—it saved a life.

The operator contacted us and explained the situation, and we were able to connect to the CTS and track its location. It was still moving and crossing through different Florida police jurisdictions. The event eventually turned into a brief chase, but the car was eventually pulled over, and the situation ended happily. Through most of the pursuit, our subscriber was being held at gunpoint, stuffed under a blanket in the backseat. Our brand had the last laugh again—this time because a wonderfully committed 911 operator knew enough to ask the question, "Does it have OnStar?" We actually flew the operator to Michigan to receive an award we specifically created to recognize her amazing contribution to such a wonderful outcome. We did it at one of our monthly all-employee meetings, and the pride and enthusiasm of our team could have filled up the University of Michigan's football stadium.

With so much going on in this category, the natural question was, "What should we be doing next?" From the very earliest days, we'd always get some reporter trying to be cute by suggesting that when we had a crook in the car, we should lock the doors, turn up the heat, and play obnoxious music as loud as we could—it would be our version of pretrial punishment. Why not, we had the technology to control the car, right? Well, maybe not exactly control it that way, but perhaps something close...

The one million stolen vehicles a year statistic had many corollaries, one of which was that those thefts caused thirty thousand high-speed chases every year, along with thousands of crashes. People, many times innocent bystanders, would get hurt in those crashes 25 percent of the time. And the bottommost of bottom lines was three hundred people were being killed annually. What if we could somehow stop high-speed chases, at least in our vehicles, wouldn't that be a great next step for OnStar to take?

This wasn't a completely new idea. We'd actually kicked it around in our earliest brainstorming sessions, but it seemed a little farfetched and had way too many moving parts to deal with when we were still figuring out the basic OnStar stuff. It also hadn't helped that we'd already had to back off the "automatic" part of theft recovery, so we'd parked the idea in the "look at it later" pile. But now it was later, and our experience had taught us was that this could be really important, so it was time to revisit the concept.

The lawyers really didn't like this idea at all, and you could honestly see why. What if we tried to slow down or stop a vehicle—a vehicle that we couldn't see, one that was likely a thousand miles away from our advisor—and something went wrong? Sure, our motives would have been honorable, but wouldn't we still be liable for the consequences that we might cause? The car full of nuns being stopped on a railroad crossing scenario was raising its head again. It would probably be better to just leave this alone; we were helping enough already.

But we weren't, really. I mean, we were doing more stolen vehicle tracking and recovering than anyone else in the world, but we could probably do more, or it was at least tempting to see if we could. By this time, Joanne Finnorn had replaced Ken Enborg as OnStar's chief legal counsel, and she had a few reservations. There was no problem with having reservations; that was only reasonable. The only lawyer I knew who might not have had any reservations was Rambo, I mean Ken, himself. But we'd run out of ex-Marines on our legal team, and now the standards had changed a little bit. Joanne was actually terrific in her role as our head lawyer; she was intelligent, mature, and extremely talented; had carried on the best of the Ken-era traditions; and added a few wonderful new ones of her own. She was deep into the details of our business, but more importantly, she'd really bought into OnStar's mission. She didn't see her role as "protecting GM from OnStar," but rather, she saw it as helping OnStar to be the best OnStar we could be.

Nobody ever wanted to do anything stupid, but stupid wasn't always that easy to define. Sometimes it might be stupid to do something, and sometimes it might be stupid not to do something. And many times it was particularly hard to figure out because most of what we were thinking of doing had never been done before. You really needed someone special in Joanne's role to help the company think through some very complex and ambiguous issues. Joanne certainly qualified as special, and she just needed some time to think this one through. After a lot of discussions and a fair amount of healthy debate, we came around to believing that this was something we should pursue, but there were a lot of "ifs" involved—if we had confidence in the technology, if we could invent a process that ensured we did it right, if we had the buy-in and support of law enforcement, and if our customers thought it was a good idea. OK, fair enough, this was a serious issue worthy of serious thought. So it was time to get to work on the "ifs."

Law enforcement really loved the idea. They hated high-speed chases and their sometimes bad outcomes more than anybody. So they were in, and better yet, they helped us invent the process that would make sure we'd do it right. Before we'd try to slow a vehicle down, it would have to be under visual surveillance by a police officer and then they'd make the judgment on whether it could be slowed safely. We'd also send a message to flash the lights of the car for a final confirmation by the officers on the scene before we'd send the slow-down command to the engine. OK, two "if" boxes checked.

Tony and his guys went out to do the research on the customer perception of vehicle slowdown, and we honestly weren't sure how it would come out. It sure seemed to me that people would like this capability, but there were some folks in the company who were concerned that using OnStar to slow a vehicle down might concern customers and was maybe a little too intrusive. Well, no sense guessing, there was a way to figure that out—go ask subscribers. The research was fascinating, with the service receiving a favorable rating of well over 90 percent. It was even better than that; the response wasn't just objectively favorable, it was emotionally favorable. And we'd also picked up something in the research that really helped us talk about vehicle slowdown in a way that made sense to everyone. Not only did people hate the fact that their car had been stolen, they took it personally, and they got angry. They'd been violated and offended. The bad guys were really bad people. They also really didn't like the fact that other people were getting hurt because bad guys trying to get away were starting high-speed chases. When you pieced it all together, it sounded like, "I've already been offended by this idiot stealing my car, and I don't want that made any worse by my car becoming the object of harm to some innocent person—so go get the moron!"

Wow, listening to customers was amazing. Their framing was perfect, and not just because it supported us doing what we wanted to, but because it was so genuine, so human, and so right. Check the customer box. Now the only thing we had left to do was figure out the technology. Walt, you're on.

Once again, Walt and his team rolled up their collective sleeves, put their heads together with a really great group of engineers from

GM's power train organization, and commenced their scheming. As usual, nothing currently in production had been designed to meet this exact need. But how exact did it have to be? We needed something to take the horsepower away from the crook, and it just so happened the engineers found existing software in some GM vehicles' power train controllers that was designed to do just that. It wasn't put there for stopping crooks; it was there to depower the vehicle if its diagnostic system sensed an eminent engine failure and wanted to keep something catastrophic from happening under the hood. The power train guys thought there might be a way for OnStar to trigger that code to activate, not because a piston was about to fly out, but because some bad guy had control of the pistons. When the engine depowered, it dropped to idle speed, which produced more than enough energy to keep the power steering and power brakes fully operational. This sounded so cool and so MacGyver-OnStar-like, but it required serious analysis and validation before we did anything with it, as there was no room for error.

A few weeks later, Walt came up to my office and said he wanted to take me for a ride. That usually meant show-and-tell, so I got pretty excited. We went down to the lab, and he told me to get behind the wheel. It was a Chevy Tahoe that had been turned into a stolen vehicle slowdown test bed. Walt sat in the passenger seat, and Dan McGarry, a great guy and one of Walt's terrific engineers, sat in the backseat with a computer on his lap. Off we went, with Dan giving me directions on where to turn until we were about to get on a section of a divided highway. Dan said the highway was intermittently under construction throughout the day and that he'd found it virtually deserted in the early afternoon because most people had found alternate routes to avoid the orange barrels. But it was open then and was about to become my "escape route" for the Tahoe that I'd apparently just stolen.

We got up to 50 mph, and Dan was right, this road was completely deserted. At some point, he clicked a couple keys on his laptop and said, "Initiating slowdown routine." A few seconds later, my outside hazard flashers had mysteriously come on, the gas pedal had no response, and a calm, prerecorded woman's voice was playing over the car's stereo speakers. She said, "This vehicle is being slowed at the request of law enforcement. Please pull safely to the side of the road and stop. The police will be with you shortly." I almost peed my pants I was laughing so hard. If I didn't use the brakes to stop, the truck was just going to coast to a stop by itself. The steering worked like normal, but you could pump the gas all you wanted, and it wasn't going to do anything. This was amazing. I asked Walt who the wise guy was who thought of the recording, but he wouldn't give them up. And, besides, it honestly wasn't meant to be funny, it's just what they thought would probably need to be played. I told you these guys were *junior* marketing experts. This was an incredible demonstration and had successfully checked lucky box number four; we'd just invented a new service.

As you might expect, with something as complicated and sensitive as this, there was a lot of real work between the demo and early law enforcement discussions and being ready for production. But everyone that came to work on this project had the same feeling—what a perfect thing for OnStar to be doing, and what a great thing for GM vehicles to bring to society. And from our PR chief Jocelyn's perspective, what a perfect piece of eye candy it was to show the world. This was going to be fun.

When it got a little more fully baked, we did a bunch of demos with select folks from inside and outside of the company. We "apprehended" Rick Wagoner, Bob Lutz, Gary Cowger, multiple members of GM's board of directors, and various other luminaries. We got law enforcement, emergency response folks, suppliers, foreign visitors, and anyone who we could think of involved, and they got their turn at being an unsuccessful car thief. This all led up to our real press event, which Jocelyn scheduled in the parking lot of RFK Stadium in Washington, DC. Joining us for the announcement were representatives from the firefighters, the Fraternal Order of Police, the general manager of Chevrolet, and John Walsh of America's Most Wanted fame. As the pre-remarks video was running, I looked at the guys sitting next to me on stage, a policeman, a fireman, and a TV star, and it occurred to me that I was living every eight-year-old boy's dream. I was absolutely sure that this was going to be our most fun press event ever.

The presentation went well, and before we turned the journalists loose to go get "caught" in the parking lot, we had a Q&A session. Afterward, a reporter from a prominent East Coast newspaper came up and asked, "Where'd you get this from?" I thought he was asking about our research insights, so I answered that way. He said, "No, who actually *did* this?" I was still a little dense and could tell that I was missing something. Finally, when he asked it again, it sunk in that he was inferring that GM couldn't have done this on its own. By his preconceived notion, we were supposed to be the lame guys, the gang who couldn't shoot straight. So who had we copied this from? Jocelyn was standing nearby, and she sensed that when his point finally got through my thick skull, I'd likely lose my composure. She was right.

I stared directly into his eyes and told him this service came from the only place it could have come from, the only people in the world who had any experience in this amazing new category—us—and that it had been developed and refined by the only technical professionals in the world who had a clue about anything as sophisticated as this, Michigan-born-and-bred GM engineers. Boy, it felt good saying that, and Jocelyn had only winced a little, so maybe I hadn't completely screwed it up. The reporter shrugged, walked away, and went out and took a demo. I don't think he wrote anything about the announcement—what a surprise. That attitude was so typical of the orientation that many members of the media had about the domestic auto manufacturers. Their personal favorites for automotive "masters of the universe" might have been Asian or European, but under no circumstances could they be from America. It just didn't fit the easy narrative.

The results of the press event were astounding. Over five hundred million media impressions in the first month, and Jocelyn explained to me that this was an "evergreen" story, which meant it would probably go on for a while longer. We saw clips show up in Europe, Asia, and South America. The story was interesting and struck most people as a pretty good use of technology and something that made sense for a company like OnStar to be doing. They were right. There'd be more stories written about this service in the future about events that hadn't even happened yet, but you could be sure someday they would. That was the one thing about OnStar that you could always count on; once we put something in motion, it was going to have an impact. We'd seen it happen too many times before to doubt the power of OnStar's people and its technology to make a real difference in peoples' lives. And if we kept doing it the right way, listening and learning as we went, it sure felt like there was a lot more of that to come.

CHAPTER 14

Take a Left and Go 8,000 Miles

In the early days of OnStar, our definition of its geographic bound-aries started and stopped in the United States—but not just the lower forty-eight, all fifty, which meant we deserved at least some credit for thinking big. Actually, there was really never any doubt that we'd also end up in Canada. Even though the laws were different and the French language requirements in Quebec were an interesting com-plication, we knew we'd have to figure it out. But venturing beyond those boundaries seemed a little beyond our reach—at least at the beginning.

But sooner than I would've expected and before we had it all fig-ured out at home, there were the beginnings of "pull signals" from other parts of GM's far-flung empire. They weren't always clear or consistent, but there were enough periodic disturbances in the force that you knew the issue was churning somewhere. Unfortunately, back then, we had enough on our plates trying to figure out Georgia, Colorado, and Iowa that we really weren't that excited about being teleported to another continent.

And speaking of other continents, we'd actually already finessed a way to shrink our definition of GM's North American region to mean the United States and Canada. Wasn't Mexico supposed to be included in that, too? Well, not when you got into the details of On-Star, which always seemed to need an asterisk to be able to explain. You see, we needed to understand the rules of the road that applied to "going global" for our little business, but like everything else, they hadn't been written yet. So we had to figure those out, and quickly, or run the risk of having the ill-suited auto industry's rules imposed on us.

While it's common to have the auto business described as being global, in many ways it's really more like a series of country markets, or at best, trading blocs, stitched together to look like a globe. Countries had their own laws that regulated almost every aspect of the vehicle business, from safety standards to emissions limits to how much local content was required to avoid otherwise onerous taxes and tariffs. There were also other important market differences, practical things like the size of roads and garages and the fact that gas cost $7 a gallon in places like Belgium. No, you typically couldn't sell the exact same car in the United States that you could in France, or Japan, or Australia, or Chile. Honestly, at one point, you couldn't even sell the same car in California that you sold in Kentucky unless you built the car for Kentucky to California's separate and more stringent emissions standards, which everybody just did.

So global in the auto industry had its unique issues, and we were just beginning to appreciate that aspiring to be global in our emerging little industry was going to have a few of its own. To begin with, you needed to understand what was necessary to make OnStar work in the first place. Once you had your arms around that, you needed to do an evaluation on a country-by-country basis to see if all of those conditions were present in the market that you were targeting. The details were actually a lot more complicated than that, but applying that basic logic and using it to sort the candidates into "more likely" and "less likely" piles was a good start.

The template was pretty straight forward and consisted of four elements. First, was there enough customer interest and willingness to pay for the safety and peace of mind services that we had experience delivering to cover our expected costs and leave room for a reasonable profit? Pretty basic stuff, but you'd be amazed how often we'd get drug off into the weeds by well-intended folks who thought that changing our service definition shouldn't make any difference in the analysis. Wasn't it almost the same thing to have the focus of the business be on finding vacant parking spots or dynamically rerouting you around traffic jams instead of safety and security? I guess so, if an Escalade was the same thing as a helicopter. They both moved people and things from point A to point B, right? It wasn't that parking and traffic weren't interesting, they just weren't anything we had any particular expertise delivering. Could we develop it? Sure, but that wasn't the same thing as leveraging what we'd already developed for the United Sates to take to other markets. It was starting something new. For this analysis, the objective was should we take OnStar to another part of the world? And if we determined that peace of mind wasn't as highly valued as parking or traffic, then there'd need to be a different analysis involving another group of people.

The second condition for evaluating a potential market was whether their cellular network was up for the adventure. That meant that there needed to be enough towers in place to provide broad geographic coverage and that the cellular companies would be willing to sell us access to that network on terms that wouldn't blow up our business model. Third, there'd need to be an accurate, comprehensive, geocoded database of the country's road network, which included a broad range of points of interest like hospitals, airports, and hotels—information down to the street address level. Finally, there needed to be an underlying emergency response network (police, fire, ambulance, etc.) that was reliable, trustworthy, and willing to allow a commercial company like OnStar to request help on behalf of its customers. If you had all four of these conditions—market interest, broad cell network, accurate digital database, and trusted 911 assets—then you'd have the underlying prerequisites you needed to start. Having them didn't guarantee success, but our experience said that trying to do something without them meant you'd be asking for serious trouble.

Mexico was a conundrum. If you researched prospective customers, OnStar's focus on safety and security services resonated very well, scoring even higher than in the United States. There was a reasonably well-established cellular network in Mexico, not as robust in rural areas as we had back home, but it could potentially work. The availability of digital map information was a little sketchier. It wasn't that there weren't companies claiming to have good data, but we knew that claiming to have it and having it were two different things. We'd learned that lesson in the United States when everybody said they had great data, and we ended up having to piece together elements of every supplier's information to create our own hybrid database before we were satisfied that it was good enough. If we were really going to get serious about bringing OnStar to Mexico, verifying that their map data met our quality threshold would be critical.

OK, customer interest, yes. Cellular coverage might work. Digital data would need to be confirmed. Now we're down to number four—a 911 infrastructure. We'd been spoiled by the incredible 911 capabilities that exist in the United States and Canada. That infrastructure, as fragmented and self-organizing as it was, was really a national treasure for both countries. People inherently trusted it as an institution and generally held the public responders in very high regard. They were the cavalry or the Mounties (literally). Did we ever have to explain to someone why it was a good thing to get the 911 folks involved in the case of an emergency or theft? Absolutely not, that frame of reference was already well established.

Unfortunately, we didn't get that same sense out of our research in Mexico. If OnStar's promise in Mexico was to connect you with the local 911 responders if something bad happened to you, then that wasn't highly valued, actually maybe the opposite. If, on the other hand, we had our own private security and response force, then that would be very interesting. But starting a militia wasn't anything OnStar was equipped to take on, and since we didn't see our mission extending in that direction anytime soon, we decided to defer anything in Mexico to a later time.

But we did look seriously at Western Europe, and when we did the analysis, it came back very positive. We'd need to develop a different kind of OnStar box to run on Europe's GSM cellular networks, but that was straightforward development work. It wasn't trivial, but it wasn't a showstopper. The main decider of whether we'd do something in Europe was going to be GM's regional president in that area, because even though we had experience in North America, there'd still be a number of very tough vehicle-related issues to manage in Europe. Late engineering and manufacturing releases were just the beginning. The European marketing guys would have to add price to their vehicles, and the dealers would have to "accept" that OnStar would have a role with their customers. We'd handled all of that at home, not easily and not without pain, and it had taken every bit of high-cover that we could muster from Harry and Rick to make it happen. So unless the top people in Europe were willing to be personally involved and provide that same kind of support, a European program would never get off the ground.

At this point, I would characterize the interest in Europe as lukewarm at best. Back then, GM didn't enjoy the same 30 percent share in Europe that it did in the United States; it was closer to 10 percent and falling. And they mainly sold small and midsized Opels (or Vauxhauls in the UK), which were more akin to Chevys than Cadillacs, or even Buicks. So they had lower volume in lower margin segments, which meant they were challenged to generate consistent returns. When they thought about OnStar, it sounded interesting, but not interesting enough to turn into a major distraction, so they decided to put a "toe in the water" and see where it went from there.

That led to the creation of a small organization, and for brand synergy's sake (and internal politics), they decided to call it OnStar Europe. Coincidentally, the president of GM Europe had just moved into that role, after having been the general manager of Delco Electronics, the group that was supplying the OnStar module for North America. As a result, he was confident he understood this space as well as anyone and decided to run the initiative on his own without officially involving us in any meaningful way. The person he appointed to run OnStar Europe was a former purchasing executive who had no experience with the technology or running a business—sound familiar? Anyway, we were supposed to "coordinate" with them, basically providing whatever support they needed if and when they *asked* for it. This was such a predictably bad big company move; create the illusion of alignment without any real mechanism to ensure that it happened. So we were to be on call, but we were busy enough that it almost felt like a blessing. And, besides, they really believed they had it under control, and the politics of trying to change their minds on that had no upside. Give us a call sometime.

We'd periodically run into the OnStar Europe guys or hear something rumbling through the vehicle engineers, but never got a request to come help. At Rick Wagoner's urging, we loaned them a really good guy, Bill Madalin, but they treated him like a double agent and kept him out of most of their real deliberations. It was clear that they liked their freedom and didn't think they needed anybody looking over their shoulder. Months went by, and at some point, the whole thing just went dark. Out of sight, out of mind probably wasn't the most effective approach, but we got comfortable with it and honestly didn't give it much more thought. That was until I was over in Europe meeting a couple of the other OEM's at an auto show, and on the way home, I somehow got invited to attend a meeting where OnStar Europe was updating the vehicle guys on their status. Hey, why not, I was already over there, and it probably wasn't a bad idea to reconnect in case somebody like Rick asked how things were going—they were still using our name after all.

I sat in the back of the conference room while the former purchasing guy made the presentation. This meeting wasn't for me; I was just an uninvolved bystander (er...I mean corporate synergy partner). By about the third slide, I couldn't believe what I was seeing. No wonder things had gone quiet; it was because this guy and his team had decided to completely abandon the mission I assumed they were on and had replaced it with something entirely different. Apparently, they'd come to the conclusion that putting stuff in cars was hard (no kidding), so they'd recast their objective as selling "connectivity." Wait, it gets stupider. Instead of at least somehow relating connectivity to vehicles like Wingcast was trying to do, their plan was to sell wireless Internet connectivity in *hotel lobbies*.

This might have actually been funny, except for two things. First, they were still calling themselves OnStar. Second, nobody else in the room was laughing. Remember, these were car guys, and this was around the time of the dot-com silliness. They were actually relieved that the OnStar initiative wasn't going to be messing with their vehicles and thought that selling connectivity sounded good to them. But didn't they see that it made absolutely no sense for somebody like GM to be involved with this? What did we bring to this party? What were our assets, our experience, and our leverageable resources? And even if we had any, which we didn't, at least explain the nature of the market and the underlying characteristics of the demand. I couldn't help myself, so I asked a couple pointed questions, got a few dirty looks and dismissive answers, and the meeting was over.

Flying home from London, I really didn't know what I should do. On the one hand, the guys in GM Europe were big boys who were supposed to know what they were doing, and we'd been explicitly uninvited from having an official seat at the table. There was a formal business review process in place; in fact, I'd just witnessed it, setting aside how superficial and bizarre it'd all seemed. Besides, who said I was the smartest person in the room? I had my reservations about what I'd seen, but I was someone without a vote. If I somehow inserted myself into this, who knew what kind of backlash that would cause.

But, on the other hand, they were using our brand in a way that wouldn't have made sense to a college freshman. If they'd been selling something that tasted like Sam Adams to customers in the United States under the Heineken brand, it would have been technically inappropriate, but not completely outrageous. But this was like selling StarKist tuna and calling it Jif peanut butter. Yikes, especially if you'd already put it on a sandwich with jelly. If they actually followed through on this strategy and the company ever sobered up and decided to bring the *real* OnStar to Europe, the brand would've been confusing and stood for nothing. So, when I got back, I registered my concerns about the brand inconsistency issue with Ron Zarrella and left it at that.

At some point, they'd spent serious enough money, like many millions of dollars, that they started to attract the attention of GM's financial oversight process. Maybe it hadn't kicked in early, but when the finance guys got on to something, they generally ran it to ground, and this was going to be no exception. How it had escaped up to this point was something I never spent much time worrying about, but it did end the right way, aside from needlessly burning through too much cash. The initiative got shut down, leased equipment for data and call centers got written off, supply contracts got unwound, and it was like it had never happened. That is, except for one thing. The smoking crater unfortunately had a name, OnStar Europe, and that name immediately became synonymous with "never again."

So now here we are. We've taken Mexico off of our to-do list, and the toxic half-life on the crater in Europe meant it'd be years before we could revisit that region again, so what was left? There were 911 issues in many other places in the world beyond Mexico, so that took out a big chunk. We'd talked to the GM Holden guys in Australia, and aside from the fact that half of my team volunteered for the hardship of living "down under," the market was small, and the Holden guys weren't that interested anyway. In terms of volume, we were down to a fragmented list of small countries, which when evaluated on an effort-per-potential-subscriber basis looked highly dubious. But there was one more place, but what a left turn that would be for our business.

That one remaining place was China. China had quickly become a very large vehicle market, and the bets that GM had made years before had positioned our joint-venture company, Shanghai GM, as a major player in the country. Apparently, back in the day, the emperor's car of choice had been a Buick when they had enough chrome on them to look like a blinged-out dragon. So when GM reentered China, Buick was a central component of its strategy, and Buick's residual brand cachet was turning out to be a valuable asset. With the government's encouragement, the market couldn't help but grow, and the partner we'd chosen for our joint venture, SAIC, was both well connected and highly capable. This had all the makings of a long and successful association.

We'd talked to a few folks about the potential for OnStar in China, and they were cordial and somewhat interested, but had their own problems to worry about. Their problems weren't the ones we had in the United States and Europe, like how to deal with over capacity and mature markets; they were just the opposite. Their problems were in trying to keep up with a market that wanted to run faster than they could, which meant you could grow your annual sales by double digits and still lose market share if you weren't careful. We understood growth issues, albeit at a much lower scale, and while they're more fun to deal with than shrinking, they could be just as difficult. So we respectfully decided not to try to push anything in China and to wait until they thought the timing might be right.

Just when you thought it was safe to go back in the water, the music from *Jaws* starts playing in your head. We got a call that the mayor of Shanghai was visiting Detroit for a meeting with Rick Wagoner, and because there was some downtime in his schedule, they wanted us to give him a tour of the OnStar Command Center. This had happened a few times before when important visitors were at the Ren Cen and had time to kill; we became the filler. Hey, no problem at all. In some ways, it was flattering to be used as an example of what GM was up to. We were proud of the command center and so confident of its predictably positive impact on guests that it was actually fun.

In China, the mayor of a city like Shanghai is powerful beyond any normal frame of reference. He was one of the country's top decision-makers and had incredible influence across his home province. Since GM's joint venture bore the name *Shanghai* GM he was someone who was very important to GM's future strategy in China. The official reason for the visit was to announce the establishment of a new proving grounds facility for SGM in China and an investment involving engines. While this trip had nothing to do with us, other than the last-minute tour, I was also invited to attend the official ceremonial dinner that was scheduled to mark the end of the mayor's visit.

The mayor arrived complete with an appropriate Chinese government entourage. We spent about forty-five minutes giving him an overview using charts that we'd translated into Chinese and then showed him the working command center itself. He seemed interested, but in meetings like these, you could just never tell. The awkwardness of communicating through a translator and the fact that they had been in nonstop, back-to-back meetings twelve time zones away from home meant that it was extremely hard to sense any real energy in the room. But the mayor did seem very interested in our emergency services and particularly our capabilities in crash response. China knew that their explosive vehicle growth meant that they were cramming the equivalent of fifty years worth of U.S. auto industry evolution into the span of about a decade, and vehicle safety statistics had predictably been under stress. As a result, technologies that had anything to do with safety were important to them. Anyway, the tour ended, everyone said good-bye, and I forgot about it until a couple of days later, when it was time to go to the farewell dinner.

Whenever you had official meetings with the Chinese, the custom was to have a banquet to recognize the occasion. When you're in China, it's done in a very elaborate and predictable way. When you're in the United States, it's like most business dinners, except it's typically much larger and involves far more formal toasting. This dinner was scheduled at GM's Heritage Center, a large warehouse-like building where GM had over a hundred historically important vehicles on display. Tables had been set up in the center surrounded by the cars, and it looked like they were expecting about seventy-five people, or ten tables worth. Everyone had precisely assigned seats, and looking at the chart, I found my way to table 10—the kiddy table. No problem with that, I wasn't even sure why I was invited in the first place, other than to fill the audience. So I settled in next to some other relatively low-level folks and knew that in about two and a half hours I'd be heading home.

Everything went as expected—toasts to the GM relationship, to the mayor, to the new proving grounds, to engines, and maybe transmissions, too. I don't remember. At the end, the mayor got up to make a few closing remarks. He said how important the relationship between China and GM was and how much he looked forward to all we'd be doing together in the future, like building new plants, designing new cars, yada, yada, yada. Then, out of the clear blue, he looked out at the audience and saw me at table 10 and said, "and bringing OnStar to China." I about choked on my cheesecake. Everybody turned around and looked toward the back of the room, smiled nervously, and then applauded the mayor's speech. Where had that come from? Did he mean it? Now what?

The final gesture of respect at the end of an event usually involves the hosts standing by the curb waving to the guests as they drive away in their car, or in this case, their bus. The GM guys gathered in a group, waited for everyone to board, and began waving as it pulled away. With his hand still in the air, Rick looked at me and said, "What did you guys do to the mayor on your tour?" I said I didn't know, but I was sure we were about to find out.

A short time later, we heard from the GM folks in Shanghai that they wanted us to begin an evaluation of bringing OnStar to China. Never in a million years would I have predicted that prior to the mayor's visit, but those kinds of things seemed to happen to us a lot. Anyway, we put together a team, and I asked Jon Hyde, our original CFO, to run the evaluation. Jon had already moved on from the finance job and was now in charge of our enterprise program management activities. In that role, he'd become very familiar with how all of the elements of the business needed to sync together for any new initiative we were launching. If this study turned into a real launch, that experience would make Jon a perfect candidate to run OnStar's first offshore venture.

Jon pulled out our four-part checklist and dug into the details. While market research in China wasn't as mature as it was in the United States, we were able to get a basic read on consumer's interest levels and willingness to pay for the services, and it looked pretty encouraging. But that was by far the most straightforward piece of the puzzle—now on to the next three.

Was there cellular coverage in China? The answer was a big yes; there were somewhere in the neighborhood of three hundred million cellular subscribers in China at that point. But it was a little funky because, in one way or another, the wireless carriers were all state-owned companies. And the only one who used the CDMA technology we were already familiar with, China Unicom, was the smallest player in the country. So if, for any reason, they didn't want to do business with us or decided to charge us an arm and a leg to use their network, then our business model wouldn't work. Thankfully, a couple of our U.S. partners, Qualcomm and Verizon Wireless, had relationships with Unicom because of their connection with CDMA technology, and Qualcomm's CEO, Paul Jacobs, and Verizon's chief technology officer, Dick Lynch, offered to help us make a high-level contact. Paul and Dick were really good guys, and both had become good friends of OnStar. As it turned out, Dick knew the Unicom CEO, so he sent him a letter on our behalf, and the next thing I knew, I was sitting in his office in Beijing. In China, it's all about having the top people support your project, because if they don't, nothing will ever happen. Dick had really helped get this off on the right foot, but that still didn't mean the negotiations weren't epically "Fred-like" in their drama. But Jon and his team hunkered down, put in an incredible amount of time and effort, and were eventually able to land the relationship in the right place.

Solving issue number three, getting accurate digital maps of China, is literally illegal. The information is considered extremely sensitive and is no kidding illegal for a commercial firm to possess in its raw form. And it's double-illegal, whatever that means, to take that data out of the country. So what is that supposed to mean? Well, it's bad if the government doesn't like what you're planning on doing with it, but if they support your project, there's a weird process that you can use to make something work. You actually have to thread a government-approved third party IT interface into the mix to "decode" the information in order to use it to deliver our services. It seemed weird and complicated, but our IT team said they were confident they could handle it.

Finally, would they let us connect to their equivalent of the 911 infrastructure? The answer to that, like a lot of things in China, was yes, if they wanted you to. The specifics of getting a straight answer to this were somewhat mysterious, but no more mysterious than anything else. There was a mostly opaque government process that would make the call, but it was the same government (sort of) that would ultimately need to issue you a business license to operate in the country in the first place. So, presumably, if an operating license got approved, you'd have to assume that so would things like this.

With all of the boxes checked, albeit in a strange way, we decided to go for it. What "go for it" meant was form a fifty-fifty joint venture with the same Chinese partner that we were using in the vehicle business, SAIC. I thought the 50 percent partner from GM would be GM China since they had all of the experience in the country, but the government said that since Shanghai OnStar (the JV name we'd chosen) was considered a telecommunications services company, the foreign investment needed to be made by an entity with operating experience in that industry. The only entity in GM that qualified for that was us, so after a lot of arm wrestling and internal gymnastics, we settled on a structure that met everyone's requirements. OnStar U.S. owned 40 percent of it, and SAISC, a sister company to SAIC, owned 40 percent as well. And just to make it a little more interesting, the remaining

20 percent would be owned by the vehicle joint venture, Shanghai GM, which itself was a fifty-fifty joint venture between SAIC and GM. There were apparently all kinds of reasons for this, although the chart that was supposed to explain it all was indecipherable. But the lawyers and accountants were sure that the venture's plumbing was set up to have our investments and operating experience having a reasonable chance of returning a fair share of the JVs ultimate profits.

Our biggest concerns beyond making the investment pay off were protecting our intellectual property and our brand. We spent a lot of time making sure we had our most sensitive technologies isolated and controlled and that we'd be able to avoid serious problems in areas like privacy. GM's local China team felt pretty comfortable that the issues could be managed, but you could tell they weren't anything you could leave on autopilot and expect would turn out OK on their own.

One thing we insisted on was that the president of the joint venture be Jon Hyde. Jon knew OnStar as well as anybody, and while he wasn't a techie, we planned on assigning a handful of really good people to the JV from our team in the United States who knew the technology inside out. What Jon brought was years of OnStar experience, good business judgment, and strong relationships with all of the senior folks at OnStar in the United States. That meant he could cut through the fog (which there'd be a lot of) on almost any issue and just get into the real work without worrying too much about organizational politics or hidden agendas.

I'd periodically get to Shanghai for the joint-venture board meetings, which let me see firsthand what Jon and his team were going through in preparing for OnStar's second launch. In some ways, it was a lot easier because of the experience we already had in the United States. In other ways, the complications of the 40/40/20 ownership structure, a twelve-time-zone separation from the experts, various never-quite-clear government issues, and normal market differences like understanding Chinese subscriber preferences and needing to add Mandarin voice recognition, all conspired to make it much more complicated.

In one of my later visits, Jon took me out in the Shanghai suburbs with a local Shanghai OnStar development engineer to give me a demonstration of turn-by-turn navigation. I was excited because I loved field trips, and experiencing a demo meant that the business was going through the important transition from PowerPoint slides to reality. The engineer was a very tall young woman, who, to English speakers, went by the name Fantasia. She was polite and nervous, but very proud of what she'd been working on. They let me drive (probably a mistake), and she helped me understand what the Mandarin navigation commands were trying to tell me to do. It worked, and better yet, we all lived through it. I hate to admit it, but one of the best parts was getting to call home that night and telling Barb that I'd spent the afternoon with a woman named Fantasia—priceless.

Jon tried to incorporate all of the lessons from our U.S. launch that he felt fit the situation he was facing in China, one of which was to try to establish the same type of family culture that we had back home. While I was in town, Jon arranged for a photographer to take his small team's first family photo. We'd done that very early on in the United States and had it prominently displayed in the command center. My guess is that someday the China team will look back on that picture the same way we do here. Wow, what a small group, and look, they're smiling—they had no idea what was coming next. Jon also built a mini command center in their call center, which was great because it had taken us nine years before we'd been smart enough to do that in the United States.

But make no mistake, Jon wasn't going to impose every OnStar tradition on his Chinese team; he wasn't in Michigan anymore. The best examples of that, to me, were when he needed to get the feng shui master in to review the list of possible Chinese translations of the OnStar logo. After a lot of deep thought, we settled on something whose characters meant "Safe, Lucky Star." Then, when they were reviewing the drawings for the office layout, the feng shui master needed to look at those as well to make sure everything was in alignment for optimal harmony. There was a structural support pole that ended up needing to be in one of the private offices, which is apparently bad for harmony. When it became clear that it couldn't be removed, the master's solution was to give that office to one of the U.S. employees—a practical solution, all things considered.

We'd spent a little over two years getting ready for China before I retired in October 2009. The business actually launched two months later, in December. What an accomplishment. There were so many moving parts, so many new issues, but so many good reasons to do this. There was no doubt that China was going to be a very large and important vehicle market for GM for a long time to come, and planting OnStar's flag on that ground made great business sense for everyone. There was also no doubt that the mayor of Shanghai's original interest in OnStar, our ability to help people when they encountered serious problems on the road, meant that we could aspire to the same peace-of-mind mission imperative in China that we had back home. The work in China promised to have every bit the same human meaning as it did here. And with time and volume, I was sure Jon and his team would have their own wonderfully emotional stories where "Safe, Lucky Star" had helped save many lives.

So it was quite a left turn that led us to our first global expansion opportunity. Why not? OnStar never really did anything the easy way. Are there more places OnStar will end up in the future? Absolutely, and the fun part will probably be in the unique way that the team will get drawn into them. Will it happen with a visit from a prominent mayor? Who knows, but I wouldn't bet against lightning striking twice, at least when your name is OnStar.

CHAPTER 15

A Fork in the Road

I'm not exactly sure when it happened, but a decade or so into the OnStar adventure, I started to wonder about what I was going to do next. It was a very strange sensation because I'd never thought about an endgame strategy for any job that I'd ever had before. I'd always just trusted that one thing would lead to another and work out the way it was supposed to. But now I was in my fifties, and I'd been in this role for over ten years. There was nothing else in General Motors that I had any interest in doing, as I honestly thought I had the best job in the company. Aside from the possibility of more money, there wasn't anything with more meaning or autonomy for me at GM, and at this stage of my life, those were worth a lot more than the money anyway. Besides, if money were your motivator, you wouldn't be working at GM because the auto industry had long ago stopped paying top salaries, no matter what the job was.

So if it wasn't about the money, and I didn't want any other jobs in the company, then why was I feeling restless? I could technically say that I'd been doing the same thing for a long time, but had it really been the same? Thinking back to those first days, so much had changed. The business had grown and evolved in unimaginable ways and that had actually been a big part of the attraction, in a maddening sort of way. OnStar never seemed to stay put for more than a couple of months at a time. It was always changing, churning, growing, and morphing, with the constant need for everyone involved to be up for learning new tricks. And the people kept changing, mostly because we were growing, but also because we'd come of age and had started to see some of the natural progressions that take place when you move from launch into adolescence. Sometimes, that was sad, like when Fred retired, but mostly, there were wonderful moments when peoples' careers blossomed before your very eyes. It was great to coach people and celebrate their professional successes, something that seemed to mean a lot more to me as I'd gotten older.

Now this was really getting confusing. So the work was interesting and continued to change and be stimulating. The people I'm working with at OnStar are talented, dedicated, and passionate about what they do. And being able to work on a mission like OnStar's, where you could literally change peoples' lives for the better, was truly a gift from God. With just a little imagination and a few patriotic songs playing in the background, you could almost feel that flag waving overhead. As corny as it sounds, this had become my own personal version of the American dream. And the good news was that I understood how special it was while it was happening, which probably gave me more strength and resolve than I'll ever know; it'd made the challenges and difficulties worth dealing with. There was so much to feel good about, but it wasn't anything you could ever take for granted. You needed to work hard for it every day, and sometimes, that work involved dealing with the kinds of unnecessary frustrations that you'd only find in a big company. They were above and beyond normal growing pains, more like self-inflicted wounds. Maybe that was the reason it was starting to feel like the right time to move on—perhaps I'd finally reached my saturation point with all of the internal foolishness.

There are a few very special times in your life that you can look back on and say, at that moment, something happened that changed everything. In my personal life, it'd been when I met Barb, or years later, in the delivery room, for the birth of my son, Chase, and three years after that, when we were blessed with the arrival of our wonderful daughter, Taylor. How could you be the same after that? In my professional life, events never seemed to rise to that same level of emotional importance, but many of them still made an impact.

John Jarrell sending me to Ft. McNair, Harry Pearce's sense of humor in dropping me into Project Beacon, meeting Fred, and Rick Lee, and Walt and so many other wonderful people at OnStar. Getting to know folks like Ernie Allen, and Dr. Hunt, and Phil Samper, and yes, even being told that I was a pimple. That certainly had stuck in the dark recesses of my subconscious, and who knows how much determination and tenacity that thoughtless comment had fueled in me over the years. But there hadn't been one event, one poignant moment, one epiphany that said it was now time to leave. It was more the cumulative effect of years of hard-to-comprehend frustrations that had finally breached the limits of my personal levee. And, coincidentally, the levee was weakening just as the frustration was building, as growing older had made me less tolerant of the politics and bureaucracy that I'd formerly just taken for granted.

Earlier in my career, I just accepted that many things just were the way they were. People at higher levels in the organization sometimes made decisions that I didn't understand or agree with. Some folks were promoted that didn't seem to merit it, while others that deserved to advance appeared to toil without recognition. You were "encouraged" to leave one job and take on another, not always direct orders, but typically with enough of an edge that you knew what the right answer needed to be. Your performance appraisals and financial rewards might not coincide with your own self-assessment or expectations. And, finally, you'd end up working for whomever someone else told you to work for, no vote required. Sometimes, it would be great, but most times, not so much. And it was especially not so much when the person wasn't someone who could help you develop, and worse yet, might not be someone who you could respect. But it never really mattered because they'd been made your boss, and it was your job to fall in line and get on with life.

While you never want to completely surrender to those rules of engagement, you do have to either accept them or pack up your tent and go someplace else. Very early in my career, a couple of years after I returned from Harvard, I'd actually gotten so fed up with one of those situations at EMD that I went looking for someplace else to work. One thing led to another, and the next thing I knew I was heading to Columbus, Indiana, to work for Cummins Diesel. Out of respect for a personal relationship that I'd developed with the GM personnel executive who'd taken care of the GM fellows at HBS, Dick Huber (unfortunately, no relation), I called to tell him I was leaving. At that point, Dick, who was head of personnel at GM's Packard Electric Division, told me to drop whatever I was doing and come to see him the next day.

Dick cleared his calendar, and I flew to Ohio the next morning for a face-to-face discussion. GM was losing fellows, particularly those coming out of HBS, and Dick wanted to understand directly from me why I'd made the decision to leave. We sat in his office for most of the day talking about everything in the world. Dick didn't try to guilt me into changing my mind; he just wanted to make sure I'd thought it through, which I thought I had. At one point, he asked if I could make up any job I wanted at EMD, recognizing I couldn't be an idiot and say that, at twenty-seven years old, I wanted to run the joint, what would it be? I said I didn't know, so he made me promise that I'd go home and call him back in a day with what I'd come up with.

I really liked Dick, and he'd just went out of his way to try to keep a frustrated kid in the company. While I'd already mentally made up my mind to move on, his suggestion did make some sense. There was no downside, unless I really hated everything about EMD, which I didn't. So I went home, came up with a suggestion, and magically (I'm sure with some behind-the-scenes encouragement of the real Mr. Huber), the folks at EMD went along with it. I ended up staying, and life went on from there. But, from that day on, if anyone believed I made a contribution to GM, it was Dick's fault. He'd made an otherwise big and impersonal company seem human, and at that stage of my career, that made all the difference in the world. One fork in the road passed.

Had there been other frustrations over the years, either at EMD or during the early years at OnStar? Oh God, yes. But I'd gained a little perspective with age, and on balance, they'd either seemed like a normal part of business life, or in the beginning at OnStar, the price we had to pay for swimming upstream against such a strong current. The pimple comment, or the strong push-back on violating engineering rules, or silly corporate financial edicts, or inappropriate HR policies, or the maddeningly poor vehicle marketing executions were just par for the course. What did we expect? We were unproven, too small to be worth anything, and a pain in everyone's neck. So the hazing we were getting was understandable, and you just had to wear it. The alternative was to take your ball and go home, except that it wasn't our ball; it was theirs. Those were the days when folks like Ron Zarrella or Phil Samper would pick me up off the canvas, calm me down until the bell rang, and then shove me back in the ring for the next round. And, at some point, I really knew I couldn't just give up and leave anyway. I'd helped assemble this team, many of whom had left other companies to come to OnStar, and if I bailed, what would that mean for them? Hey, there was no doubt the company could've removed me at any time, but voluntarily abandoning a leaky ship because I was having a bad day would've been a low-rent move.

But now the business had been established. It was generating solid and growing profits and, by some external measures, had the strongest and most respected brand in GM. We'd already introduced six generations of vehicle hardware and had used our industry-leading experience to make countless refinements in every business process. And the OnStar salaried team now numbered nearly five hundred professionally talented and emotionally committed souls who possessed orders of magnitude more insights into this category than anyone else in the world. The machine was running on all cylinders, finding more opportunities to improve, and continuously inventing new services that delighted our subscribers. It had taken a while, but the virtuous cycle had begun, and that felt pretty good.

What didn't feel very good was a continuing lack of appreciation from within the company for what *they'd* actually created. While I was never quite sure why, the needless skepticism of many GM folks seemed to rise in direct proportion with a mountain of irrefutable evidence to the contrary. It made no sense, but I ascribed at least a part of it to the never-ending revolving door of people who rotated through the corporate interface jobs that affected us most. From the time we started, we saw the comings and goings of six GM North American CFOs, four presidents of GM North America (unless you want to count Rick's rebound into that role twice), five heads of North American vehicle marketing, and five GM North American heads of information technology. Every one of these roles was an important place where we plugged into the company and where building support and confidence was critical. And while Rick did a good job of maintaining some connection to OnStar throughout this time, he had enough other things on his plate, like running the car company, that he couldn't possibly involve himself in all the political maneuvering and drama that the constant turnover in those other positions was causing.

The worst part was the continual need to "prove" to a constant stream of new people who didn't know anything about us or our business that OnStar was creating real value for GM and that it needed to be run differently from the car company to have any chance of that continuing. The valuable part should have been easy if you could read English. Look at the consumer research, done dozens of times, and all you'd see were high consumer preferences for GM vehicles with OnStar if only GM's vehicle marketing organization would ever get around to making it a part of their priorities. And we had separate financial statements for OnStar, also written in English, which showed that the bottomline was on an upward trend and approaching numbers that started with a B. "Proving" value shouldn't have needed any more time and effort than that, and it certainly shouldn't have needed constant repeating, but unfortunately, it did.

The part about proving that the business needed to be run differently was hitting on the essence of Clay Christensen's comments regarding companies not knowing where to "stick" their newly created businesses. It's just way too tempting to hand-wave the differences in a new business, and for the sake of who knows what, efficiency, consistency, politics, sun spots— just smash everything together to make it easier to deal with. Homogenizing OnStar into GM's vehicle business seemed to make practical sense. What needed to be talked about? Actually, quite a lot, but sadly, these were nuanced, strategically subtle discussions when they were done right and cartoonish religious proclamations when they were done poorly. And guess which type we usually ended up having? These were unwinnable arguments when the other side was armed with the righteous sword of "one team" or "structural cost reduction." And we were the OnStar guys, for heaven's sake; it was obvious why we felt the way we did. We were trying to protect our kingdom, our turf; we must be trying to feather our own nest somehow. Our motives for wanting to be treated differently were clearly suspect, or at least that's what fit the storyline the best.

I'd routinely get lectures from some very senior people in the company—a couple of times coming from my own bosses—telling me how "lucky" we were to have their support, that "everyone else in the company wants to stop installing OnStar," and that they were "putting themselves on the line and taking crap for supporting us in more meetings than they could count." Basically, they were doing our heavy lifting, and we should really appreciate their personal sacrifice. At one point, I'd gotten more of that than I could handle from one of the North American CFOs in a one-on-one meeting, and I just lost it. I said, "Fine, if you don't think this should be on all of the cars, then just take it off. I don't get paid a commission on this stuff, and my job is actually easier if we have fewer customers. So stop doing me any big favors. This either makes business sense or it doesn't, and if you don't think it's worth doing, just pull the plug." I think he was shocked that I'd stopped defending "my baby," as everyone had just come to expect that from me. He backed off and left us alone for a while, but I wasn't sure if it was because he finally got it or thought I was about to go postal and didn't want to be in the room when it happened.

So there really wasn't any one thing that pushed me over the edge, but there was a catalyst. It was when I was told that I was getting my sixth supervisor, Troy Clarke. I'd worked directly for Rick Wagoner for a few years since Gary Cowger had moved out of the GM North America president role to become the head of global manufacturing. The business in North America had been struggling, and Rick decided that he needed to get back into the region personally, so he added the title of North American president to his role as CEO of the entire company. Rick told me he'd have his hands full holding both positions and was hoping that I'd be OK without a lot of personal supervision. He did say never to hesitate to grab him if I needed his help, which was great because I knew he really meant it. So I tried to make good on being low maintenance, and the arrangement worked pretty well.

Eventually, the storm clouds passed (at least temporarily), and in May 2006, Rick decided to step out of the North American role and appoint the former president of GM Asia Pacific, Troy Clarke, to take over the North American job. And just like that, I now worked for Troy. Troy was an interesting guy, but I'd said that about many of the bosses who I'd cycled through before him. He was intelligent, quietly intense, and was really fond of thinking and speaking in terms of the mental models that he used to organize his approach to the business. That wasn't necessarily bad, but it made for awkward discussions when I'd need to translate OnStar to fit into one of his frameworks. In fairness, I was probably more concerned about that than he would've wanted me to be, but that was the problem with having so many bosses in such a short span of time. There was never any real rapport that developed because there just wasn't the time or a continuity of experiences. We'd not hunkered down in any foxholes together, or survived any close calls, or celebrated any improbable wins. He had no feel for my experience and judgment, nor did I really have any feel for his. But these kinds of relationships aren't level playing fields; they're asymmetrical. By definition, they're built around the concept of superior and subordinate, and I knew what role I'd been assigned. When there was a judgment tiebreaker needed, we both knew what way that was going to go.

We had a few early encounters that I'd say were fine, but uncomfortable. It was probably more because of me than him, as I'm sure I was subconsciously looking to confirm my concern that I was in for another strange and irritating boss learning curve. But, for whatever reason, rather than taking a breath and putting up with it all over again, it just struck me that I'd probably had enough of this ride and it was time to get off. That was hard to come to grips with at first, but when I'd lie awake at night thinking about it, I'd flashback to something he'd said that I didn't agree with or a predictably bad run-in I'd had with GM finance, IT, or marketing, and I'd usually end up drifting off to sleep feeling much better about my decision to go. But what's the right way to leave?

Recruiters had approached me during the dot-com days, but because of the tenuous state of our business at that point, I didn't have any desire to put much effort into the process and just told everybody no thanks. When the market blew up in the early 2000s, everything just seemed to die down on its own, but then it picked up again in about 2004. I don't know why, maybe it was because OnStar had survived the technology carnage and had become more well known, or maybe it had been the cumulative effect of all of the PR events I'd been involved with, but anyway, it still didn't seem like the right time to think about moving on, so I just kept politely declining to be considered for whatever it was they were pitching. But now the time was right, so I started to give the process some serious thought.

At around this time, something coincidentally happened inside of GM that changed everything. For a lot of reasons, GM had decided to change its executive pension program to reduce the payout for future years of service. Since GM couldn't unilaterally touch what the UAW hourly workforce was entitled to, they'd been periodically messing with the benefits of active and retired salaried employees, and this was just the latest example. Since you had to stay until you were sixty-two to qualify for that program, I convinced myself it wasn't going to matter to me anyway because there was no way I could last that long.

But the other part of the announcement actually changed that and lowered the qualifying age to fifty-five. Wait a minute, what did it say again? No kidding, I could go at fifty-five? That was just two and a half years away. Let me get this straight, if I can deal with all of the nonsense for another thirty months, then I can retire with a reasonable pension? I just had a new plan; call off the recruiting dogs and saddle up for a high-intensity sprint to the finish line. I wondered what it was going to feel like to have this settled in my mind—how about wonderful.

In early 2007, GM was awarding incentive compensation in the annual "passing out of the envelopes" ritual for executives. Each manager who had executives working for them would get worksheets where they'd look at the expected "par" value for each executive's award, what the theoretical average person should get, and then they'd get a little extra money to spread around to their high-performers as they chose. You could also take money away from someone who hadn't done a particularly good job and use that to add even more to the high-performers' awards.

Over the years, GM had encouraged more and more pay differentiation based on performance, an approach I strongly supported. We were fortunate to have really good executives at OnStar, about thirty of them in total, but you could be sure that guys like Walt always had a little bit more to look forward to on envelope day than most other people did. Even though the additional money wasn't ever going to make him rich, he understood the system and really appreciated the message of recognition and respect that it was intended to send.

Anyway, it was my turn to get my envelope. But, surprisingly, even though my boss's office was only an elevator ride away in the adjoining tower in the Ren Cen, I got a message that said I didn't need to come over to his office, that he'd just call me on the phone. That was a little different and the first time that'd happened in the twenty years that I'd been an executive. I always liked having the meetings with my guys face-to-face, even the ones that had their amount reduced from par. It was only fair to tell them in person and give them a chance to respond and ask questions if they needed to. Anyway, I didn't really know how he operated, so maybe this was just his normal approach.

I got the call, and he began walking me through how the par number had been calculated. I got that, actually the process was the same for everyone, and I'd been doing this for two decades. Anyway, he finally got to the point where he told me what my specific payout would be, and it turned out to be par—no plus or minus, just par. He kept going because there were other things in the envelope like stock options, but before I knew what I was doing, the insubordinate autopilot in me kicked in, and I just started laughing on the phone and said, "You've got to be kidding me." There was an awkward silence, and then he asked what I meant. I answered, "You can't tell me that I'm your par guy, can you?" I knew what we'd accomplished last year; we'd turned in a very strong performance, so how could this be? It really surprised me how easily this was coming out of my mouth. I should've felt a little queasy, but I wasn't at all.

There were a few awkward moments on the phone until he finally said that all officers get par, because par for an officer means you're doing great. What a crock. You're going to tell me that once you reach the officer level, everyone is magically transported to Lake Wobegon? No, everyone at GM, especially the officers, was not above average. I knew these guys, and there were many truly exceptional people in that group, but there were also some stinkers. How were we going to keep the really good ones if this was the approach? But he wasn't kidding. This was just plain weird. I honestly cared less about the few thousand dollars of difference it would have made if they'd given me a "plus-up." It was flat out the lack of respect it showed for the contribution that I thought I was making. Hey, if they saw it differently, just tell me I wasn't getting it done. I could deal with that and would actually appreciate the candor. But they weren't telling me that; in fact, my formal performance reviews were saying just the opposite. So how do I make any sense out of this? They were just making this too easy. I was becoming more and more comfortable leaving the job of a lifetime and being able to do it with absolutely no regrets.

The following summer, two years before I turned fifty-five, I made the decision to tell Troy what my plans were. My concern was that we'd never really talked much about succession planning, and they might need the time to do it right. If they were going to be comfortable with promoting somebody who was already working at OnStar, it wouldn't be that big of a deal. But if they thought they needed to bring in someone without any experience, my sense was they should at least consider bringing them into the business in another role ahead of time to get familiar with the industry and the team. This job wasn't necessarily harder than anything else in the company, just different. So why take the risk of parachuting some automotive hi-pot in at the last minute if you didn't need to?

Phil Samper told me I was nuts for telling them so far in advance. He said they wouldn't appreciate the heads-up and might actually mess with me since they knew I was planning on leaving. Other than Barb, Phil was the only person that I'd told of my plans, mainly because I didn't think it would be fair to anyone else to have the uncertainty of who would be next hanging over their head when there was nothing they could do about it. I couldn't say I knew Phil was wrong, but my feeling was that I had to at least try to do it the way I thought could be the best for OnStar. If they didn't see it that way or decided to mess with me, then I guess that was just the way it was going to have to be.

I was in Troy's office for a normal monthly one-on-one meeting, and when the other topics were covered, I told him about my retirement plans. He was a year younger than I was, and all he said was that was interesting and that he was going to have to start thinking about that for himself someday. No "Why are you thinking of that?" or "Are you sure?" just more or less "Fine, thanks for letting me know." I really tried to make the point about succession, but that didn't seem to register, at least it didn't seem important enough for him to worry about at that moment. So I'd just gotten a load off my chest, and it felt like it was lying under the table in his office to be dealt with by the janitors that evening. I guess I didn't know exactly what to expect, but I didn't think the reaction would've been a yawn. A couple of months later, he actually asked me if I'd be interested in someday being considered to be put in charge of GM's business in Canada or Mexico as a next career step, and I had to stop myself from laughing out loud. No offense, but there was nothing to those jobs; they were 80 percent ceremonial government relations and 20 percent worry about monthly car sales. The fact that he thought I'd look at them as a "step up" was sad and just confirmed that he had no idea what I was already doing for a living.

It was six months later, actually the week before GM's Christmas break in 2007, that I got a call late one afternoon to go to Rick's office. I didn't know what he wanted, so I grabbed a stack of information on everything I thought he might be interested in, from the status of China to our most recent monthly subscriber retention numbers. When I got there, he closed his door and said, "So what's this I hear that you're planning on leaving?" and he quickly followed it up with, "You know you'll take a pretty stiff haircut on your retirement by leaving so early." I said I understood the math on the reduction and was OK with that because I'd probably find something else to do anyway. And I told him I was leaving because it was just time. I would have been in the job over fourteen years when I reached fify-five, and that was probably enough. I'd run my leg of the race.

He said we both knew OnStar wasn't the same as when I'd started, and he thought I liked the business, so it must be something else. I said, "OK, since you asked, I've just had enough of how this place operates." I didn't like the skepticism of OnStar that was tolerated in the company or the fact that the vehicle marketing was allowed to be so atrocious. I said I'd been disappointed at how the position was being valued and rewarded and embarrassed to have to bring that up. And, finally, I said that I'd had it with the revolving doors of supervisors I'd been assigned to and that I needed to be in a place where I could respect and learn from the people I worked for, and at the moment, I couldn't. Hey, he asked, and I was being as honest and respectful as I could be. Actually, I had nothing personally against Rick at all; I actually liked him a lot. So I owed it to him not to cop out, but to be candid. I really did wish my comments could somehow be taken constructively.

And while we were on the topic, I said I really hoped he would start to think about whom he wanted to run OnStar when I left because that was only eighteen months away. He started to say something along the lines of "what will it take," and I stopped him and said this wasn't about trying to leverage myself into a better deal. He said OK, but that we weren't through talking about this, and he intended to set something up in a couple of months to see what we could figure out. I said fine and that I'd put together a few thoughts on who might be good candidates to consider as my replacement from OnStar and another list that would include people from GM.

Rick never did set up that next meeting, but that was understandable since he had way more important things occupying his attention during those times. He was only a little more than a year from ending his own run at GM, although he never got the peace of mind out of knowing that ahead of time like I did. This was the last formal meeting that needed to take place for me to finally feel like my decision was official. I'd thought when I first told Troy that I was planning on leaving that Rick might want to talk to me, and I was flattered that he'd taken the time to want to understand my situation. Thankfully, there wasn't much time to wallow in all of this; there was more work to do. OnStar always had a way of occupying my mind and using all of my available energy, so my sleepless nights got to revert back to their normal demons, like can we survive next week's IT code drop, or are we ready for launching the new version of turn-by-turn navigation? Ah, normalcy at last.

But the normalcy didn't really last long. By the fall of 2008, the implosion of the North American vehicle market was shaking Southeast Michigan's world to its foundation. At GM, there was a liquidity crisis looming on the horizon, actually, more like hovering directly overhead. Seats were being unbolted and thrown out of the plane in a desperate attempt to keep it airborne, and I saw a ratchet heading in our direction.

I took a vacation day on a Friday in September to join a few old buddies from EMD for a golf weekend. As I was pulling into the parking lot of the golf course, I got a call from Rhonda Miska, my executive assistant. Rhonda had been Lorrie's replacement a few years before and was just fabulous. She was incredibly professional, multitasked like nobody I'd ever met, anticipated issues faster than Radar O'Reilly on *MASH*, and was genuinely a wonderful person. Everyone loved Rhonda, and despite all of the craziness that typically characterized OnStar, she was always able to remain calm and approachable, which made everyone's life much easier, especially mine. Over the years, she'd become good friends with Barb and Chase and Taylor, and they mercifully agreed never to tell anyone that Rhonda actually ran the place.

Anyway, she called apologizing for messing with me on vacation and said Rick Wagoner needed to talk to me as soon as possible. My buddies were on the first tee, so I told them to play away, and I'd catch up with them in a few holes. I called Rick and got patched into a conference call that included GM's treasurer Walter Borst, and they told me they'd been digging into the corporate attic to see what they might be able to sell to raise some cash and had come up with a few candidates, including us. Rick said he thought OnStar was strategically important to the company and would really rather not sell it, but that under the current circumstances, everything needed to be on the table. So what did I think?

I'm not sure my answer was going to make any difference, but I told him I was confident there was value to be realized if they really wanted to try to sell us, and he said good and to expect a contact on Monday from J.P. Morgan, who would be managing the process. Marching orders acknowledged, it was time for a very strange round of golf. The next week, we connected with the guys from J.P. Morgan, and we quickly agreed that we'd keep the team working on this very small. I remembered how tough it had been on everyone at EMD when we'd been put up for sale years before. It's extremely unsettling, and since you couldn't be sure it would turn into a deal anyway, why stir the pot needlessly. So I asked Rick Lee to be on point, and we also involved Walt, Scott Kubicki, Tony DiSalle, and Joe McCusker, our CFO.

The J.P. Morgan folks were surprisingly good to deal with, and in a very short period of time, they helped us "package" the business in a presentation that took prospective buyers through our current strategy and future growth opportunities, complete with endless sets of financial projections. I was actually hoping the story could be told with the OnStar Command Center as a backdrop because it helped people who otherwise didn't know much about our business bring some real-life context to an otherwise long set of charts. Thankfully, it worked out that way most of the time.

I think the GM people were a little nervous at first that we'd feel bad and cop an attitude because they'd put us for sale, but I honestly never resented it at all. These were desperate times in the company, and OnStar was their asset to do with as they pleased. It was amusing and somewhat ironic to watch some of the very same GM people who'd been openly skeptical of OnStar's value argue emotionally for how many billions of dollars we should be able to get for this wonderful business. But it didn't matter because I'd always believed it was worth a lot, so presenting it that way to prospective buyers was no problem for me at all. And, in some ways, it could've been good to be purchased by someone willing to pay a lot for OnStar, since it was inconceivable that, if they did that, they'd act as ambivalently toward us as GM many times had.

Anyway, you couldn't have picked a worse time to try to sell this business for GM's definition of top dollar. Both strategic and financial players looked at GM's situation and were unwilling to pay full value for the asset. The financial players sensed blood in the water; GM was desperate for cash, and the private equity firms were interested in cutting a fat hog on this deal, or they'd just sit back and see what happened next. They didn't need to own OnStar for any particular operating reason, so it either needed to be a great deal where they could leverage GM's desperate liquidity problems against them or no deal at all.

The strategic players saw OnStar's short- to medium-term value being overly dependent on the questionable health of GM. OnStar relied on new GM vehicle sales for subscribers, and what happened if GM couldn't get through the current cash crunch and keep building cars? That resulted in heavy discounts being applied to OnStar's future cash flow projections to account for the uncertainty and risk in GM's underlying vehicle business. So, in both cases, this was looking like a buyer's market, and GM didn't want to sell us bad enough to take such a haircut on valuation. It was partly that, and partly by the time it all played out that fall and into winter, it was clear GM's cash hole was so large that it wouldn't be able to self-fund its way through the crisis anyway.

What we did confirm was that we had a reasonably good story to tell, one that held up pretty well to an aggressive and invasive evaluation process by a number of outside professionals. The J.P. Morgan guys said the response they'd gotten back from the prospective buyers we'd talked to was surprise at what GM had actually created with OnStar. They'd come in with low expectations that it was going to be anything real and left with a much different sense of the depth and substance of the business. I guess it really didn't matter what they thought because none of them ended up buying us. But it was gratifying to get confirmation from some otherwise smart and dispassionate people that our baby wasn't really that ugly after all.

From this point in the first quarter of 2009, everything picked up speed. The government sent in waves of people to analyze GM's business, presumably looking under every rock for efficiency opportunities, hidden assets—you name it. They never did talk to us, which surprised me a little, but wasn't disappointing considering the distraction and consternation the analysis was causing for the car business. I'm sure there'll be many books written with behind-the-scenes details of how the financial bailout and bankruptcy played out; I'm happy to say I have no detailed knowledge of those events, save the briefings the officers would periodically get on its progress. When we all heard that Rick had been asked to resign and Fritz Henderson was taking over as CEO, it wasn't completely surprising, but was still something of a shock to the system. It didn't seem fair, but we'd lost control of making fairness judgments when we couldn't pay our own bills. At least we all knew Fritz, which seemed better than the alternatives circulating through the rumormill.

Fritz took on the CEO role with all the energy you'd expect if you knew him, but it was clear he didn't relish getting the role the way he did. I'm sure Fritz saw himself as GM's best chance to get through this mess with as little collateral damage as possible. He was smart, deeply experienced in the car business, and had a lot of confidence in his own abilities, but what a tough time to finally get his shot at a job he'd been aiming at for his entire career. There were brutally hard issues to face, and multiple bizarrely complex work streams to manage, and it all had to be done under the white-hot glare of highly skeptical government overlords. Thankfully, Fritz brought his heart along with his considerable experience to the task, because he'd need every bit of that to thread the army of moving needles that the company was facing.

One of the criticisms coming back from the government's task force had to do with the ineffective and calcified culture that they thought was strangling the company. They said GM had been insulated, slow-moving, resistant to change, risk-averse, and didn't hold people accountable; traits that would need to change in the new GM. Fritz got that message, and soon after he became CEO, he sent a note to all of the officers asking for feedback on four key cultural characteristics: product/customer focus, speed, risk-taking, and accountability. We were to describe what those meant to each of us, what the obstacles were in today's GM, and how we could improve. I was now T-minus four months from qualifying for retirement, if the company survived the bankruptcy process and there was a GM to retire from, so I wondered if my input would be useful. But since I thought my experience over the last fourteen years at OnStar had afforded me a different view on this, I decided to fill out the form and send in my thoughts.

The following was my response to Fritz's request:

Product/Customer Focus

Description – What this means to me is framing important enterprise decisions with an understanding of what they mean for customers. Setting priorities for resource allocation on what will create better customer experiences and lead to deeper customer loyalty. Dedicating time and resources to developing a profound and nuanced understanding of customers and competitors, and using that to set strategy. Maintaining integrity in building and living a customer-centric brand position, and avoiding the temptations to incrementally compromise on the margin. In any new service launch, expecting that early experience will lead to opportunities to improve, and using feedback processes to ensure that it's happening. Being very clear on who the customer is and not defining the customer as the "next person in the internal process" or "the dealer."

Obstacles in today's environment – Pressure to make decisions to optimize cost or satisfy internal process objectives that individually aren't obviously bad, but cumulatively aren't good. Too many people are given or assume the role of "speaking for the customer," which tends to dilute the execution and accountability. Lack of follow-through and sweating the details on all elements of the customer experience, resulting in check-the-box executions. Rationalizing that constraints in the current business model/structure prevent exploring creative solutions or bold moves.

Future ideas for improvement – Clearer senior level–focused reviews that reinforce accountability for deep customer and competitor understanding. Reviews of specific, prioritized initiatives being pursued to address the largest gaps in customer perception.

Speed

Description – To me, speed means competitive advantage. Speed means understanding, completely, the consequences of delay on important issues and making intelligent risk and resource judgments to accelerate outside of normal process when there is disproportionate leverage. Speed means leading with care and insight, respecting the laws of nature, but not always obeying them. Real use of speed requires not diluting the concept by pronouncing everything as urgent, but also not accepting the most-recent experience as the template. Measuring progress in hours, days, and weeks instead of months and model years, and where possible, relating "time to impact" to the number of subpar customer experiences that take place until the initiative is complete.

Obstacles in today's environment – Speed is too often internally confused with risk. It's often overused as a concept, losing its meaning and becoming diluted. There is very little institutional appreciation for speed-to-market as a critical success factor for the business.

Future ideas for improvement – Create clearer alignment on important initiatives where unnatural speed will be required to be successful. Lead with an emphasis that reinforces that an improvement in a timeline in most cases is as important as an improvement in cost or other project deliverables.

Risk-Taking

Description – Risk-taking means picking spots that make a difference, deeply understanding the subject matter and thoughtfully reviewing the options, and acting in the face of uncertainty with good measurement and feedback loops. Risk-taking of consequence is not an exercise in delegation and empowerment; it's an important tool that should be used to pursue real competitive advantage. In uncertain situations, where discontinuous improvements are being targeted, the ability of the organization to take intelligent risks is critical. At a minimum, risks need to be taken consciously, with some version of after-action review that either confirms success or creates an enterprise learning that leads to better-informed next steps. Poor executions, with ill-conceived understandings of the consequences, that ultimately lead to bad outcomes should be labeled poor leadership, not risk-taking.

Obstacles in today's environment – Too many gatekeepers in the series of groups who need to be coordinated to take enterprise-wide risks. Lack of discipline and rigor applied to understanding risk-taking as a process or a tool. Risk-taking is often used as the surrogate for the "anti-process," and risk-takers become known in the extreme as either irresponsible or bureaucracy fighters. Risk-taking in business shouldn't be seen as a personality trait of individuals, but as a necessary component of many successful initiatives. Effective oversight of risk-taking requires strong general management skill sets, which don't broadly exist in the company.

Future ideas for improvement – Consciously manage significant initiatives requiring risk-taking with good measurement schemes and more frequent review cycles.

Accountability

Description – Having a deep and fundamental understanding of an individual area of the business, and creating a manageable, focused list of key measures/deliverables that will make a real difference in the success of the enterprise. While in many instances there will be a broader range of measures that are interim or process metrics meant to understand progress, accountability measures should really relate to whether the enterprise is fundamentally successful. Great progress reducing quality problems per thousand vehicles may be an important and necessary interim view of product quality, but if our products continue to sell at a significant price deficit because of poor quality perception, we haven't won by improving that measure. This measurement approach needs to be connected with leaders who personally hold themselves accountable for meeting those objectives, spending little time explaining why they didn't achieve the numbers unless the explanations become an important part of the learnings required to take the next action to improve the outcomes.

Obstacles in today's environment – Too many places where individual functional scorecards show objectives being met when overall success measures of the enterprise are clearly not being achieved. Long standing approach of rotating individuals on a two- to four-year cycle, which too easily allows for the results of decisions to be disconnected from the person who originally had the job, and too many people count on that to escape accountability.

Future ideas for improvement – More thoughtful choices of measurements. Removing leaders who deflect rather than internalize accountability for results.

I looked over what I'd written, corrected a couple of typos, and hit the send button. There was nothing particularly deep in my observations, just what I'd learned from the last decade working at OnStar. Would it be applicable to the bigger GM? I thought so, but that wasn't my call. I was a little surprised that I never heard anything back from Fritz on what I'd sent in, but there were fifty or so officers, and for all I knew, everyone had sent in something very similar. Either that or it just didn't fit what he was looking for. He did thank everyone for their feedback during one of our periodic bankruptcy update conference calls, but that was it. A few weeks later, he'd picked a few folks to participate on a cultural transformation team to advise him on what to do and how to do it, and from the people involved, it was clear it was going in a much different direction than I'd suggested. This was a tough issue, and heaven knows we'd learned many lessons at OnStar that confirmed how important it was to get the culture right and how much effort that took if you were really serious about it. And that was in a new organization. Changing something as tradition-bound as GM's hundred-year-old culture would require a massive effort.

The bankruptcy process was full of drama and something of a blur. It's amazing how fast the formal process went and how few real issues surfaced during the proceedings. It wasn't because there weren't issues, it really was a tribute to the effort and focus Fritz put on getting through it as quickly and professionally as possible. He kept stressing what a gift it was to get a second chance and that we certainly weren't going to get a third. He was right on both counts. As an otherwise unimportant footnote to history, OnStar, LLC, wasn't technically able to file for bankruptcy with the rest of GM because our financial results were positive. Since there was no real upside to talking about that, it was left unsaid, except to a handful of our key suppliers who took comfort in that legal distinction.

So on July 10, 2009, the post-bankruptcy new GM was born—amazingly, on my fifty-fifth birthday. But it really didn't feel like anything to celebrate. A lot of peoples' lives had been disrupted; folks had lost their jobs and their dealerships. People that held GM's bonds, including one of my uncles, had suffered big losses. And the common shareholders, of which I was one because GM required someone at my level to own two-times their annual salary in stock, had just been wiped out. No, celebrating wasn't in order, more like licking your wounds and realizing how fortunate it was to have at least a remnant of the company survive. Hopefully some good would come of all of this; I sure hoped and prayed that it would. There were still a lot of people counting on the new company for their livelihood, including my family at OnStar.

CHAPTER 16

Stepping Down

So here we are again, back where it all started. I sent out the note announcing my retirement and immediately went to watch Fritz Henderson's videoconference announcing the wide range of leadership changes that were about to take place. About 40 percent of GM's corporate officers were leaving, GM Europe was going to be sold, and the structure was going to be simplified into a North American business and an international operation. The functional heads of things like manufacturing, sales, and engineering would report directly to Fritz, as would some other "cats and dogs," smaller groups like parts, GM Mexico and Canada, and finally, OnStar. In this case, being in the "other cat and dog" category was much preferable to the alternative of being "stuck" in yet another inappropriate organizational structure. And it was that alternative that had almost happened, which would have been tragic.

Leading up to the announcement, I met with Troy Clarke to reengage on who was going to run OnStar. Phil Samper had been right, they hadn't done anything with the twenty-four-month heads-up on this issue, letting it slide to the last possible moment. In fairness to Troy, he wasn't sure what role he was going to have in the new GM and was pretty open about feeling a little up in the air, which actually made me feel sorry for him. He was a GM lifer just like me, thought he still had a lot to contribute and wanted to stay. Everyone knew his current position was going away, and him not knowing what was going to happen this close to D-day just seemed wrong.

Anyway, it wasn't surprising that getting the plan settled for OnStar's succession wasn't on the top of his priority list. He said he

299

thought Fritz hadn't finalized the selection for my replacement, but had decided that the new head of OnStar should work for the GM Parts Operation. *What?* The guys who worry about spark plugs, air filters, and floor mats? Those parts guys? Apparently, the logic was that Fritz had too much on his plate to have it report directly to him, so he'd park it where it would get more attention. And weren't parts kind of like OnStar? They both sold things "after the car was sold," so it seemed like a pretty good match.

My jaw dropped onto Troy's table. This was both unbelievable and unbelievably bad. The similarities between selling replacement parts and OnStar were nonexistent. And, to make matters worse, the guy they had running the parts business was not going to add any value to the OnStar business—maybe the opposite. What was my appeal process? Troy said if I had a problem with the direction that this was headed, I'd probably need to talk directly to Fritz. OK, well at least it didn't sound like it had been completely settled yet, and there were a couple of other things I felt like I needed to talk to Fritz about anyway, since it was clear he was personally making all the calls at this point. We'd gotten an annoying directive from GM's HR folks assigning OnStar a target to reduce 20 percent of our executives and over 10 percent of our total salaried employees to be consistent with everybody in the car business. But weren't their targets developed by "benchmarking" what Toyota was doing? And had somebody conveniently forgotten that Toyota didn't have an OnStar business?

The bureaucracy just never seemed to have bounds, but it didn't matter. Our "contribution" had already been "baked into" GM North America's commitments. As far as Troy was concerned, if OnStar got a hall pass just because we were growing, then our shortfall would unfairly have to be applied to people who were already making cuts. Hey, I get the human side of this, and "fairness" is a laudable goal to aspire to, but fairness to what? Fairness to the feelings of the people making the cuts or fairness to the shareholders who expected the business to be positioned to generate the best possible set of results?

Anyway, I'd reached a dead-end with Troy on this, and as long as I was headed into Fritz's office for the succession issue, I thought I might as well take a shot at this one as well.

I asked Rhonda to try to set up the meeting, and with everything else going on, I was really appreciative that Fritz made the time to see me so quickly. I'd spent a lot of time thinking about the succession issue, and I told him at this late date it would be unnecessarily risky to bring someone in from outside of OnStar because there wasn't time to do a "from scratch" transition. I identified three good candidates from inside OnStar, each with their own strengths, but all things considered, I thought Walt was the best choice. He seemed surprised at the recommendation, but after a fair amount of discussion, he said Walt was someone who he could seriously consider. It wasn't a final decision, but I'd said what I needed to, and Walt was now at least in play.

The next thing I said was I'd heard that he was planning on putting OnStar under the parts guy, and I told him I thought that would be a disaster. The businesses weren't a good fit, and OnStar was still going to need support from the very top of the company. I also said I didn't believe the person in charge of the parts business was capable of taking this on and generating the kinds of results GM was looking for. He asked where I thought it should report, and I said, "To you." The business was now big enough, it was on the brink of launching in China, and he knew that we had just decided to launch an aftermarket OnStar product through retailers like Best Buy that had the potential to make the business much larger. But potential and reality were two different things, and getting the leadership structure right would be an important element in the ultimate success of the business. It was really important to connect OnStar to someplace where it wouldn't be predictably pressured to conform to the processes or constraints of a mature, restructuring vehicle business. He said he thought his span of control was too broad to take OnStar on directly and asked me to send him back an email with other suggestions.

Then it was on to the final issue—headcount. Fritz had gone public with headcount reduction targets for the overall corporation, and while little OnStar's numbers weren't going to make or break hitting the objective, I'm sure he didn't want to set precedent where a closed-door meeting with him resulted in that group being spared cuts in personnel. So I told him what my concerns were and gave him the facts. We'd just basically recruited a number of the folks on our team; in fact, 30 percent of our employees had been with us for two years or less. It hadn't been easy getting people with the skill sets we needed to agree to work for GM or the auto industry, and if we made deep cuts now, it would be doubly hard to recruit the next wave. And with everything we knew we had coming at us, there was very little doubt that we'd find ourselves needing to add many of the positions back in the very short term. Because he knew I was leaving in two months, I hoped he'd view my input as the corporate equivalent of a "deathbed confession." These people weren't for me, this was the right thing to do for the business, and I hoped he'd really understand that.

He surprised me by punting and asking for more details. He said to go back and show him, department by department, what I'd do to hit the original target and what I'd do if the target were reduced. I wasn't sure why he wanted to get into that level of detail or how he'd make any real judgments about it anyway, but the place he was offering to leave this was actually better than the "hit the target" answer that I was half expecting. So I left his office feeling really happy that I'd asked for the meeting because Walt was now under consideration, and I had a chance to make specific recommendations on the other two issues. But I had to get on this pretty quickly because my personal shot clock was rapidly approaching zero.

We bounced emails back and forth and had a couple of phone conversations before everything was settled. He agreed that Walt would be the right person for the job, and with Walt reporting directly to him. It took a while to get to this point, like the final phone call happening about thirty minutes before I sent out my announcement email on July 30. But, drama aside, I was very grateful to have had a chance to provide my input and even more grateful that it'd been taken seriously. The potential for bad outcomes would have been too high if it'd gone another way, and the fact was the problems wouldn't have been immediately visible. The business was going to be fine in the short term no matter who was put in the role. OnStar was an annuity business with a relatively large subscriber base that had enough positive momentum to generate good financial results no matter who was in charge. But, in the medium term, and especially the long term, veering off on the wrong compass heading even a little bit ran the risk of having the whole business coming unwound. Hey, I had to keep reminding myself this wasn't my company anyway, but a team of amazing people that I'd had the privilege of leading had invested incredible energy and passion to get OnStar to this point, and it would've been a tragedy of Biblical proportions if naive or ineffective leadership turned out to be the ultimate cause of this business's decline.

On the headcount issue, I'd say it was a draw. We were still told to reduce five executive positions, but were able to lower our overall headcount reduction target by twenty-five positions, which meant a couple dozen more OnStar professionals had been spared pink slips. But they really weren't the lucky ones; they should've never been in jeopardy in the first place. The lucky party in that decision was the new GM because they'd just retained some wonderfully talented people who were almost lost to the gods of false consistency.

Walt and I spent a lot of time together in the weeks before I left. I'd specifically asked if he wanted the job before I made the recommendation to Fritz, and he said he did. My guess was that his willingness to take it on had more to do with his belief that he was probably the best person to keep the dream alive, rather than his desire for more money or influence. Walt wasn't built that way, he wasn't the guy that would claw his way over rivals, and he wasn't very political. It wasn't that he was naive; he just didn't like the waste of time and energy that most of the corporate intrigue usually was. I sure hoped that, for both OnStar and the new GM's sake, most of the silly politics were behind us because there was much more important work to be done. And, besides, the alternative of selecting leaders based upon their political maneuvering skills was just crazy and was never a model that was going to lead to sustained success for any company.

As we got later into August, someone reminded me that, on August 31, I would be attending my last OnStar all-employee meeting. That was unbelievable. First, it was unbelievable that our little monthly meeting tradition, started over fourteen years before, had actually survived for that long. There'd been so many practical reasons that had come up to cut it back to quarterly, or even annually. Didn't it cost too much? And the loss of productive time, ninety minutes a month, wasn't that just a waste? And how about needing to generate content and presentation materials, didn't I have better things to do than that? Those were all fair questions, but when you boiled it all down, it just made sense to me to keep it going. The business did move quickly, and people deserved to be kept up to speed on what was happening. They also deserved the respect to be treated as partners and not day laborers, people who were worthy of the effort and cost of holding a meeting where they could stay connected to the amazing mission that we all shared.

While the emotional overload that it caused kept us from doing it at every meeting, we did occasionally bring a subscriber or an advisor or a 911 official into our monthly meeting to retell a recent OnStar story. It had happened when we brought in the 911 operator in from Florida who'd helped save the young woman who'd been abducted at the ATM machine, and we'd done it many times before that. But there was one of those reenactment events that happened during my last year at OnStar that was probably the best example of why this long-standing meeting tradition still felt like it made so much sense.

Apparently, an eye surgeon had been heading up north by himself to go deer hunting, and as he was unloading the gear from his truck at his remote camp, his muzzle-loading rifle accidentally discharged, shooting a large-caliber projectile into his chest. Thankfully for everyone concerned, he was driving an OnStar-equipped Chevy Silverado and was able to make it back into the driver's seat to push the OnStar button for help. What transpired from that point on was an amazingly dramatic story that ended with the doctor getting help before he would have otherwise bled to death.

We made contact with the family and found that the doctor's wife wanted to come in to one of our monthly all-employee meetings to say thank you to the people at OnStar. She said her husband was going to be fine, but couldn't come himself because he was still too emotional to talk about the event. But she did say the doctor's mother also wanted to come to say thank you as well. Jim Kobus, who worked for Jocelyn and had been my wonderfully talented coconspirator in preparing for these meetings and many other media events over the years, arranged for the 911 operator who'd taken the call that day to also fly down to be with us. Since I'd been in enough of these types of meetings in the past, I knew that this needed to be the last item on the meeting's agenda because it was undoubtedly going to stir up some very powerful emotions. When we told the doctor's wife that we intended to play a few minutes of the tape of her husband's call as background for the story, she said she needed to stay outside the room while it was running, because she knew if she heard it, she wouldn't be able to address our team.

We got to the end of the meeting, and Jim ran the tape. I'd intentionally not listened to it before myself, which was probably good because I'm not sure I could have sat through it twice. At the beginning, the doctor was lucid, but obviously in great pain. We quickly conferenced in the appropriate 911 response center for his location, but his Silverado was way off into the woods and not near any named roads. The challenge was now to keep him calm until the good guys could get to him. Early in the call, the doctor asked if someone could contact his wife, and our advisor said she had their home number on file and would try to conference her into the call. A minute or so later, his wife was on the phone with him, along with our advisor and the 911 operator, while he was sitting in the truck and bleeding badly. The doctor told his wife how much he loved her and then asked her to say good-bye for him to their young children and tell them that their daddy loved them very much. This man absolutely believed he was going to die, and it's incredibly hard to listen to. But his wife tells him in a very matter-of-fact tone that he'll be fine and that he can tell them that himself when he gets home.

At some point, the doctor started to show the signs of blood loss and said he was going to get out of the truck and start walking to find help. Any movement, much less walking, would have caused even greater blood loss and certainly ended his life. Again, his wife just calmly said that he needed to stay put and that everything was fine. He told her she didn't understand how bad it was because he'd shot himself in the chest and that it wasn't going to be all right. But she didn't change her tone at all; she said it's probably not that bad, just sit still, and she'd be seeing him soon. Eventually, the authorities were able to locate his truck and got him to the hospital in time to save his life.

After the tape stopped, the doctor's wife came into the meeting room and told everyone how much she appreciated what OnStar had done for her husband that afternoon. She said she had no idea how hard it must be to make all of the technology work, but that however it had happened, OnStar had given her back her husband, and more importantly, had given their children back their dad. There was complete silence in the room when I stood up to end the meeting, and not surprisingly, very few people were making any eye contact. Here was a room filled with over five hundred steely-eyed techies working for one of the biggest corporate monoliths in the world, and they'd just been reduced to a pile of quivering jelly. I choked out a couple of words like, "Thank you very much, meeting adjourned," and everyone rose to their feet and quietly walked out of the room.

I stayed after to talk to this amazing woman and to the 911 operator. He was an older guy who'd been working in the 911 field for many years. He said he hadn't thought about that call since the day it happened—no, he said, actually the night after it had happened, because it had kept him from sleeping. He said when the doctor first asked to contact his wife, before he could say that wasn't possible, our advisor had already said she'd try. He said that never goes well, that the loved one always panics and makes things much worse, and that when the phone was ringing at the doctor's home he was praying nobody would pick up. But when his wife answered and had been so amazing on the call, he thought that maybe the doctor had a chance. He said there were three parts leading to the miraculous outcome that day—the 911 system, OnStar, and the doctor's wife—and it took all three to have the story end the incredible way that it did.

I asked the doctor's wife how she stayed so calm during the call. Did she really not understand how serious it actually was? She said, yes, she understood it was really bad and that everything inside of her was screaming and crying. But she also understood that his only chance was for her to use every ounce of strength she had to hold back the emotion and stay calm for him. Amazing. We all ended up hugging, and I went back into afternoon meetings that all turned out to be big wastes of time. Everyone had been completely overwhelmed by the event and looked like wrung-out dishcloths; the reality of what we meant to this family was just too powerful to easily digest.

So that was why the OnStar family got together on a monthly basis, not always for stories like those, but to stay calibrated on why we were all there in the first place. And, now, after roughly 150 or so of these meetings later, some of which I had called into when I was traveling over the years, my last one was actually on the horizon. What was that supposed to mean?

What it meant was that Jim Kobus came into my office as usual two weeks before the date to review the proposed agenda. We'd done it scores of times before, except this time Jim came in, sat down, and just smiled at me. Wait a minute, where's the list of topics? Where were the slides that we needed to review? He said that I just needed to chill out; everything was being taken care of. I had some sense what that meant and said even though I'd soon be retired, I wasn't without some influence, and he'd better not let anything silly happen. He just smiled again and said they'd reserved ten minutes for me at the end of the meeting for whatever I thought I needed to say, but that I had to make it brief because I wasn't in charge of this particular meeting.

This had the feeling of mischief in the making, and it got even fishier when I found out that Barb and Taylor had been invited to attend. And it got stranger yet when I learned that they'd also arranged for my mom and dad, my sister Sandy, my two brothers-in-law, and one of my nephews to be in the audience. Hey, this was work, why do Mom and Dad need to be at my work? It was a nice thought, and when I found out Rhonda and a couple of other folks were behind it all, it was just better to surrender because it was going to happen with or without my blessing. I did decide, though, that I wasn't going to let this meeting end on an emotional note—that was reserved for subscribers. No, my final ten minutes at an all-employee meeting would be used to review two "Top 10" lists—first, the "Top 10 Cool Things About Running OnStar," and finally, the "Top 10 Things To Do in Retirement." If people were going to get weepy at this event, it was going to be because my jokes were so lame.

The meeting day came, and my family and I were ushered into the first row. Pretty formal I thought, but it later occurred to me that they just hadn't wanted me wandering around and bumping into people that I wasn't supposed to know were there. The lights dimmed, and a booming voice came over the sound system. A sentence or two into the intro, it occurred to me that it was the voice of a very prominent Detroit radio personality, Paul W. Smith. Paul owned the morning airwaves in Detroit, broadcasting on legendary WJR from 5:45 to 9:00 a.m. I knew that because I showered with Paul W. every morning and many times had the pleasure of being a guest on his show to talk to him about whatever we were doing new at OnStar. Paul was genuinely a very good man—very smart, very entertaining, and sometimes very funny. He was also unabashedly a Michigan homer in the best sense of that term. He shamelessly stood up for all that was good about Michigan and the Detroit area, but also routinely called out the politicians or businesspeople who he thought needed to pick up their game or get off their self-interested agendas. I liked him so much that one year I asked him to play in our Buick Open Pro Am group with Justin Leonard. We either bonded that day or maybe it was just the fact that we protected each other from the spectators whose loved ones we'd injured with our wayward tee shots. Either way, he'd become a good friend, and I thought how nice it was of him to record this intro—maybe it was OK Mom and Dad were there after all.

A minute later, Paul W. came out from behind a curtain and emceed the next hour and a half of the event. He was great, just the right balance of entertainment and off-color jokes—why not, this wasn't being broadcasted on the radio. Then came a series of presentations that I could only describe as a mixture of wonderfully warm testimonials and Don Rickles at the Friar's Club. Harry Pearce came out first and did an amazing job telling everyone his version of the founding days of OnStar. Harry was justifiably proud of what our team had accomplished, but honestly, from my perspective, he deserved a lot of the credit for making it all possible. Then Fred Cooke—yes, that Fred—hijacked the microphone for his turn at the campfire stories. Fred described OnStar's early days as more than mildly dysfunctional and said in many ways it resembled the Island of Misfit Toys. More people presented, including Don Butler, Jocelyn, and Walt, and they had a number of people who couldn't be there in person who sent video messages instead. There was Ernie Allen, from the National Center for Missing & Exploited Children; Paul Jacobs, the CEO from Qualcomm; B. B. Hwang, who ran the LG Electronics business that had become such an important partner of ours; Dr. Hunt and Dr. Runge; Fire Chief Harmes; and finally, Dr. and Mrs. Hazen from the hunting accident. I'd never met Dr. Hazen personally, but that didn't keep me from feeling an immediate connection to him. This was like my personal version of *It's a Wonderful Life*, except there was no Mr. Potter, and it had never stopped being Bedford Falls. What a gift all of these people, including the five hundred or so in the audience, had given me that afternoon. What a blessing this had all turned out to be. General Motors had done an amazing thing, an improbable thing, in bringing OnStar to life.

It was so fitting and so touching that Harry had come to be part of this, and I actually learned a little about the early days that I hadn't known before. That was great for the OnStar team to experience since many of those in attendance hadn't even been hired yet before Harry had retired, or even Fred, for that matter. It was like watching the passing on of the story by the tribal elders, something that I'm sure made a wonderful and lasting impression on all of the people in that audience. They were being told how much their work mattered, how it had a history, and how that history brought with it an obligation to create an even more amazing future. I really appreciated all of the kind words, but in fairness, I was only the prop. My retirement had given this gathering a convenient reason to happen at this time and at this place. But the celebration was about something that was much more important than that and something that had been the creation of far more than any one person.

The meeting ended with some laughter—accomplished courtesy of my corny top-ten lists. But I started my final remarks showing a picture of the three other members of the OnStar senior staff who were retiring at the same time I was, saying, "That's what one hundred years of GM experience looks like." It was literally true; between Bill Ball, Rick Lee, and Greg Payne, they had a hundred years of service, and I thought it was important to acknowledge all they'd done to bring OnStar to life. Unfortunately, the combination of their images on the screen, and the words "That's what one hundred years looks like" didn't start a discussion of their many contributions, instead it ended up eliciting roaring laughter. Oh well, it was the thought that counted, and they did make a great warm-up act for my real funny material.

I'd sent a number of people outside of GM a copy of the email that went to the OnStar team announcing my retirement attached to personal notes of appreciation and thanks. I was surprised at how many people I felt truly deserved my personal gratitude and what an amazingly diverse group it turned out to be. There were folks like Clay Christensen and Adrian Slywotzky, Chief Harmes, Dr. Hunt, Dr. Runge, and Col. Pete Munoz, the head of the Michigan State Police. But the list went on and on, including the CEO of Verizon Wireless, Lowell McAdam, and their chief technology officer, Dick Lynch. Sure, we had what could be characterized as a large supplier-customer relationship with these guys, but over the years, it had become much closer and more personal than that. They had both really taken our mission personally, and that had made a huge difference in the way our teams worked together and the amazing things we'd been able to accomplish.

Thank goodness a lot of those types of "closer than arm's length" relationships had developed with our key suppliers because this was anything but a commodity business. I sent notes to Dave Dougherty, the CEO of Convergys; Tony Hopp, who ran our ad agency, Campbell Ewald; and to the heads of Digitas, Delco Electronics, Continental, and Minacs. But aside from the long- standing Verizon relationship, there was a more recent, but very special partnership that really deserved special acknowledgement, and that was with LG Electronics.

We'd been introduced to LG through Verizon when we were struggling to get what we needed out of our other vehicle hardware suppliers, and because Verizon was such a large buyer of their handsets, they agreed to talk to us. During our first meeting, I half expected them to politely say they weren't interested because our volume was very low in comparison with products like their flat-screen TVs and cell phones, and it also came with strings attached. The strings were an onerous set of vehicle-related validation requirements not found in the consumer electronics industry and the connection to a business where lives were at stake.

Nam Woo was running the business sector where our business would fit and didn't immediately jump on the opportunity, but in fairness to him, that was actually a good sign. As I'd said before, not everybody was cut out to work in this category, and he was just trying to digest the complexity of the technology and the challenges of our mission. Thankfully, Nam ultimately decided they wanted to take this on, and from that moment forward, I never experienced a more emotionally committed and technically capable group in my life. I really liked these guys—their products were exceptional, their work ethic was incredible, and they had fully embraced our mission as their own. Nam eventually went on to become president of LG China, but he left a legacy of leadership and personal commitment that had earned my gratitude and respect.

The final group that I sent notes to were actually a number of individual GM dealers. Wow, had those relationships come full circle. These were mainly folks who had served on our dealer council at some point over the years and had provided important encouragement as we grew OnStar. I'd come to know some wonderful dealers who'd been willing to spend their time with us on periodic conference calls or travel from time to time to attend meetings in person. We'd broken through the superficial approach that too many GM dealer meetings were famous for and constructively engaged on issues with only one purpose in mind: to make OnStar as valuable as possible for all of our constituents—subscribers, dealers, and for GM. Did that mean we always agreed? Absolutely not, but it meant we'd come to trust each other's motives and had developed a mutual confidence that we'd be able to work through any serious issues. Maybe because our initial interactions with dealers had started so poorly, these might have been some of the relationships that I savored the most.

Then there were the final individual good-byes to my family members at OnStar. I had a couple of weeks in the office after my final all-employee meeting, and I was trying to tie up a few loose ends. My long-standing habit was to get into the office about 6:30 a.m., which usually gave me at least a half hour or so to catch up on whatever emails were lurking in my inbox. It also gave anybody who needed a few minutes on an urgent or impromptu topic a time where they could just stick their head in my office and have a quick discussion. So many times over the years, I'd walk in early, only to find Walt or Scott Kubicki or the IT folks waiting for me, which usually meant something had gone wrong the night before. We'd head into the conference room with the whiteboard, where they would explain it all, and we'd decide what to do next.

Well, now that time had turned into something else. There were people coming in for a few quiet and personal moments to say goodbye. It wasn't organized or scheduled; it just seemed to happen. There were people who were relatively new to OnStar and folks who had been with the business for over a decade—OnStar Yodas we called them. It was so nice to take a breath and share a few private moments with folks who were making the effort to connect one last time. The discussions would generally start awkwardly, then we'd be laughing remembering some of the near-death experiences we'd shared together, and usually, there'd be a hug, and at least my eyes were misty at the end. These were precious, precious moments that touched my heart and reminded me yet again how blessed I'd been to travel this path with such wonderful and talented teammates.

One of the discussions took place with Kelley Kettenbeil. Kelley had been with us almost since the beginning, originally working for EDS, but then taking the plunge and signing on with OnStar before it was at all clear that it was a smart thing to do. She was very talented and extremely knowledgeable about most aspects of the business, and people just loved working with her. That led to me selecting her as my technical assistant, basically a business professional who could sit in on a broad range of meetings and help me stay on top of and follow up on all of the diverse opportunities and issues running around inside of OnStar. She'd been in that role for about eighteen months, probably longer than would be normal, but since I knew I was leaving, it just didn't make any sense to make a change so close to the end. Besides, she was doing a great job, and I enjoyed working with her. It was going to be hard to say good-bye to people like Kelley. We'd worked together literally every day, just like I did with Rhonda, and she felt more like family than a coworker. I'm not sure our final discussion had many words in it at all. She'd say two words and stop; then I'd say two words and stop. It didn't matter, as we'd probably said more than enough to each other over the years. It was just the filler before it was time for her to get up, get a hug, and head out the door. The fact that these moments had to happen didn't make them any easier.

I did decide to write a few individual thank-you notes to some of the folks at OnStar, mainly because if I had tried to say these things in person, I probably wouldn't have been able to get them out. With Tony DiSalle's permission, this is the note I sent to him on September 22, my last day in the office:

Tony,

Well, the hours have dwindled down to a precious few. A lot has gone on in our time working together, and I just wanted to say thank you very much for all you've done for me, and for OnStar, as we've shared a very special journey that has turned out to be more of an adventure than any of us could have ever known.

As you're well aware, over the years my skills in picking leaders for our marketing role at OnStar were subject to reasonable questioning—like WHAT WERE YOU THINKING??!!! It's actually a fairly entertaining list to think through at this point, in the sense that a migraine, or a hammer to the thumb, or pie in the face is entertaining. Sometimes fun to watch from a distance when it's happening to someone else or when it's far enough back in history that you forget the pain and surrender to the fact that you did it to yourself.

Then came Tony. I certainly couldn't have known at that moment that things would be as different as you turned out to make them, but it was like the Lions finally winning a game or maybe the Cubs in the World Series (OK, not that extreme). At some point, the odds said I had to break my losing streak. Thank you for making that happen. I hope you look back and smile as much as I do when I think of all we've been through since your momentary lapse of judgment in joining Fred's aptly named Island of Misfit Toys. Dealer mutinies, VSSM insurrections, agencies with game that would show up occasionally, Bat airbags, Tiger Woods, South Park—the list goes on and on. How many NADA meetings where we would pinball between folks that liked us, folks that hated us, and folks that wondered who we were—and that's just the description of the GM people!

Through it all, Tony, you brought a quiet, calm, professional determination to no kidding move the needle toward a very special place. There is no OnStar brand, at least the way we're proud of it today, without the capabilities you brought to this business. And it was honestly as much how you did it as what you did that was always so amazing to me. Far from your predecessors who always looked more like one-eyed pirates with half of their attention focused on their next "real" job in tower 200, you brought your heart as well as your head to this business and showed a commitment and resolve to always do the right thing for OnStar despite the potential for personal political consequences. That was courageous and clearly noticed by all of your teammates who desperately needed that kind of engagement, as it was sorely lacking in marketing until you got here.

So thanks for all you've done, and for all you're about to do, as the business moves into whatever the next stage is numbered—I've lost count. I know you and Walt will become co-conspirators just as you and I always have been—except he really deserves the "junior" in junior marketing expert more than I ever did.

On a personal level, you've been a really good teammate, a good man, and a great friend, and I will miss you. Barb and I wish you and

Kim and your family the fullness of God's blessings for health, happiness, and prosperity for whatever the future may hold. And if there's ever anything I can do to help you personally, either here at OnStar or anywhere else your career leads you, please let me know. You deserve whatever help I could possibly be. Please stay in touch.

With Warmest Regards,

Chet

Tony deserved that note from me, as did the others who got their own version of my thanks. The business was in a better place because of him. He needed to know that, and he needed to continue to make a difference in the future of OnStar. I knew he'd do just that and that he and Walt would become great partners in keeping this dream alive.

A month or so before we were both set to retire, Rick Lee had asked me if I wanted to go up to Northern Michigan when we were done at OnStar and spend a few days golfing at his place in Harbor Springs. Actually, it was better than that; he asked whom I wanted to invite to come along and join us. It didn't take long to figure out that the perfect foursome would also include Ken Enborg and Fred Cooke. They'd both preceded us into retirement, and we'd all stayed in fairly close touch. I'm not sure if Rick had his junior psychiatrist degree or not, but those few days were just what the doctor ordered for early OnStar withdrawal. We had so much fun hacking through the forests during the day and eating and drinking too much at night, of course accompanied by a never-ending series of war stories that always ended up with us narrowly escaping the jaws of death. It was actually amazing how we all remembered many of the events, most of them from many years before, with the clarity of things that had happened yesterday. I guess that's what "seared" into memory means.

So this is what retirement looks like. Fred and Ken seemed to be doing just fine. Ken had actually taken on some semi-full-time work at a law firm just to stay busy, and Fred was enjoying his grandchildren and shuttling between his lake house in Indiana and a place he had in Florida. We talked about what was next for Rick and I, and we both said we wanted a little decompression time before we'd see what, if anything, either one of us would get into next. I said I was thinking of trying to write down what I could remember about my time at OnStar before it was lost in my memory, but I was a little afraid that it had already started to happen. The last few days had actually rekindled my interest in doing that, just listening to the pride that these guys had in the stories they were telling. Their story, and so many others, really did deserve to be told—even if the only audience might be the few people who had lived through it all with us.

A few weeks later, I sat down to try to start writing, half expecting the session to last about fifteen minutes before I'd get frustrated and realize it wasn't going to be possible. I couldn't tell you what I had for breakfast two days ago. How in the world was I going to go back fourteen years? I kept no journals, no diary. I had no day-planner records. Where would it come from? In a process that I can only describe as stranger than I understand, one memory just led to another and another until there were times that it honestly felt like I was back there again—in those meetings, living through those disasters, celebrating those sweet, but rare early moments of success. I actually woke up a few times dreaming those same dreams from back in the day, and I could tell they were authentic because most of them didn't end well this time, either. Maybe this was God's final display of His sense of humor in this chapter of my life. If it was, he'd given me one more gift that I probably didn't deserve, but I really treasured. This had truly been an improbable and amazing journey.

Acknowledgments

It's hard to know where to start because there are so many people to thank for helping make the story of OnStar come to life. There are the people who inspired the idea for the book, provided valuable feedback, and contributed to multiple early revisions and who were often more optimistic about its prospects for publication than I was. Then there are the people who I had the amazing good fortune to share the adventure of OnStar with personally, a collection of exceptionally talented and deeply committed souls who I came to admire and treasure as kindred coconspirators and trusted friends. Finally, there are the many people who touched my life and career prior to my arrival at Project Beacon, providing the love, guidance, and perspective that somehow allowed me to have the chance to be considered for a role that was as unobvious a next step for me as it was an incredible blessing.

So first of all, to my mom and dad, for your love and the lessons that you both taught me about respect and working hard and for encouraging me to be the first in our family to pursue a college education. You provided a wonderful foundation and set me on a compass heading that ultimately made everything else possible.

To Barbara, the love of my life and my incredible wife and partner of thirty-two years, for having the sense of humor to marry me in the first place and for all of the amazing gifts you've given me ever since. Your faith in God has inspired me, your kindness and gentle spirit has sustained me, your unwavering loyalty has fortified me, and the family you created by the children who you brought into this world and so lovingly nurtured has blessed me beyond measure.

To my children, Chase and Taylor, for being a source of pride and happiness and for bringing a sense of balance and purpose to my life. And separately to my daughter, Taylor, for the determined role she played in encouraging the writing of these memories and for the special time we've spent together that's helped ease my transition into retirement.

To some special people who I knew prior to joining OnStar, for helping me learn and grow both personally and professionally and helping to shape my future, including Sandy Curcio, Sharon Dunning, John Jarrell, Frank Boatwright, John Cavanaugh, Ron Floyd, Gary Gumushian, Tim Cling, Don Vossler, Dennis Odom, Dave Morrison, Dr Alan Whittaker, Gordon Eiland, Dick Huber, Dr. Alan Gropman, Billy Cook, Lutz Elsner, Jim Young, Jay Dodd and John Gable, just to name a few. Each of them, and many others, left me much better for their friendship, support, and encouragement.

To an extremely important list of very special individuals within General Motors, for stepping up and standing tall in support of acting on GM's most noble instincts by bringing OnStar to life. They took the mission personally and displayed vision, determination, guts, courage, tenacity, and the type of integrity that made me proud to work in the same company with them. They include Harry Pearce, Ron Zarrella, Rick Wagoner, Vince Barabba, Larry Burns, Jim Queen, Ed Koerner, and Gary Cowger.

To a diverse group of wonderful people from outside of General Motors, for, in many ways, providing key support, resources, inspiration, motivation, insights, and encouragement during times when their absence would have represented a serious loss to both me and the business. They include Professor Clay Christensen, Phil Samper, Adrian Slywotzky, Dr. Rick Hunt, Lowell McAdam, Nam Woo, Dr. Jeff Runge, Paul Jacobs, Jim Mateja, Paul W. Smith, B. B. Hwang, Dave Dougherty, Elaine Minacs, Ernie Allen, Randy Farnsworth, Paul Rubin, and Dick Lynch.

To a large group of mercifully unnamed and, in most cases, not referenced individuals, for their predictable cynicism, parochial and self-interested agendas, and sad lack of vision that fueled my personal determination and provided the OnStar team with many emotionally significant, if not completely necessary, bonding opportunities.

And finally, and most importantly, my thanks to the entire OnStar family, for allowing me to stand in front of their orchestra and, from time to time, letting me feel like I was helping them make their beautiful music. And while it would be futile to try to list everyone who truly deserves to be on that list, my special thanks goes out to Lorrie Robertson, Jon Hyde, Ken Enborg, Fritz Beiermeister, Bruce McDonald, Fred Cooke, Walt Dorfstatter, Greg Payne, Kathy Murphy, Todd Carstensen, Debbie Frakes, Jocelyn Allen, Jim Kobus, Rhonda Miska, Kelly Kettenbeil, Debbie Rough, Bill Ball, Joanne Finnorn, Joe McCusker, Scott Kubicki, Terry Inch, Greg Ross, Rick Lee, Jim Smith, Dave Rockett, Steve Schwinke, Tim Nixon, Tony DiSalle, Andy Young, Ian Wild, Mike Doeden, Dennis Keith, Don Butler, Lois McEntyre, Jim Kornus, George Gulliver, Tim Cox, Jeff Jaworski, Chris Steele, Kathy Kay, Mark Timm, Sam Mancuso, Nick Pudar, Ed Chrumka, Lisa Jenkins, Sue Schneider, John Konkel, Bill Madalin, Manlio Huacuja, Matt Przybylski, Jim Piwowarski, Bruce Alexander, Ann Ross, Chris Hamer, Terry Sullivan, Bruce Radloff, Geri Lama, Steve Davis, Jim Profeta, George Baker, Jim Walenczak, Randy Arickx, Don Hotton, Chris Oesterling, Ellen Ajersch, John Correa, Sethu Medhavan, and Andy Sills. This list could go on and on, and I apologize because almost everyone at OnStar deserves to be acknowledged for his or her support to me, and the business, over our years together. But if you weren't specifically mentioned, either here or in the preceding pages of the book, then I hope you still take the pride that you so richly deserve in what all of your hard work and personal commitment has helped to make happen. May God bless you all.

34022828R00189

Made in the USA
Middletown, DE
05 August 2016